Seeing the Light

Seeing the Light

Inside the Velvet Underground

Rob Jovanovic

St. Martin's Press ᴍ New York

www.stmartins.com

ISBN 978-1-250-00014-9

First published in Great Britain by Aurum Press Limited under the title *The
Velvet Underground: Peeled*

First U.S. Edition: April 2012

10 9 8 7 6 5 4 3 2 1

Sterling Morrison:	'The unanimous opinion was that we were ten times better live than on records. We never played a song the same way twice, we never wanted to, maybe never could.'
John Cale:	'In Chicago, I was singing lead, no one knew the difference. We turned our faces to the wall and turned up very loud. Paul Morrissey and Danny Williams had different visions of what the light show should be like and one night I looked up to see them fighting, hitting each other in the middle of a song.'
Question:	'Do you see yourself as a creator, or more like a magnet that attracts other talents?'
Andy Warhol:	'More like a pencil sharpener.'
Lou Reed:	'We ended up at a terrible coffee house working six sets a night, seven nights a week, five dollars a man a night, and that lasted a week and a half and we were fired, because they hated our music so much.'
Doug Yule:	'When Lou and John or Lou and I were on stage there was a balance. With Lou gone the balance was gone. It wasn't the same.'
Moe Tucker:	'I used to go and get a temporary job for a week when I was home. I didn't need as much money as the others did for their apartments. I lived at home rent-free. We never got any royalty cheques. Maybe one or two little ones.'

Contents

Introduction

It is unlikely The Velvet Underground could have been born anywhere else but in New York City. The sleaze, dirt and danger of Manhattan translated viscerally into the Velvets' sonic world, a world that produced a monolithic urban noise that pulled at your insides and messed with your head. They were the perfect blend of art and rock, one of the truly original bands. Yet despite the inspiration they kindled in first-time listeners, they struggled during their own lifetime as they had little in common with their contemporaries of the British invasion, the growing folk rock movement or the emerging San Francisco sound. The 'Summer of Love' was an alien and unwelcome concept to the Velvets whose music was cold, hard and, more importantly, real; not a floaty fantasy or dreamy philosophy.

Few bands in the history of rock and roll have measured up to the lasting impact they made. Their four studio albums in a five-year span sent out ripples that took years to reach the shore, but when they did, the impact they had was monumental. That impact has been felt across numerous genres; rock (The Flaming Lips' frontman Wayne Coyne claims that the Velvets have 'a mystery that I'll never figure out'), glam (Bryan Ferry says the Velvets were Roxy Music's key influence), grunge (Kurt Cobain made mix-tapes for his friends with Velvets' songs on them, and Nirvana covered 'Here She Comes Now'), indie ('Hearing the Velvets for the first time saved me,' said The Libertines' Carl Barat), avant-garde ('The first Velvet Underground album only sold 10,000 copies, but everyone who bought it formed a band,' said Brian Eno) and pop (OMD covered 'I'm Waiting For The Man'). The band's original 'classic' line-up consisted of singer and principal writer Lou Reed, drummer Maureen Tucker, bassist and electric violist John Cale and guitarist Sterling Morrison. Musically, lyrically, thematically and aesthetically, their ideas of art and multimedia presentation were innovative whichever way you look at it. Though under-appreciated at the time, they were certainly a band ahead of their years.

The band produced their own version of primitive folk rock, and skilfully merged it with avant-garde dissonance, but the lyrics were real and to the point. The guitars swept from icy calm to an explosive crescendo with a maelstrom of emotive, powerful playing. Their fledging style would have few followers for the best part of a decade. 1970s punk-queen Patti Smith was one of the next generation of New York artists who embraced the Velvets. '"Heroin" is one of the more perfect American songs', she said. 'It addresses the deeply painful and destructive elements of it and also what is precious about it. All with Lou's simple, direct language.' As successive generations of musicians discovered the song they waxed lyrical about it. Art-rocker Thurston Moore of Sonic Youth said 'Singing about heroin was groundbreaking, and lyric writing was never the same afterwards.'

If the band were shocking on record, they were nothing short of revelatory when seen live. From their earliest days together they experimented with a sublime brand of multi-media presentation that was years ahead of their peers. What had been accepted as cutting-edge light shows by other bands at the time were blown away by a synthesised obliquity. Slide, cine-film, spot-lighting and strobe effects were all present at a Velvet Underground show. Usually all at the same time.

Whether it was at the Café Bizarre (where Andy Warhol first saw them and decided to take them under his wing), at the Filmmakers Cinémathèque or at one of their early university shows, The Velvet Underground were like nothing anyone had ever seen before. Reed, Cale, Tucker and Morrison would wear predominantly black clothes and wraparound shades, thus creating an image of New York rock-star cool that still endures forty years on. The fact they only did so because they were blinded by the films and slides being projected onto the massive screens behind them doesn't matter.

Often the band would spend much of the show with their backs to the audience, partly because of the light show, partly because it seemed like a cool thing to do. John Cale wailed away on his electric viola with his hair swishing around his head; the tall, lean Sterling Morrison provided steady guitar support with a mix of bluesy riffs; Moe Tucker, who from a distance was totally androgynous, stood while playing her basic drum kit; Lou Reed hardly moved at all and sang the songs in an eerie monotone. For a while this mix was enhanced by the addition of the ethereal cool of German chanteuse, and ex-model, Nico. She would contradict the band by wearing an all-white trouser suit, singing songs while sitting on a stool and playing a tambourine.

Musically they stunned – almost abused – their audiences. In the early days many people walked out because they just hadn't known what to expect and couldn't deal with it when they got it. In New York, where the folk scene still held sway in the mid-1960s, and on the West Coast, where soaring harmonies and 'flower power' was taking hold, The Velvet Underground were the antithesis of all the music that surrounded them. Those few in the audience who could appreciate the music then had the light show and the multiple layers of films and slide projectors to contend with. It could disorientate the most sober of onlookers. Who needed drugs when they could witness this?

From their placement at the very edge of urban society, documenting the underside of the city, the Velvets managed to produce what is now described as the most influential record of rock history, *The Velvet Underground & Nico* (1967). It sounds as fresh and exciting today, more than forty years later, as it did when it was recorded. Over the next four years the band would release a further three albums and undergo multiple personnel changes, but the standard of their music was kept high through a series of restless stylistic changes. *White Light/White Heat* (1968) was a feedback-laden dervish of an album, *The Velvet Underground* (1969) demonstrated the band's laid-back semi-acoustic abilities and the Reed swansong, *Loaded* (1970), was a showcase for catchy pop songs delivered in an accomplished variety of styles.

How did The Velvet Underground come to be so influential and to see their music endure so long after they originally split up? Unlike much of the music that was produced in their lifetime, theirs had no sociological or political agenda. They produced simple short stories set to sound, sometimes against a deluge of screaming feedback, which was pretty much unheard of in the mid-1960s. Sometimes the words were sparse but the music could go on for fifteen minutes. In concert a single song might be played for up to an hour.

The main reason why they have touched so many artists is that they weren't afraid to do what they felt was right. They didn't pander to any record label requests or trends of the time. Their first two albums were revolutionary in their experimentation. At a time when harmony and melody were at a premium, the Velvets produced drones and primal rhythms. They weren't just an avant-garde band, they were at the very edge of the avant-garde and the intertwining of various art forms (music, poetry, film, light shows, theatre, to name just a few) into their sphere was truly mould-breaking.

The Velvets continued a counterculture mixed-media procession that started with Kerouac and Ginsberg, passed through Dylan, continued with Patti Smith and The Ramones, and on to The Strokes. Their music stimulated the body while the lyrics stimulated the mind. In the 1970s Lester Bangs wrote that most of the people then writing the praises of the band were the same ones who had ignored them during their lifetime and just wanted to jump on the hip bandwagon had gathered momentum. The fact that bandwagons frequently change course helped the band's initial cult following grow to something bigger. As hippy-dom faded in a mess of failed promises of a better world, corporate clout took the psychedelic world out of the hands of the dreamers. The following generation almost inevitably reacted against what the 1960s had stood for, and embraced a new nihilism that morphed into punk, helped by the economic and social malaise that spread across both sides of the Atlantic during the 1970s. The fact that the Velvets had done exactly what they wanted, and how they wanted, the fact that they produced noise and feedback, and the fact that they were the anti-hippies all contributed to them becoming the inadvertent torch bearers for the New York punks of the mid-1970s.

In England it was David Bowie who first picked up on them and began covering Velvet Underground songs in the late 1960s after his manager, Ken Pitt, brought him back an acetate of *The Velvet Underground & Nico* from a business trip to New York. It was also Bowie who embraced the bisexual nature of their songs to his advantage as glam rock took off. Later, in the early 1970s, he and Reed would write and tour together.

The world's largest cult band provides an unlikely link between Ginsberg and Kerouac, and Lydon and The Ramones. They were avant-garde in the true sense of exploring uncharted territory. Their songs not only sounded different but they also expressed certain feelings, attitudes and the kind of experiences that had never been heard in rock music before.

There can be a strong argument put forward for Lou Reed being the single most important person in American rock over the last four decades. From experimental 1960s visionary to undervalued 1970s rocker and his 1980s New York album reinvention, Reed has a current adult maturity that still produces music ahead of his contemporaries.

In 2000, the BBC aired a debate which came down to the question of which band was more influential on rock music as a whole, The Velvet Underground or The Beatles? The Velvets won. They've become a blueprint for anything that goes against the grain of the times. Ask such diverse acts as Sonic Youth, The Strokes, David Bowie, The Stooges, Big Star, R.E.M., Henry Rollins, New Order, Cowboy Junkies – the Velvets were their touchstone. In the often bizarre world of rock and roll, the story of The Velvet Underground is one of the more curious tales, and this is it.

Chapter 1
1942–1964
Beginning to See the Light

'They put the thing down your throat so you don't swallow your tongue, and they put electrodes on your head. The effect is that you lose your memory and become a vegetable. I wrote "Kill Your Sons" on Sally Can't Dance *about that. You can't read a book because you get to page 17 and have to go right back to page one again.'*

Lou Reed

In New York during the late 1950s, the suburban view of homosexuality was that it was a mental condition that had to be 'cured'. Though Kerouac, Ginsberg and the Beat gang were running around the city having their taboo-busting adventures, it was all nonetheless very much underground. Homosexual men were still seen in terms of extremely effeminate stereotypes. For a middle-class family, the mere thought that their son might be gay was cause for great concern, and in many cases drastic medical attention was sought. The Creedmore State Hospital Psychiatric Unit on Long Island was one of the local institutions used for 'curing' such 'disorders'. The methods used for such cures weren't pretty or sympathetic. Many doctors prescribed electroshock treatment to try and alter a patient's brain patterns.

With its eighteen floors rising above the local surroundings like the imposing centre of some gothic horror story, the Creedmore cast a physical as well as a psychological shadow over its local environs. Inside the new patient was taken through endless secured corridors before reaching a waiting room deep inside the massive complex. After changing into a hospital gown, he was strapped to a table while electrodes were fitted to his head and a sponge was placed inside his mouth. Within seconds the power was cranked up and a bolt of electricity was sent coursing through his seventeen-year-old body. Soon he lost consciousness while the treatment was continued. When he came round some time later, Lou Reed was terrified to realise that he had lost his memory.

To put it quite simply, New York is the ultimate city, the capital of the modern world. It's been mythologised as Metropolis and Gotham City, the iconic silhouette of its skyline is ingrained in memories across the world. The steam rising from under manhole covers, yellow taxis with horns blaring, skyscrapers rising up in every direction, with streetwise guys and hip girls on the street corners. A myriad TV shows and countless movies have made the city seem like the entire human race's second home.

From Gershwin's *Rhapsody in Blue*, as famously used in the opening sequences of that consummate New Yorker Woody Allen's *Manhattan*, to the birth of Tin Pan Alley and the boom in sheet music, through early Broadway musicals, it is also the epicentre of world music. The city has been called the capital of jazz (Louis Armstrong, Charlie Parker, Duke Ellington), been a centre for Doo Wop (Frankie Lymon and the Teenagers) and the 1960s folk movement (Bob Dylan and Joan Baez in Greenwich Village), the birthplace of punk (The Ramones, Patti Smith) and new wave (Blondie, Talking Heads) and it was in New York where rap first hit the streets with Grandmaster Flash. Right up to the Beastie Boys' 'An Open Letter to NYC' on their post-9/11 album *To The 5 Burroughs*, this city has been the heart and soul of music for almost 100 years.

During the 1950s Manhattan was home to some of the world's most powerful record labels (Atlantic, Columbia, Decca and RCA), the biggest music publishers and most popular recording studios. The centre of activity was the famous Brill Building between 49th and 53rd Street. Here a hub of songwriting teams assembled to produce some of the twentieth century's most memorable music. Goffin & King, Pomus & Shuman and Leiber & Stoller among others honed their trade turning out scores of hit songs. 'Dream Lover', 'Spanish Harlem', 'Yakety Yak' and 'River Deep Mountain High' are just some of the countless songs New York exported to populate charts around the world. By 1962 the Brill Building was home to over 160 music-related businesses, with the whole structure of the industry represented over the eleven floors of just one edifice. You could find the song-writers, who would look to sell their output to the publishers; there were demo studios where you could hire musicians to produce a tape to help sell a song to the various artist management agencies also housed in the building, and when that was done you could also find the radio promoters who would help get the finished song out on the airwaves.

Once the finished product was out in the open, it was often the backing of a disc-jockey that would make or break a tune and so the DJ suddenly became a powerful figure in the burgeoning music business. One of the most influential and important of these emerging DJs was Alan Freed. Freed is most famous for coining the phrase 'rock and roll' as a term for the overt rhythm and blues that was then gaining in popularity. He'd been working in radio since the Second World War as a sports-caster and then as a jazz and pop DJ in his home state of Ohio. Under the working name of 'Moondog' he hosted the Moondog Coronation Ball – now regarded as the world's first 'rock concert' – at the Cleveland Arena in 1952. By the mid-1950s, Freed had moved from Ohio to New York and hosted a show on WINS radio, where his voice reached the growing Long Island suburbs and the first generation of teenagers.

Freed was spreading the word to a massive, rapidly expanding and hungry listener-ship. New York in the 1950s was expanding its boundaries as more people were moving out to the neighbouring suburbs of Long Island and New Jersey. It was a time when the middle classes were indulging in a blossoming new consumer culture and people were increasingly likely to spend their disposable income on records.

Rock music was in its infancy and the newly named 'teenagers' were showing their first signs of rebellion; James Dean and Marlon Brando portrayed troubled and tenacious figures on the silver screen and the still-new music of rock and roll began to fill the airwaves. Writer Jack Kerouac used New York as his East-Coast base while writing his classic *On The Road* and spearheading the Beat Generation, and as the decade progressed, more and more jazz clubs morphed into rock and roll dance halls. At the same time, black music was seeping into the mainstream as traditional blues evolved, through the electrification of the guitar, to rhythm and blues, and then to rock and roll. The latter of these genres was hijacked by white performers like Elvis

Presley and Jerry Lee Lewis who, alongside black singers like Chuck Berry, took the nation by storm, providing the teenagers with a thrilling new medium through which to enjoy themselves. Without the responsibilities of their pre-war forebears, the American youth of the 1950s was the first to have both the time and the money, to simply have fun, and rock and roll music was the centrepiece of the fun they wanted to have.

Alongside the chart toppers were the popular vocal Doo Wop groups of the New York area. Doo Wop was a vocal style that had evolved from a mixture of gospel and black pop vocal groups like The Ink Spots. The Ink Spots had been around since the early 1930s in Indianapolis, but really grew to national prominence during the Second World War, culminating with the success of 'The Gypsy', which topped the US charts for thirteen weeks in 1946.

During the late 1940s, Doo Wop started to have a real influence on vocal music. The Ravens were one of the first of these groups to have chart success, and became a massive influence on all kinds of popular musicians, as they integrated jazz and gospel into a more mainstream format. 'Ol' Man River' was one of eight Top Ten hits they enjoyed. It wasn't just their sound that was influential, many bands with 'bird names' sprung up too, with The Swans, The Crows and The Wrens. But it was The Ravens who continued to push musical boundaries and even incorporated rock and roll with its swinging saxophone arrangements.

The Jesters were one of the more successful groups to follow The Ravens, scoring several mid-1950s hits ('So Strange', 'The Wind', 'The Plea', 'Please Let Me Love You') and becoming synonymous with the new New York sound. Through Alan Freed's radio show this new music was heard across the tri-state area, and bands started popping up in suburban neighbourhoods across the region. In 1955 the five-piece black vocalists of The Cleftones were formed in Queens, going on to have terrific local, if not national success. These bands in turn led other local kids to have a go for themselves. One of those local kids who had been listening intently, and was utterly taken with the Doo Wop bands, was Lou Reed.

During the Second World War, Jewish accountant Sidney George Rabinowitz was living in Brooklyn when he met local beauty queen Toby Flutterman; both were native New Yorkers. Sidney changed his surname to Reed, they married and soon started a family. Their first child was born on 2 March 1942 and they named him Lewis Allan Reed, five years later a daughter, Elizabeth (known to everyone as Bunny), joined the family. In 1953 the conservative, middle-class family moved to Freeport, Long Island, a predominantly Jewish suburb.

Toby wore her hair fashionably short, became the model of 1950s domesticity and doted on her son, hoping for great things with him such as becoming a doctor or lawyer. Sidney, meanwhile, expected his son would eventually take over the family business, as was tradition. 'My parents were self-made millionaires,' Reed explained in 1976. 'I know what it's like to have money.'

The move to Freeport brought more of a change for the eleven-year-old Lou than a move of just twenty miles would probably indicate. The hard-city atmosphere in the shadow of Manhattan's skyscrapers was replaced by an overdose of suburbia. The streets were quiet and local parks were plentiful. Just miles from the self-proclaimed capital city of the world, Long Island could be called the ultimate suburb. Just as New York City sets the standard and trends for major cities around the globe, so life on Long Island has helped shape suburbia too. A city apartment was exchanged for a new house on Oakfield Avenue with a large lawn perfect for ball games. The newly-found idyll soon proved to be boring for the teenage Reed, however.

Lou Reed attended first the Atkinson Elementary School and then Freeport High, which was just a few minutes' walk from the family home. At the insistence of his parents, Reed had started classical piano lessons before leaving Brooklyn, but by the time they reached Freeport his musical attention had wandered, and he was now voraciously collecting seven-inch rock and roll singles. Like millions of other children his age, he wanted to have guitar lessons instead of piano ones. Sidney and Toby eventually relented and bought Lou a Gretsch Country Gentleman guitar, and booked him in to have lessons in the back room of a local musical instrument store. At his first lesson the instructor tried to show Reed how to pick his way through 'Twinkle, Twinkle, Little Star'. But Reed had other ideas. He rummaged around in his satchel, pulled out a copy of the latest Carl Perkins' single and said, 'Show me how to play this.' The instructor explained that it was only three simple chords, and showed him. It was Reed's first and last guitar lesson, but those three chords would carry him a long way.

In 1954 Reed was deeply affected by the death of his then-favourite musical hero. Twenty-five-year-old black R&B singer Johnny Ace accidentally shot himself in a game of Russian Roulette. Johnny Ace, real name John Alexander, had his first hit in 1952, 'My Song', and followed up with eight more hit singles including 'Please Forgive Me' and 'Never Let Me Go'. It was while playing a holiday show in Houston that during a short break he started playing around with his gun backstage. Ace put a single bullet in the revolver and was messing around when the gun discharged. He died later from his injuries on Christmas Day, and Reed was so shaken he wore a black armband in mourning for weeks afterwards.

By High School, Reed was becoming an avid writer and carried around notebooks of poems and notes. He was better suited to mental rather than physical pursuits. He tried his best to make the school's football team, but as he was quite thin he opted for basketball instead. At the age of thirteen he started having homosexual fantasies, which spilled over to his writing. Childhood friend Allen Hyman recalls that 'Some of his [Reed's] stories and poems were starting to focus on the gay world, there was a lot of that imagery in his poems.' For a conservative middle-class neighbourhood, homosexuality was definitely a taboo subject.

It didn't take much for the bored minds of suburban communities to get worked up about something. What became known as the 'Commager Affair' was one of many examples of rampant McCarthyism across Long Island. Henry Commager was a noted historian who had a school speech cancelled because he was deemed to be 'controversial'. He was just one of countless innocent Americans whose careers were tarred by false accusations of being Un-American. If Reed's homosexual feelings had become common knowledge it's likely he'd have been similarly pilloried. Despite the growing cultural diversity of New York, its suburbs were not a place where you wanted to stand out in the 1950s.

Reed was also exploring the world of cinema. After his parents bought him a motorcycle he would ride around, pretending to be James Dean or Marlon Brando. The emerging cultural image of the American teenager was perfectly timed for Reed, whose reportedly moody behaviour and escalating questioning of authority fit his anti-establishment motor-biking image. Musically, he was interested in the likes of Little Richard, Paul Anka and the staple sounds of 1950s radio.

Reed's appetite for all musical genres covered rock and roll, blues, R&B and Doo Wop vocalisations. He and a cousin often ad-libbed songs at family gatherings. Reed's early musical inspirations included The Ravens, The Diablos, The Cleftones and The Jesters. 'I used to go crazy for records like that, the street group sound,' he admitted. 'My favourite song was Elisha and The Rockways "Why Can't I Be Loved".' When The Velvet Underground had formed, Reed commented on the musical tastes of the late 1960s: 'Everyone's going crazy over the old blues people,' he said, 'but they're forgetting about all those groups like The Spaniels. Records like "Smoke From Your Cigarette" and "I Need A Sunday Kind Of Love", "The Wind" by The Chesters, "Later For You, Baby" by The Solitaires. All those ferocious records that no one seems to listen to anymore are underneath everything we're playing.'

Reed would rush out and spend his allowance as soon as the latest singles were released, and he soon had quite an impressive collection. He set about trying to get together his own band, and by the age of fifteen he'd formed one and named it The Shades. While not exactly a band, he described it thus: 'Just one guitar and two guys singing. I was in the background. I wrote the stuff, I didn't sing it. We would play shopping malls and some really bad violent places.' Bob Shad, an A&R man for Mercury, came across them, and agreed to take them into the studio. The singer was Reed's High School friend Phil Harris, and Reed wrote a handful of tunes including 'So Blue' and 'Leave Her For Me', which were chosen to be used on a single. The former was very typical of its time, saxophone intro, a dramatic spoken-word break in the middle, gang-style harmonies and a simple guitar line. 'So Blue' was almost identical, but a little faster. Both tracks were typical mid-1950s fodder, lots of 'oooh-aaaah' backing vocals reminiscent of the vocal groups that Reed loved so much.

In the studio, Harris allegedly had to stand on a box in order to be able to reach the microphone, but he did a reasonable job of apeing the vocal deliveries he'd heard on the radio. Shad assembled a decent studio band for the session and pulled off something of a coup when he managed to get legendary sax player King Curtis[2] to play on both songs. It's not surprising that his sax work is the highlight of both tracks.

The Shades had to change their name to The Jades to avoid confusion with another band with the same name, and their single was issued in 1957. Though Reed readily admitted he was just copying what he heard on the radio, the single failed to gain much attention. '[local celebrity DJ] Murray the K was going to play it,' deadpanned Reed, 'but he was off sick that day and it never aired.' Reed's first royalty cheque was for just 75 cents. Up against the likes of The Everly Brothers' 'All I Have To Do Is Dream' and The Coasters' 'Yakety Yak', these adolescent musings, while commendable for a first attempt, never really stood a chance. Undaunted, Reed continued writing and practising his guitar work. His favourite player at the time was James Burton, who played in Ricky Nelson's band on the *Ozzie and Harriet* TV show.

His longing to be a rock and roller, his early homosexual leanings and his general rebelling against his parents (knowing that being gay and wanting to be a rock star were at odds with their hopes for his adult life) all built up until Sidney and Toby decided that drastic steps would have to be taken. They were suspicious of rock and roll, and wanted him to take up what they considered to be a respectable job, like an accountant or a doctor.

As homosexuality was very much a taboo subject, it was just not discussed and not understood. Extreme measures were often taken against people suspected to be gay, such as severe beatings. Reed knew that he just had to get away from it all. 'I came from this small town out on Long Island,' he said. 'The most boring place on Earth. The only good thing about it was that you knew you were going to get out of there.' He hatched a plan with Allen Hyman that they should both go to the same college, Syracuse, in upstate New York. Reed biographer Victor Bokris reported that shortly before leaving home he wrote a song called 'You'll Never, Never Love Me', a number that was apparently aimed at his parents, though it's never been released. It was just the first of many songs that have been interpreted as being about his psychiatric treatment.

Though both Hyman and Reed were accepted into Syracuse, Reed changed his mind at the last moment and accepted an invitation to attend New York University in the Bronx instead. The Bronx campus was located close to the clinic where he was undergoing his post-electroshock therapy, so it made sense not to travel the 200 miles to Syracuse. When the therapy was over in the spring of 1960, he quit New York University and enrolled at Syracuse for the following autumn semester.

Many miles away from his parents and Freeport, Syracuse housed around 20,000 students on a 600-acre campus. Studying music, literature and philosophy, he soon adjusted to campus life. Allen Hyman was entering his second year, had a car and was well involved in the social scene, so Reed had a ready-made entry into the campus night life, but he did rebel against his friend's attempts to get him to join Hyman's fraternity. The majority of the students were from wealthy families and destined for well-paid white-collar work as doctors and lawyers. The campus was usually wet, with snow and rain for much of the year, and the architecture was so Gothic-looking that it had been used as the basis for the *Adams Family* mansion. The town of Syracuse was a busy industrial setting, without much time for artists and poets.

Reed managed to hold down a spot presenting a jazz show on the college radio station, but was fired after complaints that his selections (Ornette Coleman, Hank Ballad and James Brown) were just too unorthodox for the conservative student listenership. There was little sign in the singles charts of the cultural and social changes that rock music would bring over the next decade. Both Connie Francis and Brenda Lee had two number one singles each, and the chart-topping Elvis songs were gentle ballads: 'Are You Lonesome Tonight?' and 'It's Now Or Never'.

In his first year at college, Reed began to experiment sexually. He had his first affair with an unnamed male student, though it wasn't consummated, and he was also seeing a girl at the same time. 'I couldn't figure what was wrong,' he admitted. 'I wanted to fix it up and make it okay. I figured if I sat around and thought about it I could straighten it out.' In his second year at Syracuse he met Shelly Albin, who would become his muse for several years to come, and long after they later split up. When he took her home to meet his family for the 1961 holidays, they must have thought his homosexuality had just been a passing phase, or that the electroshock therapy had worked.

For the first two years of college, Reed spent more time on the pretty mid-westerner Albin, drugs (he soon moved on from smoking joints to taking LSD) and music than he ever did his academic studies. His grades were poor and he got into several scrapes over smoking pot on campus, before being eventually put on probation. It wasn't until a new lecturer arrived to take the creative writing classes in the autumn of 1962 that Reed's interest in his college courses was really awoken. It was the poet Delmore Schwartz who had come to Syracuse to take the post.

Like Reed, Schwartz had been born in Brooklyn, but unlike Reed he stayed there while his parents' marriage dissolved. Schwartz's early life scarred him and he went through a series of doomed relationships as he turned increasingly to find comfort in liquor and amphetamines. Through the turmoil of his private life he still managed to build up a reputation as an incredibly gifted young writer. In the late 1930s, his book *In Dreams Begin Responsibilities* was widely praised by the likes of Vladimir Nabakov and T.S. Eliot. It tells of a young man's dream about going to a movie theatre and seeing an old film of his parents' courtship. At the end of the film he thinks his future parents are going to split up and he eventually gets escorted out of the building. The story ends as he wakes from this dream on his 21st birthday. By 1962, Schwartz's stock had fallen after a number of short-lived teaching positions had seen him zig-zag from campus to campus before settling down at Syracuse.

In Dreams Begin Responsibilities had a profound effect on Reed. 'It was really amazing to me,' he recalled. 'To think that you could do that with the simplest words available in such a short span of pages and create something so incredibly power-ful. You could write something like that and not have the greatest vocabulary in the world. I wanted to write that way, simple words to cause an emotion, and put them with my three chords.'

As well as the teacher-student relationship, Schwartz took on a father-figure role to Reed and would often hold court around campus. He would delight the impressionable students by telling stories of the great writers and poets that had influenced him. Schwartz could start drinking with Reed in the morning and when they moved to bars later in the day he would sometimes order five drinks at a time. 'Schwartz was my spiritual godfather,' said Reed. 'He was my teacher and friend. He was the smartest, funniest, saddest person I'd ever met. He had a large scar on his forehead he said he got duelling with Nietzsche. He was the unhappiest man I ever met in my life, and the smartest, until I met Andy Warhol.'

Through his poetry, Schwartz pointed Reed in the right creative direction to the likes of Ginsberg and the other Beats, which helped Reed find his 'voice of the streets', bringing out his ability to tell stories in a simple language. 'That alone made the whole wretched college experience have some value,' claimed Reed. He was also turned on to the writings of William Burroughs and especially his landmark 1959 novel *Naked Lunch*. Reed was inspired by Burroughs' unusual subject matter (the lifestyle of heroin addicts, talking typewriters, time travel and viruses) and juxtaposition of images. 'He could write about everything,' said Reed. 'In some ways his surreal world was much more real than other people's, which is what New York's punks appreciated, along with the risks he took to do it.'

Schwartz saw Reed's potential to be a great poet, but Reed turned his back on a pure writing life and threw himself into his music. While he still loved traditional rock and roll, he was also aware of the folk movement gaining momentum across the universities of the country, and it was this direction that he started to explore. The first band Reed was involved in at Syracuse was an unnamed folk ensemble which did some busking and played at small bars around the campus. As would become apparent in his writing over the next couple of years, Reed was being influenced by the new folk sensation that was sweeping the country. Bob Dylan was changing people's perceptions of what 'pop' music could say, and he was doing it with the simplest of instruments, his acoustic guitar.

Reed didn't sing in the folk band as he was unhappy with his voice, so he played guitar and harmonica instead, just like Dylan. He was writing prodigiously and soon afterwards formed a rock band with old friend Allen Hyman. Using the first initials of their first names, 'Lewis' and 'Allen', they became LA and the Eldorados. Reed was convinced to sing and play guitar, Hyman was the drummer and fellow students Richard Miskin (bass and keyboards), Bobby Newman (saxophone) and Stephen Windheim (guitar) were added to the line-up. They were soon earning over $100 a night at fraternity parties and college dances, playing Chuck Berry covers and the occasional Reed original.

Most of the time Reed seemed to enjoy the spotlight, but his mood swings could also return and he'd decide he didn't want to play. The rest of the band would sometimes have to physically drag him to gigs. He could be obnoxious, and often they'd be banned from returning to the venue, though Reed later offered that this was because they sounded so bad. One night he punched through a glass door just before the show was due to begin. 'Of course he couldn't play,' recalls Richard Mishkin. 'We took him to hospital and there were lots of stitches.'

To get around the bans they would often play under assumed names like Pasha and the Prophets, until someone realised who they were and then they'd have to change names again to keep playing on the circuit the following week. There was a good music scene at Syracuse, with Felix Cavalieri (later of The Young Rascals) and Mike Esposito (later of The Blues Magoos) among their fellow students.

While at college, Reed's fascination with free jazz grew. He would often travel down to New York City to track down where the Ornette Coleman Quartet was playing. Reed couldn't afford the entrance fee so he'd try and grab an aural vantage point at the stage door or by an open window. Coleman's approach to free jazz was something that would be carried through Reed's entire musical career. Reed continues to play 'free' interpretations of his songs and guitar parts to this day, including the 2010 live tour of his 1975 solo effort *Metal Machine Music*.

During this period Reed's own material was taking shape, and he had written a piece called 'The Gift' (it shared a title with one of Delmore Schwartz's poems),[2] which drew on his difficult separation from Shelly Albin in the summer of 1962. She had gone home half-way across the country and he'd write to her almost every day. 'The Gift' would later be recorded as a song by The Velvet Underground and tells of a lovelorn character posting himself to his girlfriend in a box, with a tragic outcome. Reed was reading William Burroughs, Raymond Chandler and Herbert Selby Jnr, a mix of influences that would mesh with his musical tastes and spawn his lyrical output for the next half a century. He also penned 'Fuck Around Blues', 'Coney Island Baby' and 'All Tomorrow's Parties' around this time. The latter two would be recorded and released in the following years.

During a visit to New York he took Shelly into Harlem, where he met a drug dealer at the corner of 125th Street. This trip would become the basis of another song 'Waiting For My Man' (sic), and then he would surpass all of his previous work with a song called 'Heroin'. He didn't realise it, but he'd written what would be seen as two of the most influential songs of his generation.

Chapter 2
1965
We're The Velvet Underground

'Originally we were just jamming around and lived in this unheated apartment and Angus [Maclise] lived in the unheated apartment next door. He had just come back from India. He didn't want to be in a group though, he thought it was fun to play music now and then whenever he felt like it; so Angus couldn't be the drummer, though we were good friends.'

Sterling Morrison

Lou Reed learned much at college that wasn't on the curriculum. He had expanded his experimentations into drugs and sex, his writing had blossomed under the unique tutelage of Delmore Schwartz and he met two other students who would have varying degrees of influence on his musical direction: Sterling Morrison and Jim Tucker.

Holmes Sterling Morrison was born in West Ferry, Long Island on 29 August 1942, and was brought up in a middle-class Catholic family by his mother Ann and step-father William. William was a tough-guy cop and nicknamed 'Wild Bill'. Sterling was the eldest of six children and took the responsibility that his position brought very seriously.

Sterling was taking trumpet lessons by the age of seven, and picking up a guitar when he was 12. This instrumental change-over came after Morrison's trumpet teacher went into the military. 'I floundered until I decided rock and roll was my ruling passion and that I should learn to play the guitar,' recalls Morrison. He soon discovered that he loved the sounds of Chuck Berry and Bo Diddley. He also grew to love the blues, especially T-Bone Walker and Jimmy Reed.

As a responsible older brother he would collect his youngest brothers and sisters from school, but this was at odds with the image he wanted to portray of himself, especially as he went through his mid-teens. Out on Long Island he would listen to all the New York City radio stations and DJs like Alan Freed[1] to absorb a broad musical education, with plenty of black R&B thrown into the mix. 'If my parents had owned a piano then I would have played piano and lived happily ever after as a keyboardist because I like polyphonic music,' said Morrison. 'As soon as I picked up a guitar I knew that was what I wanted to play. That's what you need to play rock and roll for one thing, but also I liked it. I liked being able to play various notes at the same time.' The switch to guitar wasn't a popular choice with his parents, though. 'They always considered it a colossal waste of time and leading me to juvenile delinquency,' recalled Morrison. 'But I was already there so I couldn't blame that on guitar playing. I was a biker type and hung around with nasty black people and nasty white people and black rock 'n' roll music.'

When he was 17 he met Martha Dargan, who he would later marry. 'I heard about him before I met him,' recalls Dargan. 'I was in 10th grade and he was in 12th grade. He was my brother's friend and I used to see him across the street at our High School. He had a terrible black car, very tough and we used to call him "rocky", which meant tough. He wore wrap-around sunglasses and the car had the grill taken out so it looked like a shark. He'd be across the street smoking cigarettes, which was about as bad as it got at our High School.'

When their brother's friends visited the Dargan household, they were picked out by Martha and her sister as potential boyfriends. 'I remember telling my algebra teacher Mr Fisher that I was going to marry Sterling Morrison,' said Martha. 'And I hadn't even got close to him, that was much too scary.'

Morrison would go up to Syracuse to visit a friend from back home, Jim Tucker. Morrison wasn't actually enrolled at Syracuse when he met Lou Reed, but he spent a lot of time around the campus and took classes even though he couldn't get a scholarship. One day he was visiting Tucker, who had a dormroom below Reed, when Morrison heard this 'ear-splitting bagpipe music' coming from above, then he heard a guitar being cranked up. Ever inquisitive, Morrison decided to go upstairs and introduce himself. The two quickly found that they loved a lot of the same music. Soon afterwards Morrison also started attending Delmore Schwartz's[2] classes. 'Delmore was a brilliant poet, but he had a clinical case of paranoia,' said Morrison. 'He thought he was being persecuted by Nelson Rockefeller, and eventually he decided that Lou and I were both Rockefeller's spies.'

'Maybe I'm trapped by certain beliefs, but in the early 1960s, on college campuses, you went one of two ways,' said Sterling Morrison. 'Either you were a very sensitive young person, who cared about air pollution and civil rights and anti-Vietnam, or you were a very insensitive young person, who didn't care about civil rights because all the blacks he knew were playing in his band or in his audience. I was a very insensitive young person and played very insensitive, uncaring music. Which is Wham, Bam, Pow! Let's Rock Out! What I expected my audience to do was tear the house down, beat me up, whatever. Lou and I came from the identical environment of Long Island rock 'n' roll bars, where you can drink anything at 18, everybody had phony proof at 16; I was a night crawler in High School and played some of the sleaziest bars.' But he was still able to get up and take his younger siblings to and from school the next day.

Reed graduated from Syracuse in the summer of 1964 (stories that he was run out of town by the local drug police are most likely little more than myth-making), and then hung around to try his hand at a journalism (Reed: 'They said my writing was biased and that I wasn't objective') and drama course. These didn't take his fancy and he returned to his parents' house on Long Island. On returning home, Reed was immediately called before the draft board, which was choosing candidates to send to south-east Asia and join the US forces fighting in Vietnam. In a stroke of twisted luck for Reed, he went down with hepatitis and was very sick when he went before the board. He also had his previous 'mental' treatments to fall back on, and his interview was over in about 15 minutes. 'I was pronounced mentally unfit,' he said, a decade later.

Reed's parents had wrongly assumed that he would continue his education or take a position at his father's firm. They were shocked and disappointed when he took a position at New York's Pickwick International record label, situated on the western shore of Long Island, just across the river from the famous skyline of Manhattan. This low-budget, high-speed operation revolved around a small team of writers who were required to mimic the latest musical trends of the day and release sound-a-like singles for unknown acts to cash in on the latest fads. Sometimes the label would take a couple of well-known songs and pad them out with average quality filler to be able to sell it as an album in the dollar-bargain-bins.

As The Beatles had just taken America by storm with an appearance on *The Ed Sullivan Show*, and The Rolling Stones had just released their debut album, it was a good idea to rip off some sounds of the British Invasion, and the Pickwick production line did what they were told. According to Reed, 'There were four of us locked in a room and they would say, "Write ten California songs, ten Detroit songs".' The whole set-up was a cut-price attempt to cash in as a second-, or third-class version of the Brill Building. It was writing to order, and once when a customer wanted a song where the main character was killed in the last 30 seconds, Reed penned a tune called 'Let the Wedding Bells Ring'.

'This guy at Pickwick had this idea that I appropriated, because it was such a good idea, which was to tune all the strings on the guitar to the same note,' explained Reed. 'It sounded fantastic. And I was kidding around and I wrote a song doing that. I overloaded the amp and record stations sent it back and thought that there was something wrong with the recording because it was distorted. Can you imagine? I mean, this is all for real. This is not made up.' From then on, Reed would be open to unusual instrumental tunings, feedback and distortion – all factors in the seminal Velvet Underground sound that would follow.

Working at Pickwick was something that Delmore Schwartz would have been appalled by. He hated rock music, and had warned Reed about selling out his ideals. The tenure at Pickwick violated both of these. One night Schwartz had been drunk and Reed was trying to get him home from the bar when Schwartz announced that when he died he would come back and watch Reed closely, and if he sold out he'd haunt him. It was something that Reed took seriously, and was on his mind as he beavered away at the studio. In his brief time at Pickwick, Reed penned upwards of 30 songs of his own and with the other writers. The 1965 LP *Soundsville* included Reed's tune 'Cycle Annie'. That song was listed as being by The Beachnuts, which Reed sang, and he provided The Roughnecks' 'You're Driving Me Insane' on Pickwick's *Out Of Sight* album. These were all songs that had nothing to do with the kind of material he'd soon be writing for himself.

As well as recording their own crude songs, the writers were required to write material for other artists. Reed soon penned numbers for Roberta Williams ('Tell Mama Not to Cry') and The Intimates ('I've Got A Tiger in My Tank'). The $25-a-week job not only meant that Reed didn't have to work at his father's accountancy firm, but it was also providing him with a valid link into the music business, even if it wasn't the way he'd imagined it. If nothing else it was helping Reed attune his song-writing skills. The ability to turn out different styles in a short space of time sharpened his lyrics. 'I really liked doing it. It was really fun,' said Reed. 'But I wasn't doing the stuff I wanted to do.' He found an unlikely path towards doing what he wanted through a song he wrote called 'The Ostrich'.

Reed had noticed that ostrich feathers were in vogue in ladies' fashion magazines, so he jumped on the craze and wrote a song about a fictional dance called the ostrich. Loosely based on a theme like 'The Twist', the production and overall sound echoed Phil Spector's wall-of-sound – though sadly the quality of the song didn't. The vocal style is unmistakably Lou Reed, and he hypes the tune during the intro claiming that, 'We've got something new to show you, it's going to knock you dead', while the initial melody is reminiscent of 'And Then He Kissed Me'. A b-side, 'Sneaky Pete', which included ear-splitting high-pitched gang-style backing vocals, was rushed out so a single could be issued. Despite 'The Ostrich''s limitations, Pickwick decided it was the most promising of Reed's songs. As soon as the label thought it had an outside chance of being a hit, they wanted to hastily assemble a band to play some live shows under the manufactured band name of The Primitives. As the writer, Reed was chosen to be the singer, and fellow staffer Terry Phillips was included, along with a couple of his friends who had nothing to do with Pickwick: Tony Conrad and John Cale.

Conrad shared an apartment on Ludlow Street in Manhattan with Cale, and the two had been invited to a party, where they met Reed and the others from Pickwick. Talk turned to The Primitives and the need for a few more faces to fill out the line-up. 'We both had long hair and some guy approached us and told us we looked very commercial,' recalls Cale. 'He said would we like to meet this band called The Primitives.' Both Conrad and Cale accepted the invitation to be involved, even though they didn't really know what was required. They agreed to go to Pickwick later that week to talk things over. Walter De Maria came in as a temporary drummer. His drumming career was short-lived and he later became a well-known sculptor. 'We had a meeting in their warehouse and recording studio,' said Conrad. 'The studio was a cement basement room with an old Ampex tape machine in it.' Cale and Conrad listened to 'The Ostrich' and agreed to play in the band to promote the single at a couple of high schools. 'John was really impressed with Lou because he was struck by his ability to improvise rock and roll,' remembers Conrad. 'After a while the record wasn't going to break. We'd play the two numbers, "The Ostrich" and "Sneaky Pete". It was really terrible.' Reed eventually had had enough and quit Pickwick in February 1965, but he kept in touch with Cale. Soon afterwards, Conrad moved out of the Ludlow Street loft and Cale invited Reed to take over rent of the spare room. It was the start of what would be a ground-breaking musical partnership.

John Davies Cale was born a million cultural miles away from New York. He arrived into the world on 9 March 1942, a week after Lou Reed, in Garnant, South Wales. This was during the darkest hour of the Second World War. The United Kingdom was under sustained German air attack. The village was predominantly a mining settlement on the banks of the River Amman, 50 miles from Cardiff. Cale's first language was Welsh, English only came second when he started being taught it at school from the age of seven.

Cale's maternal grandmother lived with his family, and gave his mother a rough time because she'd married an Englishman, and refused to have English spoken in the house. Like most of the men in the village, Cale's father, William, worked in the coal mine while his mother, Margaret, was a school teacher at the local primary school. 'I was her only child,' said Cale. 'She made me her career for the next 20 years. My mother was very careful about showing me that you always had to look behind what people were doing and not take it at face value. My father was a very quiet man, I learned patience from him.' But little else. Cale wrote in 1999 that, 'I feel he did not play the role of a father, and I know nothing about him. I don't know where he came from, I have no photographs.'

Along with English lessons at the age of seven, Cale was forced to take piano lessons (and piano exams four times a year), but he just wanted to go outside and play like any other child. When he got to the age of 11, his mother told him he didn't have to take the lessons anymore, he would have to concentrate on schoolwork instead. While he had complained about the music lessons, he went into outright rebellion against the enforced extra schoolwork. It was out of the frying pan and into the fire.

Cale had strong facial features and grew into a tall, gangly youth. Socially he was kept to a strict regime of schoolwork and family life, and he had few friends of his own age. He still played the piano when he was not hard at work studying. He was musically talented and he'd jotted down a few short piano pieces of his own. One day a couple of researchers arrived at Cale's school from BBC Wales radio looking for talented children, and his teacher pointed out Cale. He played a piece called 'Toccata' in the style of Khachaturian. The researchers were impressed. He'd written the score on a scrap of paper, which the two men took away. A few weeks later they returned and asked to record Cale playing his music, but they had lost the score. Cale could remember part of the piece so he started playing and improvised his way through the two-and-a-half minutes. He later said that this single event changed his life. He hadn't realised improvisation could be so easy. From then on, it was all he wanted to do.

At Ammanford Grammar School Cale acquired a hunger for knowledge. He would go in as early as possible and soak up as much as he could. Having few friends meant he threw himself into music and study, and he excelled at both; playing the organ in church on Sundays and taking up the viola at school. For sport he took up long-distance running and seemed to enjoy the solitude. Cale's often lonesome formative years may owe more than a little to his relationship with his father. 'He did not show me how to be sociable,' said Cale. 'I ended up designing a covert life.'

At the age of 13 he was invited to join the Welsh Youth Orchestra as their violist. He had been playing in a string quartet, but joining the orchestra provided him with the first opportunity to really bond with children of his own age. When the group toured during the summer months it was the first chance that Cale had had to get away from home. Usually they played concerts around Wales but also took longer trips to Holland.

Though classical music was the staple of his life, Cale was inspired by hearing rock and roll on the radio, and he dreamed of going to New York. Little did he know it but he was listening to the same presenters as Lou Reed and Sterling Morrison. 'I heard it on Radio Luxembourg, from about 1954,' he recalls. 'Every Friday night at seven. Alan Freed played all the Top Ten hits from America. Little Richard, Elvis, it was great.'

When he reached college age Cale opted to study in London, but only as a stepping-stone to be able to cross the Atlantic. He'd already sent off for the prospecti of Harvard and Yale. In the autumn of 1960 he enrolled at Goldsmith's Teachers College in south-east London. He had no intention of becoming a teacher, but attending the college allowed him to take classes in musical composition and debate philosophy with his lecturers.

On graduation he had applied to Tanglewood College in Boston, Massachusetts. The college was set in an impressive campus with landscaped views designed to be inspirational to young artists. Cale was interviewed for a scholarship there by none other than the famous American composer Aaron Copland, who was visiting London. As soon as Cale had his letter of acceptance from Copland he was waiting in line at the US Embassy in Grosvenor Square to get a Green Card and an entrance to the United States. Within days of his passing-out ceremony at Goldsmith's, Cale was saying goodbye to his parents and flying across the Atlantic.

Cale was set to embark on the summer compositional masterclass run by Yannis Xenakis.[3] Xenakis, the Romanian-born, Greek-French composer was best known for his use of mathematical probabilities relating to the recurrence of notes and rhythms. His *Métastasis* (1954), *Pithoprakta* (1957) and *Achorripsis* (1958) gained him wide acclaim in avant-garde circles. Cale notes that Xenakis was the most important person he met at Tanglewood. He gave lectures about probability theory and composed mathematically based music, which Cale found hard to play.

To end the course, Cale was allowed to perform one of his own pieces. During his piano recital he suddenly jumped up and smashed an axe into a table at the centre of the stage. It caused a shock, it caused a reaction; that was exactly what he wanted. Later in New York he would find that this was a stereotypical piece of Fluxus art.

Fluxus art was often based around an event or happening, and was art for art's sake, with no hint of commercialisation. Fluxus member Al Hansen[4] took it to the extreme when he performed his classic 'piano drop'. The entire piece would consist of his pushing a grand piano from the roof of a tall building. The music of the piece was provided by the sound made by the crashing instrument, the splintering wood, the breaking keys and the strings snapping and hitting against each other.

In the early autumn of 1963, Cale headed to New York. This

was always the centre of the America that he was drawn to, from the earliest days of listening to the radio back in Garnant. 'If you're sheltered, your life via the radio becomes one of imagination,' said Cale. 'Sunday jazz, Radio Moscow: that's how I found out about the Beats, Lenny Bruce and the beehive of activity that was Manhattan.' Once there, he soon hooked up with John Cage, who he'd previously corresponded with and garnered encouraging responses. They embarked on an 18-hour piano marathon, playing a piece by Erik Satie 840 times in a row.[5]

After sleeping on fellow students' couches for a while, he began looking for an apartment of his own. To pay his deposit, he cashed in the return part of his flight ticket and took an apartment on Lispenard Street, just south of Canal Street in lower Manhattan. He was in America for the foreseeable future as he had no means of buying another ticket to get home and soon found a job at a local bookstore to pay the rent, and then set out to track down another of his musical heroes, LaMonte Young, whose work he had performed back at Goldsmith's. Cale was invited to join Young's 'Theatre of Eternal Music' and set about practising being able to hold a note on his viola for as long as possible. The classical and the avant-garde had truly met.

LaMonte Young was a 29-year-old composer in 1964. He'd studied at Los Angeles City College, and had played saxophone with Ornette Coleman and Don Cherry, among others. It was a period of studying electronic music under Karl-Heinz Stockhausen that changed his attitudes though, and he became primarily a composer of experimental music, often incorporating Asian music. He radically used drones in his work and also gave performers unusual instructions rather than standard musical notation to read. One score pointed out that the performer should release a butterfly during the recital, in another the performer was told to build a fire. Billy Name, an associate of Andy Warhol, later commented 'LaMonte Young was the best drug connection in New York. When you went over to LaMonte and Marian's [his wife] place, you were there for a minimum of seven hours.' No doubt some of the musical ideas were concocted during these marathon sessions. It was here that Cale was first introduced to marijuana. 'There was a lot of smoking, a lot of smiling, a lot of nodding heads,' he recalls. 'Nobody understood a word I said because of my Welsh accent.'

Another member of the group was violinist Tony Conrad. Conrad was a 24-year-old Harvard graduate, his mathematical background perfectly suited the drone music that the group would produce. When Conrad's roommate moved out, Cale moved in. The location was 53 Ludlow Street on the Lower East Side. It was a rough-and-ready neighbourhood, populated by immigrants and bohemians all looking for cheap digs. The apartment was ideal financially, but lacked its own bathroom and had no heating or electricity. A series of connecting leads took the power they needed from an adjoining dwelling. Ludlow Street would be featured on the sleeve of The Beastie Boys album *Paul's Boutique*. The fold-out cover showed all four streets at the intersection with Rivington Street.[6]

Cale and Conrad spent their time working up material for an offshoot of the Theatre of Eternal Music called the Dream Syndicate, and listening to the radio. Conrad pointed out not using a musical score was a way of offering classical music the chance to dispense with 'compositional authoritarianism' and allow an improvisational collaboration, which was the basis of free-jazz. 'Our "Dream Music" was an effort to freeze the sound in action,' he explained. 'To listen around inside the innermost architecture of the sound itself. It had something to do with composition, since it became a commentary on the temporal site of the composer, in relation to the sound itself.' Despite the artistic merit of this work, Cale knew it wouldn't pay his bills. 'Doing these long pieces isn't going to get you out of your problems,' he thought, and decided to set about learning to write songs.

So while Lyndon Johnson was being elected President, a year after the assassination of John F. Kennedy, Cale and Conrad met Reed via the Pickwick International. After the demise of The Primitives they decided that they could make other music together, not just pre-packaged pop. By now Reed had a handful of songs, some dating back to his Syracuse days, that weren't Pickwick material by a long shot. He tried to get Cale to sit and listen to them, but Cale wasn't interested because they were on acoustic guitar, which he hated. He hated Bob Dylan, Joan Baez and the whole folk movement. 'Every song was a fucking question!' Cale roared. He wanted answers, not questions; he wanted songs to say something real.

Eventually Reed wore Cale down. The Welshman relented and agreed to sit through Reed's acoustic songs, but he wasn't expecting to like them. His opinion of straight folk songs remained, but he was impressed by the words that Reed had constructed. The lyrics were literate but simple and hard-edged, an unusual combination and miles away from what was going on in popular music at the time. 'The first time Lou played me "Heroin",' recalls Cale, 'it totally knocked me out.' Reed also played Cale 'I'm Waiting For The Man', 'All Tomorrow's Parties', 'Wrap Your Troubles In Dreams', 'Prominent Men' and a new song called 'Venus In Furs'. Cale was so impressed that he agreed to sit down and work on some new arrangements with Reed. He immediately added his viola to grate against Reed's guitar, giving the songs a newly intimidating feel. Cale had removed the bridge from his instrument which meant he could bow across several strings at the same time and make a great deal of noise when it was amplified. When Cale realised that Reed had tuned all of his guitar strings to the same note at Pickwick, he was impressed. That was exactly what they'd been doing with the Theatre of Eternal Music. Reed wanted to explore his sometimes risqué lyrical ideas, while Cale was keen to explore the music and his curiosity about how classical and pop music could be fused together. Finally Cale had found someone who could work with him in the spirit of New York.

Chapter 3
1965
Prominent Men

*'As soon as The Beatles hit we were completely flabbergasted.
I was, Wow, I missed out on all of that. And then I met Lou.
There was this literary bent at the basis of all of it, plus, with
all the drugs that were going on, Lou and I really understood
[each other].'*

John Cale

Soon after starting a daily work schedule on the new songs
with John Cale, Lou Reed bumped into Sterling Morrison
on a subway train. The two hadn't seen each other since
Reed left Syracuse, and in the meantime Morrison had been
jumping from place to place. After a year or so hanging around
at Syracuse he'd skipped to Albany, where he spent some time
selling vacuum cleaners while he figured out what he wanted
to do with his life. Next stop was Illinois, where a friend of
his was at college. Another year in the Midwest was spent
sleeping on the floor in an attic for minimal rent and washing
dishes for spending money. When he eventually decided to
study English, he enrolled at Manhattan's City College along

with Martha Dargan's brother, with whom he shared an apartment on West 84th Street. By now he was going out with Martha
and had developed into a self-taught guitar player. 'I was going
to art school on Long Island and would go into the city to see
him at weekends,' recalls Dargan. 'It was the party place on
weekends for us girls.'

During the brief Subway meeting, Reed suggested that
Morrison bring his guitar along to Cale's loft and join in a jam
session. Initially Morrison and Cale didn't get along, but once
the mutual mistrust had evaporated they worked well together.
'At first he did not like or trust me,' wrote Cale in his
autobiography, *What's Welsh For Zen*, in 1999. 'He had such a
chip on his shoulder. I didn't know what his problem was.'

Morrison is sometimes mistakenly overlooked within the trio
that also comprised Cale and Reed. His meticulous playing and
incisive mind gave the group valuable insights into what a tune
required, and his expert playing would provide it. Cale and
Morrison also spent time working on material outside of the
group setting. Both had inquisitive minds and wanted to push
the limits of what was sonically possible. The majority of this was
too extreme for Velvet Underground consideration and anyway,
lyrics would have spoilt the aural experimentations of repetitive
drones and simple recurring themes. 'Stainless Steel Gamelan'
was one such piece and sounded like an improvised steam train's
bell being carried along on a bed of droning guitars – for ten and
a half minutes.

By the mid-1960s, rock bands were taking over, and usually
wore some kind of costume or uniform to make themselves more
entertaining and fashionable. Paul Revere and the Raiders wore
costumes of the American Revolution; The Yardbirds, The

Monkees and The Animals all dressed the same. The loose ensemble at the Ludlow Street loft were on the outside looking in. 'In 1965 the pop music scene was going to go without us,' recalls Morrison. 'John had no pop involvement whatsoever, and Lou and I had given up. It was impossible. The bands all had matching suits and dance routines, it was a very cosmetic time. So we said, "Well, we don't have matching suits and it's very unlikely we'll be able to work out these dance routines, so I guess we've had it." So Lou, John and I, having concluded that we'd had it, were free to pursue anything we wanted.' That's exactly what they did, and the basic acoustic songs that Reed had written began twisting into something quite different.

It was a slow process, though. Day by day they practised and refined the songs, but during this time they had virtually no money to live on. They survived by eating oatmeal and giving blood for a small fee. They also posed for pictures for cheap tabloid newspapers. 'My picture came out and it said I was a sex maniac killer that had killed 14 children and tape-recorded it and played it in a barn in Kansas at midnight,' recalls Reed. 'When John's picture came out in the paper it said he had killed his lover because his lover was going to marry his sister and he didn't want his sister to marry a fag.' Other income arrived from busking, sometimes at 125th Street and Broadway. Then they decided it might be a good idea to get a drummer. 'We had one theory that said that all bands tend to sound alike because all the drumming is alike,' remembers Sterling Morrison. 'We said our drumming is not going to be like anyone else's.'

Whereas Lou Reed and Sterling Morrison had rock and roll and the blues at heart respectively, and John Cale brought an avant-garde, classical slant to the sessions, the real wild card was the free-spirited drummer Angus Maclise. Maclise lived in an apartment down the hall from Cale and shared some of the Welshman's musical sensibilities. 'Angus was the most rabidly artistic of us all,' recalled Morrison. 'It wasn't long then before I met Piero Heliczer and learned what the underground film scene was about, the things we did changed the direction of my life.'

Maclise was a Connecticut native, four years older than Cale, who had undertaken an eclectic series of musical training regimes throughout his life. From Haitian drumming at the age of seven, through three years at the Dolmetsch School in Surrey, England, where he studied Medieval European Dance Music, to a decade of practising Latin drumming and Jazz technique at the Buddy Rich School before he landed with the Queens Symphony Orchestra in the mid-1950s.

But drumming was far from Maclise's only artistic output. He was friends with Piero Heliczer, the Italian poet and filmmaker. The pair formed the Dead Language Press, which published Maclise's early poetry. These publications gained him a critical fan base, which included the highly influential underground composer LaMonte Young and the members of the left-field Fluxus art movement.

Sometimes Maclise and Young would play live music in front of projected films, often at a sympathetic venue called the Filmmakers Cinematheque on Lafayette Street. Maclise was now living on Ludlow Street and rehearsals would take place in his unheated apartment. 'When Angus played the bongos it was just like poetry,' said Piero Heliczer. A neighbour, Marian Zazeela, joined the group (and later married Maclise), as did guitarist Billy Name. The music they played was described as 'Indian Drone Music'. At one of the multi-media shows, Tony Conrad was present, joined the group soon afterwards and they took the name Theatre of Eternal Music. When Name left, he was replaced by another Ludlow Street resident, John Cale. Cale soon found that he was doing more than just musical experimentation with Reed. 'Before I met Lou, I had snorted, smoked and swallowed the best drugs in New York, courtesy of LaMonte, but I had never injected anything,' wrote Cale in his autobiography. 'Now dime and nickel bags of heroin were added to the menu.' Cale couldn't bring himself to place the needle in his own arm, so Reed took care of it. Cale's first reaction was to throw up.

While playing with the band, Maclise was also working on other projects. In 1964 he wrote a film score for *Chumlum* by Ron Rice. Most of this was recorded with Maclise playing a strange instrument – a cembalum. It was a stringed instrument, which was played with sticks. This was not his only film work, as he later provided the music for films by the likes of Warhol associates Gerard Malanga and Jonas Mekas.

Maclise drifted from project to project, and generally had a peripatetic nature. After trips to London and Paris, he set off for India. When he returned, Reed and Cale were living on Ludlow Street and Sterling Morrison was jamming with them at ad-hoc rehearsals. Of course they didn't have a drummer, so Maclise agreed to play with the group. On his return he also immediately set to work on another multi-media show with Piero Heliczer at the Filmmakers' Cinématèque called *The Launching of The Dream Weapon*. Unlike the earlier Theatre of Eternal Music, this show upped the ante by adding dancers and poetry to the film and light shows that accompanied the music. The music was provided by the new quartet of Reed, Cale, Morrison and Maclise. Initially they didn't have a name, but through the early summer of 1965 they played other shows under various names, which included The Warlocks and The Falling Spikes. Maclise would play whatever and whenever he wanted. Once he arrived half an hour late for a performance so he stayed behind and played by himself for half an hour after the rest of the band had departed.

'If you told Angus there was a rehearsal at two o'clock on Friday, he wouldn't understand what you were talking about,' recalled John Cale. 'He would just come and go, wherever and whenever he pleased. The music was very different from what people later heard. It had a Beat-poet quality, these interesting pitter and patter rhythmic patterns behind the drone.'

It was Maclise who came up with the final name for the band when he found an old paperback book called *The Velvet Underground* at Tony Conrad's apartment. The book, by Michael Leigh, showed whips and leather boots on the cover and the blurb claimed, 'Here is an incredible book. It will shock and amaze you. But as a documentary on the sexual corruption of our age, it is a must for every thinking adult.' Sterling Morrison was less than overwhelmed by the hype. 'It was about wife swapping in suburbia,' he deadpanned. The text itself within the book didn't bother the band, they just liked the title.[1] They considered themselves part of New York's underground film-making clique rather than the world of rock and roll, and they wanted to have the word 'underground' in their name, so that was that.

'We said, "That's nice",' recalls Morrison about the band name. 'It's abstract and the word underground meant something, and so we said sure, why not? – never figuring we would rise above our particular little echelon at the time, so that was fun. It was outrageous: the only people playing in New York City at the time were ourselves and The Fugs. We were lurking around the old Cinémathèque living in the Lower East Side with around $25 a month combined.'

The Fugs have, in hindsight, been credited as the folk version of The Velvet Underground, combining Bluegrass, country and folk. They began playing galleries and clubs during the early part of 1965, playing at the opening party for the new location of Izzy Young's Folklore Center on 6th Avenue and having Andy Warhol visit their shows.

With a drummer on board, a band name they all liked and no money at all, they decided to make a demo tape in July 1965 to see if they could get any interest and maybe some cash. 'We all roomed together at one point,' said Sterling Morrison. 'That was the best, we could write faster.' Using the old tape deck that Tony Conrad had left behind when he vacated the Ludlow Street loft, they laid down various versions of six songs, four of which would later be recorded for the debut Velvet Underground album. As was his wont, Angus Maclise was missing the day that they recorded the demo tape, so the other three went ahead without a drummer.

The first song on the tape, 'Venus In Furs', was a million miles from the powerful version that would later be recorded for the album. The initial arrangement used only acoustic guitars and was sung by John Cale, not Lou Reed. Opening with the memorable couplet 'Shiny, shiny, shiny boots of leather/Whiplash girl-child in the dark', this song would become embroiled in the Velvet's mythological standing as some kind of sexually deviant band. The effect was a slow, medieval-sounding track that reminds the listener of some ancient strolling minstrel, maybe the sound of a lyre. This nebulous arrangement strangely fits with the lithe lyric, which told the S&M story of the dominatrix, her slave Severin and the black prince, taken from the book of the same name. 'Taste the whip, now bleed for me' was not the kind of lyric you would hear on the radio in 1965, where 'Ticket To Ride' and 'My Girl' were topping the charts.

Reed took over the vocal duties for 'Prominent Men', which was the kind of song that Cale had long despised. Basically a Bob Dylan pastiche, Reed sang in an unusual nasal style and even threw in a folksy harmonica to add to the protest-singer feel. The lone acoustic guitar accompanies the Reed/Cale vocals on the chorus, which claims: 'Prominent men tell prominent lies', before another blast of Dylanesque harmonica. Not surprisingly, the song was soon dropped from their repertoire.

Reed's writing was not sensationalistic at all, and he generally kept away from the usual teenage preoccupations of the pop charts. 'I'm Waiting For The Man' took listeners down to the gritty New York Streets. Not Fifth Avenue, but up to Harlem and the intersection of Lexington Avenue and 125th Street. It's a location that Reed later admitted he had really used to score drugs for himself. This wasn't a subject that he himself thought would be that shocking and he didn't understand what all the fuss was all about. He rightly argued that if he had been writing a novel rather than a rock song, no one would have batted an eyelid as he took the listeners back to his apartment to see him shoot-up with 'Heroin'. John Cale neatly summed up 'Heroin' by saying, 'It was about a tough social situation – and it wasn't sorry for itself.'

This lack of self-pity and the reportage nature of the vocal delivery made the song even more shocking. It didn't necessarily promote or attack the use of drugs, it told the story of what happened when you shoot up. The early version of 'Heroin' has a similar arrangement to the final one. Overall it's only the lo-fi nature of the recording environment that causes any significant differences. It's also the first song on the tape to feature John Cale's viola, which teases the song along a strange and haunting path. 'I'm Waiting For The Man' allowed Sterling Morrison to show off some of his best blues licks and give the song a completely different feel to the recorded version. Reed used a nasal vocal unlike his usual delivery and seemed to indicate he was more influenced by Bob Dylan at the time than he would later admit. Lyrically, it was complete.

'Wrap Your Troubles In Dreams' did have some rudimentary percussion as one of the trio sounds as if he is slowly and deliberately hitting a nail with a hammer. John Cale takes the vocal duties (which Nico would handle later, and record for her own debut solo album, before the song was dropped from The Velvet Underground's set list). It's a slow, dour effort and wasn't a great loss when the band chose not to record it for their first record.

'All Tomorrow's Parties', which, again, was later sung by Nico, is here sung by Lou Reed with strong backing vocals from John Cale. One arrangement here was an almost-jaunty, fast-paced take that sounded like a George Formby song. Other takes on the demo tape are slower and more restrained, showing that the band was still experimenting with how their new songs should be best presented.

Numerous takes of each song were included on a 90-minute cassette that they assembled to try and gain some interest. It's rumoured that a copy found its way to The Rolling Stone's manager Andrew Loog Oldham, but that avenue led nowhere. After these demos, Morrison and Cale talked Reed into taking over the majority of lead vocal duties because his voice and delivery better suited the material, especially when he shunned the Dylan-styling of the acoustic numbers.

One song that seems to have been lost forever and included Maclise was the intriguingly titled 'Never Get Emotionally Involved with Man, Woman, Beast or Child'. Moe Tucker confirms it was recorded in the summer of 1965, but it has yet to see the light of day.

'When Angus Maclise was around I remember sitting at the apartment one night when Sterling learned to play "Green Onions",' said Martha Dargan. 'They were getting together a business called The Flower Barrel to make some money while going to college. I remember them playing at the Village Gate with Angus, that was much zanier and far out. They were playing real Velvet Underground songs to a small, half-filled auditorium on a Sunday afternoon.'

Eventually the band got the chance to be paid to play a gig and earn some money after months of living in semi-poverty. The proposed show was arranged by journalist Al Aronowitz, who asked them to play at a High School in Summit, New Jersey, with a couple of other bands: 40 Fingers and the Myddle Class. This simple change of fortune actually led to the break-up of the original line-up. Angus Maclise, true to his art-for-art's-sake roots, reacted by saying, 'You mean we start when they tell us to and we have to end when they tell us to? I can't work that way!' He announced that even though the payment would be just $75 to be split four ways, he'd rather quit the band. Which he did.

To fulfil the show they needed a replacement, and fast. With just days to go, Sterling Morrison remembered that his friend from Syracuse, Jim Tucker, had a younger sister who played drums and had been in an all-girl group. Her name was Maureen 'Moe' Tucker. She was a couple of years younger than Cale and Reed, having been born in Jackson Heights on 26 August 1944. Her parents, James (a house painter) and Margaret (a clerical worker), had brought up a middle-class Catholic family.

Moe doesn't recall there being much music around the house while she was growing up. The first record she can remember buying is 'Smoke Gets in Your Eyes' by The Platters. Hearing the African beats of Olatunji formed the desire in her to be a musician, she revealed. 'That's what got me more tuned in to rhythm and percussion, but the music of Bo Diddley and the Stones was what got me actually wanting to play drums. I never really went to rock and roll shows. I saw Bo Diddley, of course: he was playing about 40 miles away, I had to go. That was about 1963. I've seen The Stones. But I don't go to concerts – it's too much trouble and it never sounds good.'

She would often listen to WINS at night, and was especially fond of Murray 'The K' Kaufman's *Swinging Soiree* show. He took over from Alan Freed, and similarly, was a champion of black and Latin artists. From 1958 to 1965 he was king of the New York airwaves and thus a powerful figure in the music business. Kaufman was a massive boost to The Beatles' stateside assault in 1964, broadcasting from their hotel room and hosting their show at Carnegie Hall.

'Murray the K was the biggest DJ in New York,' said Moe Tucker. 'He used to open and close his show with this African music and it was always the same song. Every time I'd catch it, I'd say, "Oh man, this is great!" But he never said who it was. It was really frustrating. One night he mentioned it for some reason: "That was Olatunji 'Drums of Passion'." So I ran out and got it the next day. In 1962, I was in the High School library when an announcement came over. "Anyone who would like to sell candy to help pay for an African drummer named Olatunji to come to assembly to play, please go to the office." So I ran to the office for that. So, in our silly little Levittown, Long Island school, we got Olatunji and his full troop with 10 or 12 musicians and 10 or 12 dancers. It was just stunning. I've loved him for a long time. I asked the teacher for the next class after the assembly if I could get a pass so I could find him and get his autograph. She did let me go and I got an autographed picture, which I still have on my bulletin board here.'

Olatunji's 1960 album *Drums of Passion* has now sold five million copies worldwide and influenced countless drummers. The Nigerian percussionist produced simple, but highly effective beats to accompany his chants and has now become a cornerstone of what Western listeners call 'world music'.

Tucker started playing drums in 1963. 'I had one snare drum,' she recalls. 'One day my mum came home from work with a second-hand drum kit, which was a complete piece of garbage, but I was delighted. I played along to the chart stuff of the time, which was good stuff back then: The Stones, The Beatles, Bo Diddley . . .' At first, she didn't have much money to spend on records so she just bought the ones she wanted to play along with. 'I was just having fun, I wasn't thinking I wanted to be a drummer,' she explains. 'I loved the music so much it wasn't enough just to listen.'

Eventually the love of playing led to joining a band with some work colleagues. This three-piece band gigged under the name of The Intruders, mainly belting out Beatles' and Chuck Berry covers. It was far from a glamorous introduction to the world of rock and roll. In fact, the night after playing a Long Island bar, the drummer of the next band was shot by a stray bullet.

'I played in a cover band for a couple of months,' she recalled. 'We practised, practised, practised and then played one show at a Long Island bar. The lead singer was very hard to deal with and the band just sort of fell apart.' Though Jim Tucker had kept her updated with the bands of Sterling and Reed, Tucker had never heard them play. So when she heard they needed a drummer she was nervous because she really wanted to join them, even though she didn't know what she'd be letting herself in for.

Like Maclise, Tucker was an esoteric drummer and pretty much self-taught. At Morrison's suggestion, Reed travelled out to Long Island to give her an impromptu audition for the gig. 'I had known Sterling since I was 12,' recalls Tucker. 'I was 19 at the time, living at home and keying stuff into computers.' She was also planning to attend Nassau Community College on Long Island and played a little bit of guitar, but practising her unorthodox drumming took up a lot of her free time. 'I was just playing drums very nicely in my room with no intention of making a career of music, no intention at all,' she continued. 'The opportunity came up to play with them and sure, what the hell? This'll be fun.'

Tucker had also previously met Reed when he dropped by to pick up Jim. Moe had a few days' warning that Reed would be coming over to hear her play. She knew the band was desperate for a drummer, but not so desperate that they'd take someone who couldn't keep time.

Reed asked her to play a couple of songs and was impressed with her drumming. He asked her to join the band, initially for just the one show.

'I always play standing up because I can then get that style and sound I want. If you're sitting, you can't use the bass drum as a cymbal,' explained Tucker. 'You ride along on the bass drum very often. When I was first playing with the Velvets we did a lot of improvising as opposed to structured songs and I always hated cymbals. There are so many drummers who are technically much better than I'll ever be, but they're just so damn busy. I always think that the drummer's just supposed to keep time – that's basically it. Before the show I went into the city a couple of times to practise so I could actually hear the songs.'

The show that Tucker had been drafted in for also had the local band, The Myddle Class, on the line-up. The Myddle Class were an energetic garage band who had demoed songs that were later recorded by The Monkees' session musicians.

This time organiser Aronowitz had chosen a triple bill, with The Velvet Underground as the middle slot. Aronowitz had made a name for himself through his columns in the *New York Post* and *Village Voice* as he interviewed everyone who was anyone. He was well connected with the big names of the day and would let stars such as Brian Jones and Carole King come and stay at his New Jersey house if they wanted to escape the bright lights of the big city.

Aronowitz was taking something of a gamble to book The Velvet Underground, a band whom no one had ever heard of, with a drummer who had hardly had a chance to practise with the rest of them. During their career the band played at some strange venues. This trend seems to have been set from their very first gig under the name The Velvet Underground, playing at a High School gymnasium. Thirty miles west of Manhattan, and in a sleepy little suburban town (much like the ones Reed et al. had grown up in) was how they started out on 11 December 1965 at 125 Kent Place Boulevard.

The evening began at 8pm, and at $2.50 a ticket The Myddle Class had a good local following and so they headlined, while the exotic newcomers from New York, the Velvets, were placed second on the three-band bill. Of course no one knew what to expect. 'At Summit we opened with "There She Goes Again", then played "Venus In Furs" and ended with "Heroin,"' recalled

Sterling Morrison. 'The murmur of surprise that greeted our appearance as the curtain went up increased to a roar of disbelief once we started to play "Venus" and swelled to a mighty howl of outrage and bewilderment by the end of "Heroin".'

Indeed, as the curtain was raised the kids in the audience, many of whom had parents accompanying them to the show, were shocked. The Velvets all wore black, Cale and Reed were wearing shades, the drummer played standing up – and was it a boy or a girl? Cale's frenzy at his viola was not what a middle-of-the-road pop crowd was expecting. Before 'Heroin' was finished many of the crowd had left. 'I remember that my drums basically fell apart during our three-song set,' recalled Tucker. 'One item broke per song. I don't remember what broke exactly, probably the snare stand became loose and I couldn't make it tighten anymore, or the bass drum leg fell out.'

Tucker recalled that, because of her crumbling drum kit, they were lucky to only be playing three songs. 'The audience didn't like us,' she revealed. 'They were there [to see] the local heart-throb kid and had no desire to listen to us. We never planned our appearance, we just wore what we wanted – we never sat down and said, "Let's all wear black." So our image was probably there from that first show.'

As they left the stage the Velvets were confronted by irate members of The Myddle Class, who had just lost half of their audience. Cale apologised on behalf of the rest of the band, but Al Aronowitz wasn't disappointed at all. 'You gave them a night to remember,' he remarked. In fact, he was quite taken by the band and soon offered them more work, this time at Café Bizarre in New York City. Despite only thinking she'd be in the band for a single show, Moe Tucker was asked to continue at the upcoming Café Bizarre shows that were pencilled in to begin just days later.

'I was in New Jersey the first night,' recalls Martha Dargan. 'I remember standing in the parking lot after the show [when] someone asked Lou for his autograph and I said: "Woo! Lou, your first autograph!" And he got mad at me because he was supposed to be cool.'

To play a series of shows in New York the band needed to prepare more finished material, and fast. But the band members never took drugs to inspire the songwriting: they would take amphetamines to keep working, but not psychedelics. 'We needed more of our own material so we sat around and worked,' said Sterling Morrison. 'I remember we had the Christmas tree up, but no decorations on it. That's when we wrote "Run, Run, Run".' Cale and Reed also worked up an experimental piece called the 'Black Angel's Death Song' and they practised a few cover versions, including Chuck Berry's 'Little Queenie' and Jimmy Reed's 'Bright Lights, Big City' to pad out a longer set list.

'We ended up at a terrible coffee house, working six sets a night, seven nights a week, five dollars a man a night,' recalled Lou Reed. 'That lasted a week and a half, and we were fired because they hated our music so much.' The Velvets' early sound was certainly an acquired taste and despite claiming that their music was hated, it did reach out to the avant-garde. Important connections were about to be made.

Café Bizarre was located on West 3rd Street in Greenwich Village. It consisted of a long room with sawdust on the floor. 'There was nothing bizarre about it,' quipped Lou Reed. 'It was a dump.' The band were contracted to play a series of sets every night. Forty minutes on, twenty minutes off, until the place closed. It was a time when little was expected of them and they felt free to experiment. 'We never said to each other, "Don't do that, play this",' said Moe Tucker. 'Everybody just played what they wanted.' The experimental aspect of the band was summed up simply by Tucker's drum kit. 'I had a bass drum on its side,' she explains, 'no pedal, and one cymbal that was like a garbage-can lid that had been run over six times, and a snare and a floor tom.' She was even more limited at the Café Bizarre engagement as the management insisted she couldn't use a drum kit, only a tambourine. This attitude emphasised the underlying conservative nature of this supposedly free-thinking culture: a full-size drum kit would be just too 'crazy' for the dinner-crowd. 'We tried to get gigs in the Village that summer,' recalled Sterling Morrison. 'It was supposed to be the avant-garde there, the clubs didn't want us.'

John Cale played with all kinds of side-projects,[2] but had ambitious, if unconventional plans for the band. 'When I played viola on "Venus In Furs", it wasn't until then that I thought we had discovered a really original, nasty style,' he explains. 'The idea was that we could create this orchestral chaos on stage and Lou could improvise. We would record performances, we would never make records. Every concert would be different.'

The Velvets weren't exactly growing up in public because for most nights at the Café Bizarre there was almost no public there, while the few souls that were in attendance sat at their tables talking and drinking as the band played in the background.

'We were paid in food: it was like $5 and dinner, which was fine for me – and welcome for them because they were pretty desperate, I'm sure,' recalled Moe Tucker. She was working a nine-to-five on Long Island, then travelling into Manhattan after work. 'We played for half an hour, then took a break and then played again, got home late, then went to work next morning,' she continued. 'At that point I still wasn't officially a band member.'

Before the end of their tenure at Café Bizarre, the band made perhaps the most important contact of its career. The celebrity creator, artist, designer and film-maker Andy Warhol came to see them and decided he wanted to be their manager. Barbara Rubin, a New York filmmaker and scenester, became the unknowing catalyst in this scenario. She had connections with Warhol and his arty hangout, The Factory, and with the likes of The Byrds and Donovan. Rubin had seen one of The Velvet Underground's first shows at Café Bizarre and wanted to film them in action. She asked Gerard Malanga, one of Warhol's assistants, and Paul Morrissey, another filmmaker who worked closely with Warhol, to assist her on the project Morrissey suggested to Warhol that he might also want to come along and see this new band. One of the most memorable connections in the history of twentieth-century culture was about to be made.

Chapter 4

1965–1966

Reflect What You Are

'Andy was a problem-solver. Anything that came into his grasp was turned into something. Andy was like, "If we're going to get high, we're going to be legal." He'd come back with all these medical magazines with all these inserts for pills.'

John Cale

At the end of 1965 Andy Warhol was already an American icon and destined to be one of the most important US artists of the twentieth century. Indirectly he was about to have a tremendous influence on rock music, an influence that would continue through to the likes of David Bowie, Talking Heads and Roxy Music in the 1970s. He'd been born in Forest City, Pennsylvania to Czechoslovakian immigrants with the surname Warhola, in 1928. After graduating from the Carnegie Institute of Technology with a degree in Pictorial Design he moved to New York in 1949, where he dropped the 'a' from the end of his surname.

Within a decade he was one of the most renowned designers in the city. Initially he drew illustrations for major New York magazines and branched out into freelance advertising campaigns. His work for the Lord & Taylor store and I. Miller shoes got his name recognised in influential advertising circles. By 1960 he was painting. His distinctive brightly coloured portraits of celebrities (such as Marilyn Monroe, Elvis and Elizabeth Taylor) were produced alongside enduring images of American trash-culture (cans of Campbell's soup and bottles of Coca-Cola). Beyond painting, Warhol used screen-printing to make multiple, repeating versions of his work and tapped directly into the consumerism of modern art.

While Warhol didn't 'invent' Pop Art, he managed to infiltrate popular culture and mainstream consciousness though it. Jasper Johns had exhibited beer cans several years before Warhol was unveiling his multi-image collages of celebrities and household goods. It was his transferral of these goods from the corner store Seven Eleven to the hip New York galleries that was his greatest achievement, and the way in which he put his indelible stamp on the movement. He showed America its own image in reflection, that the trashy, mass-produced, consumables could be, and indeed were art. He further confused matters by also using political images like an electric chair or the exploding atom bomb.

After receiving critical acclaim for his work Warhol turned his attention to filmmaking and gave up painting for the best part of a decade. By now he had his own studio/hangout 'The Factory' set up at West 47th Street, where he filmed early black-and-white silent movies with succinct titles like *Eat*, *Kiss* and *Blowjob*. These often unscripted clips were simple, frequently single-shot efforts which just focused on the action from the title. Warhol would tell someone to sit on a chair and eat some fruit while he filmed them, simple as that.

Warhol's success as an artist meant that everything he did was closely followed. This was a time when America began to worship the cult of celebrity. It didn't matter what you had achieved to be famous, it mattered who you were and who you were associated and seen with. Warhol was quick to sense this sea change and made the most of the people who came to visit him at the Factory. By filming them he made them famous. They weren't actors, they just did natural things while Warhol filmed them. That was how they joined the fast-expanding ranks of 'the celebrity' to the point where they were called Warhol's Superstars. It didn't take long for 'real' celebrities to start coming to the Factory to be filmed by Warhol. Dali, Dylan, Ginsberg and everyone who was anyone came for their screen tests, where Warhol would hold a close-up of their face and that was that.

Having conquered visual art, made an impression in the underground film circuit and been hailed as an iconic designer, Warhol's thoughts turned to the world of rock music. Paul Morrissey and Warhol had already had discussions about a music project at a club out on Long Island. The club's owner wanted to pay Warhol and his entourage to frequent the venue and give it some much-needed publicity. Warhol's idea then switched to include him having his own band – he would be their manager – which would play at the venue.

The night Warhol and his crew swept into the Café Bizarre, Warhol immediately saw the opportunity for himself and the Velvets. They had their distinctive all-black clothes and shades. It was an image, and image meant everything to Warhol. He wasn't put off by the ambivalent reaction from the 'tourist' crowd at the bar; he saw past the music and asked Morrissey to approach the band at the end of the night. Morrissey cut straight to the chase and offered to buy them new equipment and to get them a New York residency, while also financing their future albums. Just like that. They'd also be managed by Andy Warhol, who was an instant ticket to fame and celebrity. Lou Reed couldn't quite believe what he was hearing and the band agreed to visit Warhol at The Factory the following morning. 'I got The Velvet Underground into Café Bizarre and they walked out with Andy Warhol,' snapped Al Aronowitz. 'If I had signed a contract with the Velvets I could have sued the shit out of Warhol.'

So the following day The Velvet Underground visited The Factory for the first time. This ex-industrial loft occupied the whole floor of a former factory, hence the name. Located at 231 East 47th Street it was the hub of New York art. Warhol had assistants printing silk-screens and making collages, and the whole space was covered in silver foil.

'It wasn't that Andy was going to be the manager but we went to The Factory to look around,' recalls Moe Tucker. 'It was great; I always had a fun time there. I didn't know what to expect before we got there but everyone was so funny.' The place was filled with the comings and goings of drag queens, art critics, filmmakers and junkies. It was quite a scene. 'I didn't make any effort to impress Andy Warhol,' said Sterling Morrison. 'It wasn't like a visit from some big record producer, he was just an artist that I knew little about, except in terms of notoriety.' They discussed what Warhol wanted to achieve and how he wanted to go about doing so. 'Andy Warhol told me that what we were doing with music was the same thing that he was doing with paintings and movies and writing; i.e. not kidding around,' recalls Lou Reed. 'To my mind nobody in music was doing anything that even approximated the real thing, with the exception of us. The very first thing that I liked about Andy was that he was very real.' They soon reached an informal agreement to work together the following year, 1966.

The Velvet Underground played at the Café Bizarre through late December and over the Christmas holidays, but they weren't keen on having to play there on New Year's Eve. They managed to negotiate their way out of it when the manageress took a dislike to one of their songs. One night she warned them that if they played 'The Black Angel's Death Song' again she'd fire them. Sensing the opportunity, they started their next set with a raucous version of that very song. They were fired.[1]

On New Year's Eve the band made their first television appearance. Instead of playing at Café Bizarre they spent New Year's Eve partying. They joined the Warhol entourage at a James Brown concert in Harlem and then used Edie Sedgwick's limo to rush over to The Factory before midnight to see a TV special. Walter Cronkite had visited them during the making of a Piero Heliczer movie, *Venus In Furs*, back in November. Titled *The Making of an Underground Film*, the show featured Cale, Morrison and Reed playing an instrumental version of 'Heroin', with Heliczer adding a new saxophone accompaniment to the song. Aired on CBS, it would be the only time during Reed's original tenure with the band that they were shown on network television. The New Year was seen in amid much optimism and hope: the band had a manager, a growing range of material and a lot to look forward to. 1966 was going to be quite a year.

The New York Society for Clinical Psychiatry held its annual dinner on 13 January 1966. The venue was the upmarket Delmonico Hotel on Park Avenue and the guest speaker was Andy Warhol. Months earlier when he'd been invited Warhol had agreed on the condition that he could 'speak' through films. In the meantime he'd met The Velvet Underground and he wanted them to 'speak' for him instead. He hadn't told the organisers, though.

Warhol was there to meet the black-tie attired guests in a dinner jacket of his own and he showed films around the room during the opening cocktail reception. Then, as the guests sat down for dinner, he unleashed The Velvet Underground. While the band assaulted the diners' eardrums, a film crew burst into the room. Factory-ites Edie Sedgwick and Gerard Malanga ran around the audience shining bright lights into the faces of the near-200 guests and bombarded them with a list of dazzlingly blunt questions. 'Is his penis big enough?', 'What does her vagina feel like?', 'Do you eat her out?', 'Why are you getting embarrassed? You're a psychiatrist, you shouldn't get embarrassed!'

The cameras zoomed in on the faces of the reddening psychiatrists, many of whom stood up and walked out. If any of the guests had thought they were going to study Warhol, they were to go home disappointed: he had neatly turned the tables to both study and film them. With harsh lighting casting dramatic shadows behind the band, and with electric-candle chandeliers hanging above the guests, The Velvet Underground took to the stage. While the band played, they had a whip dancer on stage. The tuxedo-attired crowd were literally speechless. 'That was hysterical!' recalls Moe Tucker. 'Those poor psychiatrists sure had something to talk about for a while afterwards, they were flabbergasted. I just sort of sat back and said, "What the hell are we doing here?"'

Warhol's name being what it was, the 'gig' was given a lengthy write-up in *The New York Times*, something the Velvets alone would have found nigh-on impossible in January 1966.

Grace Glueck wrote that while the psychiatrists worked their way through roast beef and small potatoes, the Velvets provided a sonic backdrop of 'High decibel sound . . . a combination of rock 'n' roll and Egyptian belly-dance music.' Dr Arthur Zitrin commented, 'We've had everyone appear at these annual dinners. I'm program chairman for next year. How the hell are we going to follow this act?'

In January 1966 the US album chart included an eclectic mix of genres in its Top 10. The Rolling Stones' *December's Children*, the *Beach Boys Party*, the *Best of Herman's Hermits*, the *Sound Of Music* soundtrack and two Herb Alpert albums (*Whipped Cream And Other Delights* and *Going Places*) were all selling very well. But all of these were very different from the kind of music that The Velvet Underground would be presenting around the country throughout the coming year. Their music would have more appeal to the arty crowd, and with Warhol acting as mentor they were the perfect band to become ensconced at The Factory.

The Factory was more than just Andy Warhol's artistic headquarters, it was the epicentre of sometimes twisted relationships, psychological dramas and intrigue. Warhol used his base as a looking glass on the world, like a spider sitting at the centre of a tin-foil web. He made films featuring the protagonists of the relationships he observed, while taking diet pills amid the swirling sex and amphetamines. Mind games were played, which suited Lou Reed but not the other Velvets. 'There were several layers at The Factory,' explained John Cale. 'There was the gay community for a start. Lou understood that and enjoyed it. Sterling and I, less so. Moe just tut-tutted a lot.'

'Lou loved the transvestites,' added Factory regular Mary Woronov to *Uncut* magazine. 'He loved the craziness of the amphetamine addicts.'

The group had gone from near-starvation on Ludlow Street right into an affluent, artistic menagerie of people who understood what the Velvets were doing right away. Andy Warhol gave the band rolls of his cow prints to use as wallpaper in their apartments. When they left the new occupants probably wouldn't have known what was on the walls.

'As an art student I was well aware of Andy Warhol,' said Martha Dargan. 'But at first I was more aware of Gerard Malanga. He was the scout to find the band for Andy. They always played till 4am, which was a little late for a girlfriend and I remember waiting for them to pack up, night after night. When we started hanging out at The Factory, there was always music. When The Beatles' *Rubber Soul* album came out, we were at The Factory on a rainy Sunday afternoon. People were lying around on couches, reading *Vogue* magazine. Andy would be working on the floor and we'd have to be careful, walking in between his work.'

Martha spent her weekends at The Factory mainly waiting to find out where that night's hip party would be taking place, as did many others. 'Moe and I were always horrified at what we saw around us,' she adds. 'But we were also having the time of our lives and there was always music around.'

Moe Tucker also spent her weekends at The Factory because she was working on Long Island during the week and lived in Levittown. She wouldn't rehearse with the band per se, but they would fool around and maybe Reed would present a new idea for a song that they'd work through. Hanging around at The Factory, Tucker felt she should be out of place. She had little in common with the other women there but, strangely, she felt right at home. Later on she would spend her free time at The Factory typing up Warhol's taped notes for his book, *A: A Novel*. In return he paid her $50 a week, plus he covered her tab at Max's Kansas City for food and drink. It was a heavenly agreement for Tucker, but she refused to type up any swear words uttered by Warhol. Paul Morrissey had to go over the manuscript later and fill in the missing words by hand. 'Maybe Andy just understood my feelings because we were both Catholic,' laughs Tucker. It was just one example of the respect in which she was held at The Factory. While she didn't partake in the drug scene that was all around her, she didn't lecture anyone about it either. Everyone just co-existed happily.

On just the second day at The Factory, John Cale was seduced by Edie Sedgwick and he soon moved into her classy Upper East Side apartment. The arrangement lasted less than two months though, as Cale came to appreciate the delicate emotional frame of mind that Sedgwick balanced and he left soon after, before he was roped into becoming 'her nurse', as he put it. For her part, she had just left Andy Warhol and had her mind set on getting together with Bob Dylan.

Much of the time at The Factory was just spent hanging out, waiting to find out where that night's party would be taking place. Invariably the whole gang would go out together, often to The Ginger Man, where Edie Sedgwick had an account and would pay for everyone's meal. The band members took this as a lifeline: having eaten nothing all day, they would hungrily devour the steaks and hamburgers on offer. Sedgwick loved being the centre of attention. She was seen as the counter-culture's queen of decadence, the Warhol superstar and fashion shoot icon. Often she was photographed for the likes of *Vogue* magazine and appeared in Warhol films such as *Vinyl, Bitch, Prison* and *Poor Little Rich Girl*. For a while in the mid-1960s she and Warhol were inseparable; she even dyed her hair silver to match his wig. She met Bob Dylan at The Factory and he reportedly wrote 'Leopard-skin Pill-box Hat' and 'Just Like A Woman', on his 1966 album *Blonde On Blonde*, about her. She fell in love with Dylan, but when she found out that he had already been married in secret she was devastated. Her drug use escalated and she went downhill fast. '[Drugs] were just there,' said Sterling Morrison in 1975. 'We didn't make a secret about them, that's all. It is part of the everyday experience of millions. Some of my best friends took drugs, as the saying goes. Seems like all of them did.'

Edie Sedgwick died in 1971 at the age of 28. Sterling Morrison recounted a story where he was riding in a limousine with her and she'd just bought a really expensive pair of shoes. She opened the box in the back of the car and decided on the spot that she didn't like them after all. Then she wound down the window and dropped them out of the car. 'That's the essential Edie,' he said. 'Not a happy person.'

Andy Warhol never told The Velvet Underground how they should play their songs and he never tried to influence their style. Any suggestions he had were merely little hints to try this or that. Like many of the artists that surrounded him in The Factory, he was more interested in collaborative arrangements and being able to help guide people in a certain direction of their own. The only real impact he made on The Velvet Underground's music was a suggestion that they use a second lead singer in addition to Lou Reed, and even this idea had originated with Paul Morrissey. Warhol's influence was purely spiritual.

The idea of a second singer took off because of a fluke of timing. German singer, and ex-model, Christa Paffgen (aka Nico) had arrived in New York over the New Year holiday and early in 1966, she just happened to walk into The Factory. She had briefly met Warhol and some of The Factory crowd a couple of years before and had promised to visit them, if she ever got the chance. Warhol thought she would be perfect as the female vocalist for The Velvet Underground and he presented the idea to the band.

Nico was born in Cologne on 16 October 1938, just days after Hitler's troops had marched into Czechoslovakia. While her ancestry has often been reported differently (Victor Bokris reported that she had Spanish and Yugoslav parents, was born in Hungary in either 1943 or 1940), it's widely accepted that her parents were German and her father was conscripted into Nazi service during the Second World War. There, her family life descends into myth and conjecture. It's generally agreed that her father received serious head injuries during the hostilities and was then either sent to a German concentration camp (never to return) or shot dead by his commanding officer rather than being allowed to return home with brain damage. Nico was just four years old when this happened, and she and her mother moved to her grandparents' house across the country. Life was tough for them: they would watch the red sky at night as Berlin burned in the distance under the continued allied bombing raids.

In 1953 her mother found Nico some work at a Berlin fashion house as a model. Her modelling career soon took off and she was taken under the wing of Coco Chanel, necessitating that she and her mother move to Paris. While on vacation in 1959 she was visiting a friend's villa in Rome when she caught the eye of the enigmatic film director Federico Fellini. He was transfixed by her looks and immediately offered her a walk-on part in his classic movie *La Dolce Vita*. Nico literally walked into her part in Fellini's most famous film. Translated as 'The Sweet Life', it has gone down in cinematic history as his masterpiece. Centring on a reporter's travels from news story to news story, the film catalogues a series of Italian nights and dawns. Fellini used the film as his social comment on Rome's decadence and the underlying loneliness that the reporter witnesses in a series of social situations.

The following year Nico's modelling took her to New York, where she had some success, but she longed to be a famous singer or actress. In an attempt to improve her movie aspirations, she enrolled in Lee Strasberg's Method School and joined the same class as Marilyn Monroe, but that avenue didn't lead anywhere. Disappointed, she headed back to Europe and, in the first of many relationships with famous rock stars, fell in with The Rolling Stones' Brian Jones. The Jones' relationship allowed her her big chance as a singer. No doubt swayed by her looks as much as her voice, she recorded a single for Andrew Loog Oldham's Immediate label. The resultant single was 'I'm Not Sayin'', a Gordon Lightfoot song which was produced by future Led Zeppelin guitarist Jimmy Page. The song even had a promotional film clip recorded for it, which showed Nico singing by a river, looking wistful.

Back in Paris for a while she met Bob Dylan, who wrote a song for her to record: 'I'll Keep It With Mine', and it was here in France that, albeit only briefly she met Andy Warhol and his associate Gerard Malanga. By the time she arrived back in New York in late 1965 she had also had an affair with French actor Alain Delon[2] and shortly after gave birth to a son. Delon often denied he was the father, but saw fit to provide money anyway.

So in the first days of 1966, back in New York, Nico looked up Warhol at The Factory and waltzed in with a burning ambition to be a singer, a couple of singles under her arm and a young son in tow. 'She looked like she could have made the trip over right at the front of a Viking ship,' observed Warhol. In her trademark deep Germanic-English accent and wearing a turtleneck top and trouser suit, she cut quite a sight at The Factory, giving the scene an air of European mystery and panache.

'Nico's the kind of person you meet, and you're not quite the same afterwards,' said Lou Reed. 'She has an amazing mind.' She didn't always say very much and if you asked her a question, she might be silent and then answer it several minutes later. 'You couldn't exactly go to the store and buy ten Nicos', said Mary Woronov. Paul Morrissey suggested to Reed that Nico should sing, but Reed wasn't keen, and neither were the rest of the band initially. However, as they expanded their set they realised that Nico's unorthodox vocal style could open some interesting aesthetic avenues, and so she was allowed to link up as an auxiliary member of the group. Her accent, looks and detached aura of confidence led to comparisons with Marlene Dietrich and the whole decadent Berlin nightclub scenes of the 1920s and 1930s.

John Cale said that because Andy Warhol brought Nico to the band they accepted it as they always trusted his suggestions and ideas, and she did give them a completely new dimension. Her vocal style aligned with Cale's Welsh lilt gave a further European edge to the music and her feminine presence meant that certain songs might acquire a different meaning. Reed later wrote 'I'll Be Your Mirror' specifically for Nico and they gave her an old song to sing, 'All Tomorrow's Parties'.

Her desire to be famous prompted her to ask for more material to sing and she had some support from Paul Morrissey, who doubted Lou Reed's ability to carry the band alone as the lead singer. Morrissey believed that Nico had more stage presence than the diminutive Reed. For her part, Nico wasn't afraid to use her womanly charms with whoever she thought held power within the group, and she'd soon had short affairs with both Cale and Reed.

When Nico and Reed split up, partly because Reed didn't like the idea of a woman being an equal centre-of-attention in the band, she handed him a scathing put-down at The Factory. Reed said 'Hello' to her, and she didn't reply. At least not right away. A few moments that seemed like hours later, she simply responded, 'I cannot make love to Jews anymore.'

Andy Warhol suggested to Reed that he write a song about Edie Sedgwick. 'She's a femme fatale,' said Warhol. Reed took Warhol's words to heart and came up with a song called just that, 'Femme Fatale'. He thought that Nico should sing it, as her voice suited the song perfectly; he also gave her another new tune, 'There She Goes Again'. 'Nico showed up at The Factory,' recalled Sterling Morrison. 'Andy said, "Oh, here we have Nico. Would you like her to sing with you?" We said, "Well, we couldn't dislike it." That's how we became The Velvet Underground and Nico. She just came kind of creeping in. We knew that it couldn't last, because we didn't have that many songs she could sing.'

Chapter 5
1966
Uptight

'We had The Dom and a three-year lease, believe it or not. It really sickens me still when I go to St Marks Place because more than anyone we invented that street. There was nothing going on there. Absolutely nothing. The Spa at one end and just Polish-type stores, and Khadija Design, and the Bridge at the other end. No one had been there very long. Khadija had been there longer than anyone. It was an African clothing store. That was in 1964. Somehow we showed up at The Dom looking for a big room, and we said, ah, Dom, this is it. No one went down to St Marks Place. No people coming in off the street. There was no point in being there. It appeared to be a disaster.'

Sterling Morrison

Andy Warhol announced The Velvet Underground to the world. With the new line-up ready to go and new songs being written all the time, Warhol introduced them in a television interview on New York's WNET. In his understated voice he whispered that 'We're sponsoring a new band and it's called The Velvet Underground and we have the chance to combine music and films and art all together.' To the wider world it was going to be an interesting proposition. What would the outcome be? What effect would Warhol have on the music scene? At the time the conditions were perfect for Warhol to try and make his mark. As Dylan had said, the times were a-changin'. Surely the band couldn't lose in this situation as Warhol would provide them with money, equipment, a place to work and complete artistic freedom. Lou Reed called him a protector, while John Cale described him as a catalyst. Warhol encouraged their sometimes obscure subject matter even though he wasn't really into the music: it was the overall concept that he was most interested in. To him it was three-dimensional art with an audio soundtrack. It was his typical modus operandi of putting disparate elements together and then standing back to observe what came out of the mixing pot.

With Warhol's name attached to theirs, the band would find new horizons open to them. They already had a small down-town bohemian following, but they started to attract the slick uptown hipsters, the socialites and fashion editors. A Velvet Underground show was one of the few places in New York City where the two worlds would come and mingle together. The people with, and without money crossed any vague class barriers that existed in New York. All of this thrashed together at The Factory.

The Factory was a laboratory of the avant-garde where Andy Warhol could observe and document society. Warhol was an expert at letting ideas and themes bounce around him; he was a catalyst, sometimes for himself, sometimes for others, and he loved to watch how things took shape. 'It was like heaven,' said Lou Reed of his early days at The Factory. 'I would hear people say the most astonishing things, the craziest things, the funniest things, and the saddest things. I used to write it all down.'

'We hung around The Factory all the time,' adds Sterling Morrison. 'We never felt glamorous, we were only there because we were The Velvet Underground.'

'I never knew very much about Andy,' recalled John Cale. 'There was a constant flow of people, a big social scene. We would go up about two in the afternoon and then figure out what the rest of the day might be like. Everyone was very campy, there was a lot of game-playing going on. Lou felt at home in that environment, I didn't really. I had a lot of respect for Andy, I liked to watch him frolic around.'

Nico had been rehearsing with The Velvet Underground from 3 January 1966 and their first show together was planned for 13 January.

The band's initial shows were advertised under the title *Andy Warhol – Uptight* and were hosted at the Filmmakers Cinémathèque. 'European Son' was debuted there, Creedance Clearwater Revival's 'Suzie Q' was covered and they even let Nico sing 'I'll Keep It With Mine'.

The Warhol entourage hit the road for the first time on 9 March when they took the short drive to Rutgers University in New Jersey. In contrast to their usual stage garb the band all dressed in white so that when the films were projected onto them the band members would blend into the screens and become invisible.

Though they had hardly played together, they soon hit their stride. Reed was pleased with the choice of Tucker as the drummer, saying, 'She turned out to be fantastic. There is only one human being who can play that way.' Her distinctive style was at odds with conventional drumming wisdom. 'I always hated songs where if you rolled at every opportunity, there would be a constant roll throughout the song,' she explains. 'Or if you crashed a cymbal at . . . every place where you felt like you should do that. So I consciously avoided it. While you're crashing you can't hear the vocal and you can't hear the guitar part. I just always felt like the drums shouldn't take over the song. They should always be under there, obvious, but not taking over the song so that suddenly you realise all you hear is drums.' She also handled the dynamic of the rest of the band very well. Nico was sometimes aloof and said very little, while the three men could be hard to handle. 'She always said there was no reasoning with any one of us,' said Sterling Morrison, who wrote the nightly set lists. 'She said that we were all crazy, and there was no sense in arguing. I think basically the band had three uncontrollable person-alities and if you throw drugs into the confusion then you really have problems.'

Nico was fitting in well and they added the drone of 'Melody Laughter' for her to sing and sometimes, if they felt in a generous mood, they'd let her tackle slow versions of 'I'm Waiting For The Man' or even 'Heroin'. When she wasn't singing she could wander on and off stage, sometimes playing keyboards if there was one sitting around. 'The only friction was when Paul Morrissey thought Nico should sing everything,' said Sterling Morrison. 'The problem was what to have Nico do when she wasn't singing.'

'Part of her modus operandi was being misunderstood,' adds John Cale. '[She had] this very naïve, beatific view of the universe on one hand, and [was] very tough and dominant on the other. She didn't put up with shit from anybody.' 'Childlike' is a term often used to describe Nico: sometimes she appeared unaware of her own beauty and singing ability, sometimes she was statuesque, a 'dominant policewoman' in the words of John Cale.

Sterling Morrison played steady guitar rhythms and Moe Tucker would keep things together with a solid beat. She needed to be the constant in a sea of chaos because both Cale and Reed were prone to shoot off on wild tangents, sometimes in opposite directions, for a few minutes during a song and they all needed something solid to tie it all together; somewhere they could all come back to after they'd exhausted their sonic explorations. Despite the ferocity of his playing, Cale never thought that he made enough of the viola, which he saw as a very powerful instrument. He also played bass and piano. Reed spun off-the-cuff stories of the underground. 'Lou is the only guy I've ever known who could improvise words that actually made sense when analysed afterwards,' said Cale.

The dynamic between the Velvets and The Factory crowd was finally coming together. Though he never directly interfered with the music, Andy Warhol was always around with an idea or suggestion about anything and everything else. Sterling Morrison said Warhol was the most important influence on his life. 'It sounds crazy,' he said, 'but on reflection I've decided that he was never wrong. He gave us the confidence to keep doing what we were doing.'

'One of the best ideas [Warhol] came up with,' said Lou Reed, 'was that we should rehearse on stage, because the best music always takes place in rehearsals. So why not rehearse on stage, which was the best idea anyone came up with.' Another Warhol suggestion was to generate some publicity by playing at the trendy *Paraphernalia* clothes shop that designer Betsey Johnson ran and designed for. The Velvet Underground played in the shop and drew a large crowd, inside and out. They eventually also drew the attention of the police, who stopped the show.

The *Uptight* university shows were being booked on the premise of them being an underground film presentation. After Rutgers they spread their wings further to appear at the University of Michigan Film Festival in Ann Arbor. The trip necessitated a several-hour bus journey packed with the *Uptight* production crew. Ingrid Superstar recalled to author Victor Bokris that, 'The effect of the music on the audience is like the audience is just too stunned to think or say anything . . . I asked a few people in Ann Arbor, who had come to see the show a couple of nights in a row, what they thought, and they formed an opinion slowly. They said that they thought the music was very way out and supersonic and fast and intensified, and the effect of the sound it produced vibrated all through the audience, and when they walked out onto the street they still had these vibrations in their ears for about 15 minutes.'

The 1,500-mile round trip to Ann Arbor had been made in a hired minibus with a trail of supporting cars but the effort was finally worth it. 'Ann Arbor went crazy,' recalled Andy Warhol. 'At last the Velvets were a smash. We had a strobe light with us for the first time. The strobes were magical, they went perfectly with the chaos music. The Velvets played. I'd sit on the steps in the lobby during the intermission and people from the local papers and schools would interview me, ask about my movies, what we were going to do. "If they can take it for ten minutes, then play it for 15," I'd explain. "That's our policy. Always leave them wanting less."'

'In our very early days we did a lot of jamming with structured songs scattered here and there,' recalls Moe Tucker. 'When we played at art shows those audiences weren't into it. As we started playing clubs we had more appreciation and a positive response. We'd make a set list but didn't always follow it exactly.' Finding the right audience for the band was a hard task to carry out. Though the use of the Andy Warhol name brought much-needed publicity, it didn't really help an unsuspecting audience know what it was in for. 'I remember looking at them [a young audience] and thinking they're too young and innocent to be exposed to our music,' said Sterling Morrison in 1975. 'I didn't think there was any reason why they should like our music and I hoped they wouldn't. I needn't have worried: they didn't.'

The trip home was less successful though. After a problem caused the main bus to pull over at a gas station, the whole entourage soon found themselves on the wrong side of local law enforcement. 'The police told us to get out of Ohio by noon,' recalls Moe Tucker. 'The attitudes were amazing now I think back to it. We were just sitting on the bus, the guys had long hair, the gas station attendant saw Paul [Morrissey] . . . and he called the authorities. Suddenly we were surrounded by troopers, just because of the length of the guy's hair!'

Once safely back home, Warhol and Morrissey discussed plans for the band and decided that a high-profile New York residency would be the next logical step. Having all the equipment in one place night after night would help enormously, as the lighting rigs and film projectors were difficult to lug around in a minibus along with the band's gear.

Paul Morrissey was explaining to Andy Warhol the problems of getting a venue when they were interrupted by a couple of gentlemen named Jackie Cassen and Rudi Stern, who had been unable to avoid overhearing the conversation on the next table. Miraculously they knew of an empty venue called The Dom on St Mark's Place, and it was free for the next few weeks. They hacked out a deal almost immediately and Morrissey rushed off to get the all-important advertisement hyping the show in the next issue of the *Village Voice*.

'This was before there was an "East Village",' explains Sterling Morrison. 'Then, it was just where old people and poor people lived. The Dom can be credited for making St Mark's Place a sleaze hole.'

At The Dom, Warhol changed the name of the show to the *Exploding Plastic Inevitable* (a phrase borrowed from the back sleeve of Dylan's *Bringing It All Back Home* album). Rehearsals for the new show included the band tackling The Who's 'My Generation', along with most of the songs which would later make up their debut album. The shows at The Dom were booked for most of the month of April. The venue had been a Polish restaurant with a very dark interior and a single glitterball suspended from the ceiling. Tables, covered in blue-and-white checked plastic tablecloths, were pushed close together to allow a stage to be set up. From the convenient balcony at the back of the room Warhol added four film projectors. 'We all wore shades because we didn't want to look at the audience,' said John Cale. 'We didn't want to see them at all, we just wanted to go and hit them with this music.' They also wanted to save their eyesight from the potential damage of Warhol's visual barrage. 'There was a guy on a spotlight, turning it on and off, and other people running other banks of lights,' recalls Moe Tucker. 'They knew the songs and they knew the moods of the songs, and they had the same sort of ideas that we had. So they would play to the songs. And there'd be films being shown behind us, on a great big screen, not a little home projector.'

The films included Warhol's screen tests and various silent films like *Empire State*, which showed a cloud floating across the sky, *Kiss*, which was simply a couple kissing, and *Vinyl*, which featured Gerard Malanga being waxed in a leather mask. Nico would stroll across the stage with the provocative scenes being projected behind her and stand there motionless while she sang. 'When we were onstage we had no idea what would happen and we liked that,' said John Cale. 'We didn't want to control it. We didn't care if anybody saw us; we just wanted to make this noise and get through on a more psychological level.' At The Dom everyone involved was paid exactly the same amount per show – around $100 each.

'I went to The Dom every single weekend,' said Martha Dargan. 'By then I was living in the city and every Friday and Saturday night I was there, it was terrific. It was very hard to walk across the dance floor if you'd had two beers, there was the mirrorball and the films and the noise, it was really packed. One night the place was filled with Hell's Angels – they really liked The Velvet Underground.' The mirrorball splintered strobe and coloured lights across the room, the films mingled with the lights and the music droned the whole experience into a dizzying spiral of the senses.

The advert that ran in the press for the opening week claimed 'Live music, ultra sounds, visions, light works, colour slides, discotheque, refreshments, food, celebrities and movies'. The haste of preparation for the engagement showed as the rear wall was still being painted white while the first films were being projected onto it. At $2.50 a head, over 400 people paid to enter on opening night, netting over $1,000 on entrance fees alone.

John Wilcock, writing for *The East Village Other*, was present on opening night, 1 April 1966. 'Occasionally a couple would get up and dance but most people preferred to watch,' he wrote. 'Art has come to the discotheque and it will never be the same again.'

The club was packed from the first night and it was a massive success, making $18,000 in the first week. Cash was retained in a series of brown paper bags. The money was about to come in very handy because the band wanted to book some studio time to record their debut album.

The band weren't paid a wage for the shows, they were just given money when they needed it. 'We didn't even talk about money – I just knew that when Sterling needed money, he got it,' said Martha Dargan. 'Moe was funny, she'd go over to Andy and say, "Okay, you son of a bitch, where's my money?" And start yanking on his jacket and he'd laugh. At that point no one was even thinking about money.'

With the money saved from The Dom shows the band could afford a limited amount of studio time at a fairly cheap and run-down (it had holes in the floor and only four microphones) facility, Scepter Studios at 254 West 54th Street. Four days were booked during the last week in April, with the sessions taking place during normal nine to five working hours. To further save on costs they employed Norman Dolph, a 27-year-old Yale graduate and Columbia Records sales executive, to engineer the sessions while Andy Warhol was the named producer.

The engineer and producer roles were pretty skewed in this instance. Dolph actually put some of his own funds forward to pay for the sessions, with the plan being for him to then help sell the tapes to Columbia and take a cut of the profits. Warhol's production input didn't go far beyond financial and a few encouraging nods from the control room, more of a film producer's role than a music producer's one. '[Warhol] would be sitting quietly in the back of the room, making the occasional wry comment,' recalls Dolph. 'He was more of a presence really.' The band would run through a take and ask for Warhol's opinion, and he'd invariably say it was great and they'd do the next song. His only real request was that they 'Do the song with the dirty words ["Venus In Furs"]. Don't change the words just because it's a record.' His enthusiasm for their more exotic material meant a lot to the band. Having someone with such a highly regarded artistic reputation believing in their work was a great boost.

Most of the basic tracks were recorded during eight or ten hours, spread over the first two days; the third day was used for a listen-back session and the fourth was for mixing. As there was no record label input into the sessions and minimal help from production and engineering sources, the band could pretty much do as they pleased. The songs were played just as they had been during live performances with very little extra arranging. The option to add some piano to the tracks was available as there just happened to be one in the studio at the time. 'My idea was to keep the sound simple,' said John Cale. 'But by overlaying the instruments' simplistic patterns the accumulative effect of the sound would be incredibly powerful. I was highly intrigued by the whole Phil Spector Wall-Of-Sound concept, but obviously I had to modify it for a four-piece. We were really excited: we had this opportunity to do something revolutionary, to combine avant-garde and rock and roll, to do something symphonic.'

The most intense part of the sessions occurred when Lou Reed sang 'I'm Waiting For The Man' and 'Heroin'. He insisted on providing a live vocal while they played live in the studio at the same time, which is an unusual and difficult proposition. Usually the vocal is added after the music has been perfected and often different instruments are recorded individually. He also wanted them done in one pass. 'They plugged straight into the board [for "Heroin"],' recalls Moe Tucker. 'They didn't have their amps with them in the studio, so of course I couldn't hear anything . . . When we got to the part where you speed up, you have to speed up together, or it's not really right. It just became a mountain of drum noise in front of me. I couldn't see Lou to watch his mouth to see where he was in the song. And I just stopped. I was saying, "This is no good, we need headphones or something." So I stopped, and being a little wacky they just kept going, and that's the one we took.'

'It's just two chords,' explains Lou Reed. 'When you play it, at a certain point, there is a tendency to lean in and play it faster. It's automatic. And when I first played it for John, he picked up on that. Also, if you check out the lyrics, there are more words as you go along. The feeling naturally is to speed up.'

Martha Dargan was present at the studios and spent her time wandering around the empty offices in the building. She also helped out with Moe Tuckers disintegrating drum kit. 'I remember [Martha] holding my snare drum so it wouldn't slide away while we recorded "I'm Waiting For The Man",' said Tucker. 'It wasn't in the stand, I had laid it on the floor. At the time I'd never been in a studio, so I didn't know it wasn't the most upscale of studios but it did the job.'

Nico was far from happy with the way the sessions were going. She still had dreams of being a female version of Bob Dylan, something the band was dead set against. 'I want to sound like bawwwbbb deeelahhhn,' she whined, but the band made her sing in her slow monotone voice on 'All Tomorrow's Parties' and 'I'll Be Your Mirror'. Her audible dismay on the take of 'Femme Fatale' is real – she was sulking because the others had made her redo it until she sounded like they wanted her to. 'You see, Nico had two voices,' explains Sterling Morrison. 'One was a full-register, Germanic, *götterdammerung* voice that I never cared for and the other was her wispy voice, which I liked.'

The final day of recording saw them run through the rest of the original material that they'd played at The Dom the night before – 'The Black Angel's Death Song', 'Run, Run, Run', 'Venus In Furs' and 'European Son'. During 'European Son', John Cale dragged a screeching metal chair across the floor and Lou Reed dropped a mirror, which shattered on the floor in perfect time. 'I remember John running, pushing a chair in front of him and Lou dropping a mirror, which I thought was really funny,' recalls Dargan. 'I got in trouble for that, because they were serious and I was partying!'

'It was a complete shambles,' recalls John Cale. 'Norman Dolph is in the booth making comments like, "Great! Dynamite! We got it!" And we're all looking at each other, going, "Where is it written that he gets to say "This is a take"?'

Dolph took the finalised tapes to Columbia and had an acetate pressed up for the label's executives. This acetate contained versions of the songs that never got any further than the label's offices. Dolph soon realised that they'd be going no further when he got a handwritten reply to the acetate which basically said, 'You have to be fucking kidding!'[1]

The swift rejection of the album surprised Dolph, who also received a letter questioning his sanity. The band tried it at other labels and though Elecktra dismissed the songs as being unacceptable, MGM immediately signed the band and paid them an advance to go and tidy up the recordings in a Los Angeles Studio. Dolph, being out of pocket from his input, was paid off by Andy Warhol with one of the artist's paintings. The engineer sold the painting for $17,000 in 1975.

Though the album could have been ready in April 1966, frustratingly for the band the process dragged inexplicably and it would be a year until it was actually released.

Chapter 6
1966
Run Run Run

*'This music [The Velvet Underground & Nico] was savagely
indifferent to my feelings. It didn't care if I liked it or not.
It couldn't give a fuck. It was completely preoccupied with a
world as yet unseen by my suburban eyes.'*

David Bowie

As the Velvets and a Factory entourage flew to the West Coast
they were entering a completely different world. 'Monday
Monday' by The Mamas & The Papas was the top-
selling single in the country. The Byrds and Love had large,
dedicated followings on the West Coast and The Grateful Dead
had just played their debut show and moved to Haight Ashbury
in San Francisco, an area that was fast emerging as the centre of
the new hippy movement. The Californian acid vibes were about
to meet some cold New York City negativism head-on. The West
Coast was colourful, The Velvets wore black. The flower
children dropped acid, the East coast was all amphetamines. The
hippies went around barefoot, the Factory crowd arrived
wearing boots. 'You had very sensitive and responsible young

people suddenly attuned to certain cosmic questions that beckon us all and expressing these concerns through acoustic guitars and lilting harmonies and pale melodies,' said Sterling Morrison. 'I hate these people.'

The Castle was a rambling mansion situated high in the Hollywood Hills. Bela Lugosi lived across the street in a house that looked like a pyramid and had been designed by Frank Lloyd Wright. Bob Dylan had been staying at the Castle right before the Velvets' entourage arrived. The area reeked of Hollywood greenbacks, but the Castle was surrounded by a lot that had fallen into disrepair: the pool was full of algae and the gardens were severely overgrown. The Castle itself had high ceilings with tall windows that afforded views of the hillside. Edie Sedgwick had brought along Chet Powers, aka Dino Valenti (who composed 'Get Together', later used by Nirvana for the introduction to their song 'Territorial Pissings'), and they stayed in the supposed haunted room, which had a pentangle outside. Here they were visited by The Doors' Jim Morrison, who took Nico up into one of the towers before tiptoeing along a parapet, risking a potentially deadly fall of over 100 feet.

Though no one had heard a Velvet Underground record before, quite a buzz was created when news spread around Los Angeles that Andy Warhol was bringing an exciting new band to play for two weeks. Warhol's party prepared for a series of shows at The Trip, the self-styled 'New Shrine of Pop Culture', on Sunset Boulevard in West Hollywood. There was a real air of anticipation hanging over the venue on 3 May as the band opened their West Coast engagement. Frank Zappa opened the show and local rock luminaries such as Jim Morrison, Sonny and Cher, Ryan O'Neal, and members of The Byrds and The Mamas & Papas were in the audience. It's been claimed that after seeing the leather-trousered

Gerard Malanga perform his whip dance on stage that Morrison borrowed the look for his lizard-king persona. Factory regulars Ronnie Cutrone and Mary Woronov played out the whip dance with Malanga during 'Venus In Furs'. 'Because it has three basic characters – the Dominatrix, the slave Severin, and the Black Russian Prince, who kills the slave,' explained Cutrone. 'We basically played only for our own enjoyment – no crowd participation, we didn't say a word to the audience during the hour and 45-minute set. Not "Thank you", not "Glad you could come out".'

'Not since the *Titanic* ran into that iceberg has there been such a collision as when Andy Warhol's Exploding Plastic Inevitable burst upon the audience at The Trip,' wrote Kevin Thomas in the *Los Angeles Times*. 'For once a happening really happened and it took Warhol to come out from New York to show how it's done.'

The band played with their backs to the audience for some of the show, and before and after it they were shooting up and taking amphetamines, which was quite in keeping with the majority of their audience. 'I thought they were wasting their money,' said Moe Tucker of the rampant drug use. 'In our case,' counters Sterling Morrison, 'drugs got in the way some, but nobody had any real problems. The real problem was that whereas the 60s were associated with grass and acid, we were associated with bad drugs – speed and junk. Beer, though, was always my drug of choice.'

A reporter known only as 'Burton' was at The Trip for *Hitline* magazine, but was far from impressed. 'A tasteless, vulgar review that should never have opened,' he/she wrote. 'Two dancers gyrated disgustingly in front of the lights . . .' he/she added, before closing by saying that the real hipsters were intelligent enough to know the difference between 'real art and just bad taste'.

The audience were predominantly seated at tables and many of the men were dressed in suits and ties. Cher walked out part of the way through the night and was quoted as saying, 'It depressed me: it will replace nothing, except maybe suicide.' Warhol and the Velvets certainly knew how to split opinion.

'I love LA,' said Andy Warhol. 'Everybody's plastic but I love plastic. I want to be plastic.' Moe Tucker wasn't so keen on the plastic, though. 'Plastic is the only word I can think of to describe California,' she said. 'I never thought we could convert them, but perhaps we could throw it in their faces a little bit. At that time if someone had said to me, "What do you do for a living?" Tthe last thing I would have said was, "Oh, I'm a musician." I was having fun and enjoying the music and unlike Lou or John, who knew from being young that they were going to be musicians, I just had a different slant on it. I worked full-time until we went to California. After that I'd get temporary jobs for quite a while to make cigarette money.'

The Trip residence was cut short after only three nights when the local police closed down the club because of an invalid liquor licence. The Warhol posse was left high and dry, far from home and with no money coming in to pay the bills. Luckily their contract with the club owners stipulated that if the band stayed in town, ready to play if the club re-opened, then they would still be owed their wages of $500 a week. So there was nothing to do but sit it out in Los Angeles for ten days.

'We had a horrible reputation,' recalls Sterling Morrison. 'Everybody figured we were gay. They figured we must be, running around with Warhol and all those whips and stuff. After about a week and a half waiting for The Trip to re-open, I moved to the Tropicana. There we partied with Buffalo Springfield, who were staying there too, and various others from the LA music scene. I rode all over the place on a motorcycle that [author] Kurt von Meier lent me, but as often as not was at the Castle anyway. It's just that I wasn't stuck up there.'

During this downtime the group met an aspiring young manager called Steve Sesnick. He hadn't got any experience as a manager, previously he'd been a college basketball player, but he was eager to become involved and did have part-ownership of the Boston Tea Party club in Boston. 'I liked Steve a lot,' said Moe Tucker. 'He was fun to be around.' The band had a two-day session booked for them by MGM at TTG, a Hollywood studio, later in the month and so it made sense to stay in Los Angeles until then. They were also being courted by Bill Graham to drive up and play at his Fillmore Auditorium in San Francisco and Sesnick acted as a go-between, buffering Graham and Warhol. They eventually agreed to travel up after the Hollywood session at the end of May.

TTG's resident producer was an up-and-coming talent by the name of Tom Wilson, a charismatic character who loved life. At 6' 4" the African-American made an imposing figure, but his energies seemed to be spent more on chasing women than working in the studio. As a Harvard graduate he founded the Transition jazz label in the 1950s and worked on producing jazz programming for a range of radio stations. In 1963 Wilson signed on as a staff producer for Columbia and began an impressive career working with Bob Dylan and Simon & Garfunkel. Some of Wilson's most important contributions came when he added band musicians and electric instruments to what were bare folk arrangements. He helped guide Dylan towards his mid-1960s' electric breakthrough and by putting backing musicians onto Simon & Garfunkel sessions he provided them with hit singles. Wilson was also behind the signing of Frank Zappa.

When the Velvets arrived in Los Angeles for the sessions Wilson was still working on Zappa's *Free*, that is when he wasn't chasing women. '[Wilson] always seemed to be chasing the chicks,' laughs Moe Tucker. '[I thought] "What do I know about producing?" I guess he was doing his job amid this parade of beautiful girls. I felt like, "Are we actually recording here? What's the deal?" There was never anyone around looking over our shoulders.'

TTG studios had started out life as a Knights of Columbus hall in 1927. From this Catholic men's fraternal society morphed the low-key facility that played host to a wide variety of 1960s' pop: The Ventures' 'Wild Thing', the Beach Boys' 'Help Me Rhonda' and the Mothers of Invention debut album, to name but a few.

The set-up at TTG Studios couldn't have been more of a polar opposite to the previous scene back at Scepter. Situated at 1441 N. McCadden Place, near Sunset and Highland in the heart of Hollywood, it was well equipped and had been home to recordings by The Doors and Jimi Hendrix: Tom Wilson was the well-respected producer on hand to guide them through the process.

They planned to re-record three of their oldest songs, all of which they had been unhappy about at Scepter. 'Heroin' was given a slightly modified introduction and Reed changed the opening line from 'I know where I'm going' to 'I don't know where I'm going', something which infuriated John Cale. 'You fucked up the whole song by changing the premise,' roared Cale. 'The song is not about drug taking, it's about a person who hates himself, and the reason he hates himself is not clear to anybody because there's this conviction in the first-person line: it gives the game away in the first line.'

'I'm Waiting For The Man' had its opening line changed from 'waiting for my man' and John Cale put guitar strings on his viola, which gave even more intimidating power to 'Venus In Furs'. The overall effect was a considerable improvement and the takes of these three songs were later used on the album alongside the New York takes of the other songs.

While in San Francisco, Gerard Malanga walked into an all-night restaurant dressed in black leather and carrying his whip. He was arrested and charged with possession of a dangerous weapon. The shows themselves also drew all kinds of attention, which caused some jealousy on the part of Bill Graham towards Andy Warhol. He felt that the Velvets should bow down to him on his own territory, but they set up parties and didn't invite him and generally made their own scene around town. It didn't help matters that the band showed open contempt for the West Coast music scene as a whole.

'We had vast objections to the whole San Francisco scene,' said Lou Reed. 'It's just tedious, a lie and untalented. They can't play and they certainly can't write. I keep telling everybody and nobody cares. We used to be quiet, but I don't even care anymore about not wanting to say negative things: things have gone so far that somebody really should say something. You know, people like Jefferson Airplane and Grateful Dead are just the most untalented bores that ever came up. Just look at them physically, I mean, can you take Grace Slick seriously? It's a joke! The kids are being hyped.'

Despite the animosity between the parties, Graham had built the Fillmore into an institution in a very short space of time. It was only in February 1966 that he'd presented a trio of Jefferson Airplane shows there. By March he was gaining a degree of notoriety and was arrested when police tried to arrest some kids at a show. Local press supported Graham and the charges were dropped. In the following two or three years he helped catapult the likes of the Grateful Dead, Santana and Moby Grape to national prominence.

Starting on 27 May the band were headlining over Frank Zappa's Mothers of Invention again. At rehearsal they further enraged Bill Graham by rubbishing his 'light show', which consisted of a single slide of the moon. 'We actually built the light show at the Fillmore Auditorium,' explains Sterling Morrison. 'Bill Graham didn't, nor did any San Francisco entrepreneur. We said, "That's not a light show, Bill, sorry." That's one of the reasons that Graham really hates us. Right before we went on, he looked at us and said, "You motherfuckers! I hope you bomb!"' The band reciprocated the animosity and ended their set with a raucous 'fuck you' to Graham. At the end of 'European Son' the three guitarists put down their instruments to create a cacophonous wall of feedback and set about battering Moe Tucker's drum kit. John Cale was a little over-enthusiastic and sent a cymbal spiralling into Lou Reed's forehead. Graham was irate with this sacriligious behaviour and rushed backstage to confront the band. As he entered the dressing room he saw Reed sitting there with blood pouring from the gash in his head and immediately left the room. 'Something about insurance reasons,' smirked Cale.

'The Mothers were following us around California,' recalled Sterling Morrison. 'During the show, Zappa would keep putting us down, like on the mike he would say, "These guys really suck." He always had an audition group. The reason for this was they didn't get any money. He would say, "If you're really good, I'll let you play." This guy's an operator. The audition group that night happened to be the Jefferson Airplane, whom he was managing. They wanted publicity and the Mothers wanted publicity because they were so many people capitalising on our show that night. We were just a neutral party – we were going back to New York to greener pastures, supposedly.'

To help with expenses on the way home from San Francisco, the band were booked in to play a week at Poor Richard's club in Chicago, starting on 21 June. Steve Sesnick travelled with them, but Nico and Lou Reed didn't. Nico had jetted off for a vacation in Ibiza and Reed flew straight to New York, checked into the Beth Israel hospital and was diagnosed with hepatitis. He was kept in for over a month.[1]

These two absences meant some swift line-up juggling was required because not many bands can play on when the two principal vocalists are missing. In Chicago it was very hot: the temperature was over 100 degrees and feelings were running high between the police and the black community. Poor Richard's had previously been a church and had little ventilation; the conditions inside were stifling for all.

At the shows, John Cale took over the lead vocal duties, Moe Tucker switched to bass and, most surprisingly, Angus Maclise[2] was tracked down and he agreed to play drums. The songs were given new arrangements, with Maclise predominantly playing bongos and Cale on keyboards. They sounded great. Across the country Reed was unable to hide his growing paranoia that he was losing control of the band, even though no one had put him in charge in the first place. The heat in the club was almost unbearable and the crowd could almost have died of thirst, such were the queues to buy drinks. Larry McCombs reviewed the Chicago happenings for *The Boston Broadside* and wrote: 'There's an electrified violin [sic] making horrible bagpipe sounds against the noisy background.'

'In Chicago, I was singing lead – no one knew the difference,' said John Cale. 'We turned our faces to the wall and turned up very loud. Paul Morrissey and Danny Williams had different visions of what the light show should be like and one night I looked up to see them fighting, hitting each other in the middle of a song. Danny Williams used to carry this strobe around with him all the time and no one could figure out why till we found out he kept his amphetamine in it.' Later the same year Williams, an experimental filmmaker and Factory fixture, mysteriously disappeared. His clothes were found by the side of his parked car on the New England coast. It was believed he had died whilst swimming, although his body was never found.

As the band entered the second half of 1966 they all grew increasingly frustrated at the hold-ups surrounding the album's release. When Frank Zappa's album was released ahead of theirs, they grew even angrier. The label also seemed happy to spend all of its promotional funds supporting the Zappa album, palming off the Velvets by saying they had Warhol to provide all the promotion they needed.

When the band came to play back at The Dom in October, they found out that it had been bought out and renamed the Balloon Farm. The previous owners were gone and so was their option of making it their regular New York base. 'When we came back, we went back to our room since that was our thing,' recalled Morrison. 'We owned it for three years, and when we came back we discovered it was now called The Balloon Farm. Actually, our lease had been torn up and the director of the Polish home had been bribed and bought off, and so our building had been taken away from us and later sold to the Electric Circus for around $300,000 . . . so I discovered early in life that when you have something valuable, someone is going to try and take it away from you'.

This was really the beginning of the end for the five-piece band and Andy Warhol's involvement with it. Without a regular New York venue, the chances of them raising their profile in their home town or being able to earn a decent, regular wage were severely diminished. There was nothing else for it but to head out on the road. 'We needed someone like Andy,' explains John Cale. 'He was a genius for getting publicity. Once we were in Providence to play at the Rhode Island School of Design and they sent a TV newsman to talk to us. Andy did the interview lying on the ground with his head propped up on one arm. There were some studded balls with lights shining on them and when the interviewer asked him why he was on the ground, Andy said, "So I can see the stars better." The interview ended with the TV guy lying flat on his back, saying, "Yeah, I see what you mean."'

The Velvets' 'tour' lasted from Halloween to Christmas and took them out through the Mid West and back through Canada. The *Cincinnati Sunday Pictorial Enquirer* reviewed the 3 November, 1966 show by saying, 'The room is huge, dark, crowded. Pinpoints of coloured light dart from around the walls, reflected from a mosaic-mirrored ball that hangs from the ceiling. At the far side of the room, on stage, is The Velvet Underground, polka-dotted, pinstriped, booted, wide-belted, dark-spectacled musicians. With them, twisting, turning, leaping, getting the message, is dancer Gerard Malanga. Walking among the tables toward the stage is Nico, tall, casual, stunning in black velvet pea jacket and loose-legged lavender pants. Whether anyone was turned on or off by the event, whether anything happened besides the happening itself is beside the point. Dig?'

'We worked the Masonic Hall in Columbus, Ohio,' recalls John Cale. 'A huge place filled with people drinking and talking. We tuned up for about ten minutes, tuning, fa-da-da, up, da-da-da, down . . . There's a tape of it. Played a whole set to no applause, just silences.' As the tour wound its way through college campuses and sports halls, the shows were advertised a day or two in advance in the local papers: 'Belkin Production presents in person Andy Warhol with his smash N.Y. scene The Exploding Plastic Inevitable Featuring The Velvet Underground & Nico, as featured in *Life* magazine.'

The songs played at these shows were increasingly becoming sonic operas that could last for a long time. 'Melody Laughter' fused 'The Nothing Song' and 'Day of Niagara' by the Theatre of Eternal Music and could last from a couple of minutes to almost an hour. It had no set lyrics, just Nico moaning and groaning her way through it. John Cale would play bass, piano and organ and could be seen franticly sawing away at his viola, constantly changing between the instruments during the song.

The strange venues and situations that the band found themselves playing in continued. One of the last shows of the year was played near Detroit at what was billed as 'The World's First Mod Wedding Happening'. The Velvets were listed fourth on the bill below 'ANDY WARHOL', 'NICO – Girl of the Year' and 'Gerard – Superstar'. The event took place on the last of three days of the Carnaby Street Fun Festival at the Michigan State Fairgrounds Festival on Sunday, 20 November. The bride and groom had volunteered to take part and were given a vacation in New York and a Warhol screen-test as gifts. Eighteen-year-old Randy Rossi wore a white minidress and white thigh-high boots. Her mother was heard to comment, 'It's not the kind of wedding we had planned for our daughter.' As the couple arrived in a black Rolls-Royce, the Velvets played and the car was destroyed. 'That was lunacy,' laughs Moe Tucker. 'We were playing but [Paul] Cézanne was recruited to beat the hell out of a car with a sledge hammer, during the ceremony and during our set. I don't know what the significance was!' The Velvets improvised the music along the lines of 'Here Comes The Bride'. Four-and-a-half thousand fans attended the event, which included all elements of an EPI show – films, strobe lights, whip dancing and music. Andy Warhol gave away the bride and afterwards sat around autographing cans of tomato soup. The Yardbirds also played and covered 'I'm Waiting For The Man', even though it had yet to be released. Then it was back home to New York and the hope that their album might at last be released.

Chapter 7

1966–1968

There She Goes Again

*'Those were primitive times. Driving around in a van, being
stopped by the police and being accused of kidnapping children
because the girls we had with us were too young and didn't
have notes from their parents. We were right in the middle of
Ohio, taking enormous amounts of speed, driving all the way
back from Cleveland to New York, overnight. Madness.
Absolute madness.'*

John Cale

In November 1966 the band found the time to quickly go back into the studio with Tom Wilson at Mayfair Sound in New York. The purpose of this extra visit was to record one more song for the album. The Velvets had been encouraged to record something that could be a potential hit single, so they put down a relatively new song 'Sunday Morning' to give it a modicum of commercial clout. Andy Warhol had suggested that Reed write a song about paranoia and after a boozy night out, and that's what he did. As he crawled back home with John Cale at six o'clock one Sunday morning the song came to him, and he and

Cale wrote it as soon as they got back to the loft. Tom Wilson also suggested to Lou Reed that he write another song for Nico, to also be released as a single, which would help the album commercially. Reed thought 'Sunday Morning' would be that song, but when they came to record it in the studio he refused to let Nico sing and took over vocal duties himself. As the writer he decided that he should also be the singer on the single. It was this paranoid control-freak side of his personality that would eventually drive the band apart.

The session at Mayfair was memorable because of the poor state of the building. John Cale recalled having to walk around holes in the floor to try and find a safe place to set up.

Though it was ultimately issued as a single in December 1966, 'Sunday Morning' failed to break through commercially. It failed to chart, and it's speculated that very few copies were ever actually pressed. The band was growing increasingly impatient with MGM/Verve about the lack of news regarding a release date for the album. Verve did manage to issue Frank Zappa's *Freak Out*, which got the jump on *The Velvet Underground & Nico* because Zappa's manager knew how to manipulate the company and insisted on their album coming out before the Velvets'.

Andy Warhol's lack of understanding of the music business, along with production problems for the record's sleeve, meant the album was delayed for almost a year and the momentum was lost. It made sense that Warhol designed the cover and he came up with the tantalising slogan 'Peel slowly and see' beside a single banana and his stamped signature. The cover didn't even have the band's name on it. What really made it different, however, and led to the delays, was that he wanted the banana image to be able to be peeled off, revealing a bright pink peeled banana image underneath.

Warhol photographed a banana, made a silk screen of it and then printed off a few copies. Like much of his work it became an iconic image of twentieth-century art and one of the best-known album covers of all time. The whole concept was to cheekily symbolise male genitalia. Other ideas that were considered included the reprinting of the worst live reviews of the band and photos of the faces of post-plastic surgery patients. Needless to say the record label wasn't too happy about either of these suggestions.

The peelable banana caused problems when a special machine had to be designed to manufacture the cover and after countless hold-ups the bananas were eventually applied by hand. The first pressing of the album not only had the peelable banana but also a gatefold sleeve: both these innovations were dropped on subsequent pressings to save on the high production costs. Later editions also had the band's name on the cover, because although having the Warhol stamped signature denoted that the whole concept of the album from the music to the packaging was art, some thought that it was an album of Andy Warhol music.

On the back of the sleeve the band were featured in five head-and-shoulder photographs. 'Everyone got the chance to pick their own picture but me,' recalled Moe Tucker. 'I was working and couldn't go into the city that morning, and Paul Morrissey picked it out. And I thought, "Oh my God, what did he pick?" because his taste is a little bit different to mine, but when I saw it I was really relieved.'

Delays in the official release of the album just meant it had longer to permeate through the record industry. In late-1966 Ken Pitt, the manager of a 19-year-old English singer-songwriter called Dave Jones, acquired a copy on a business trip to New York and took it back for the singer. 'Andy Warhol's music is as bad as his painting,' said the manager. Jones, who later changed his name to David Bowie, thought, 'Oh, I'm going to like this', and he said it was a revelation. 'Everything I both felt and didn't know about rock music was opened to me,' recalls Bowie. 'The music was savagely indifferent to my feelings. It didn't care if I liked it or not. This was a degree of cool that I had no idea was humanly sustainable and it was ravishing.' Before the album was released Bowie was already including 'I'm Waiting For The Man' in his set list with his band, The Riot Squad.

Another Englishman to be excited by this unreleased gem was The Beatles' manager Brian Epstein. He was said to have taken a promo copy with him when he took a vacation with John Lennon, and that he played it constantly. Later he met Lou Reed in New York and considered taking on the band's European management duties. 'We had a lot of dealings with Brian Epstein,' said Sterling Morrison. 'He loved the first album, and it was his favourite record for a long time. We had a lot of talks with him, riding in his car around Manhattan. First he wanted to sign us and have us be his only American group.' The Velvets refused the offer as they were happy being managed by Warhol, who could guarantee more publicity in the United States, but more talks continued in 1967 and the European issue was raised. 'So then the second round of talks was about Three Prong Music, our publishing company,' continues Morrison. 'He wanted it to merge with Nemperor, The Beatles' publishing company. We fretted and fretted over this and decided that if Epstein thought the stuff was so great, maybe we should hang onto it. We couldn't see any advantage to being part of Nemperor – who was ever going to record our stuff? So that was the end of that. But then the third offer Epstein made was to put together a big European tour and we said that was fine and then, on the eve of the final signing, Epstein died.'

With Epstein's death, the hope of any European success faded too. The band decided that they should concentrate on home territory first anyway, so when Verve said the album would be out in the spring, they set their sights on making 1967 the year they finally made it.

Andy Warhol, ever the master of hyperbole, had posters plastered all over Manhattan proclaiming Nico as the 'Pop Girl of 66'. Now, however, it was 1967. The superstar of the previous year was trying to go it alone and was singing downstairs at Stanley's, under the old Dom on St Mark's Place.

It was being made clear that any new Velvet Underground material was unlikely to be written specifically for her, and she had always wanted to be a solo star anyway. She was increasingly being ridiculed at Velvets' rehearsals for singing off-key, so she took a step away from the band with these weekly shows. Besides, she needed the money. Initially she asked Lou Reed to accompany her on guitar but he refused point-blank and sarcastically suggested that she should sing along to a tape machine. Which is exactly what she did.

The sight of the beautiful but ultimately sad-looking German sitting there on stage with a battered old tape deck was a pitiful one and before long she had a series of people volunteering to help her out. She played on a bill with Tim Buckley, was given a song by Tim Hardin and was joined on stage by Sterling Morrison, John Cale, Ramblin' Jack Elliott, Lou Reed (after he decided that he'd been too cruel and sat in for a few shows) and 16-year-old Jackson Browne, who'd just arrived in New York.

Jackson Browne had travelled from California to see the relatively unknown 19-year-old Tim Buckley play in New York. Paul Morrissey was aware of Buckley, and hired him to play with

Nico. Every night Browne would be watching from the front row. He caught Nico's eye and the two started an affair. Browne revealed that he too had been writing songs, and when Morrissey heard them he also got Browne to accompany Nico on stage. Browne learned her Velvet Underground tunes and she sang some of his songs.

Encouraged by Warhol and Paul Morrissey, who thought she had more chance of making it with a solo career, Nico would sing her Velvets' songs, her early singles and the new songs donated by generous songwriters, plus a couple of unreleased tracks, 'Wrap Your Troubles in Dreams' and 'Melody Laughter'. Warhol suggested that to give herself an enhanced air of detachment she should sing inside a Plexiglas cube.

The rest of the band continued to work on new material most days, though Moe Tucker was still working for some of the time and didn't play on the five-song demo tape that was pressed up as an acetate for MGM. It was in John Cale's still-unheated loft that they worked through the coldest months of the year, despite the fact that the last album still hadn't been released and was still gathering dust in the label's vaults.

All of the songs recorded in early 1967 lasted for less than three minutes and 'There Is No Reason' went on for not much more than two. It was an acoustic lament: the singer of the song has been hard done by and Reed complains that there was no reason for him to be treated so badly. 'Sheltered Life' also shows an immature character, this time listing all the things the protagonist hasn't done in his sheltered life. It was the only one of this batch of songs that Reed takes a solo song-writing credit for, though he should maybe have disowned the overly-comic kazoo solo. He would later re-record it for one of his solo albums in the 1970s. 'It's Allright (The Way That You Live)' echoed some of the semi-ballads from *The Velvet Underground & Nico* and 'I'm Not Too Sorry (Now That You're Gone)' was an echo-y metallic-sounding take which featured some blues guitar effects from Sterling Morrison. The only one of these songs to later be used by the band was 'Here She Comes Now', which at this point was little more than a rough melodic idea with viola and some sparse words from Reed.

In March 1967 *The Velvet Underground & Nico* was finally ready, and arrived in the shops under the Verve imprint of MGM. The album is now regarded as one of the most important albums of all time,[1] but then it was so far under the radar that few people outside of New York City even knew it existed.

As soon as the album hit the shops, it hit a problem. Eric Emerson, who had appeared in some of Warhol's films, saw the back cover and kicked up a fuss. It showed a concert picture of the band and his face could be seen on a film projected behind the stage. He hadn't been asked to give his permission and so he threatened to take MGM to court. The album was immediately pulled from the shops and then later returned with a sticker over Emerson's face.[2]

The music that finally reached the ears of the American fans (it would be a further six months before the album received its UK release) caused a reaction. In some cases it was very good, and others very bad. The era that the album was documenting had already changed and it seemed to be out of its time. Set starkly against the backdrop of New York City, *The Velvet Underground & Nico* provided a slap in the face to the sound of the West Coast. It was a culture clash between triply hippy flower power and alternative, tough streetwise Easterners. The West Coast sang of magic castles and everyone being high and happy, the Velvets put forward a picture of loneliness, drug-induced paranoia and masochism. The album swung from one extreme to the other. The cacophony of 'Venus In Furs' and 'European Son' contrasted sharply with the delicate tones of 'Sunday Morning' and 'I'll Be Your Mirror'.

The late addition of 'Sunday Morning' as the opening track, though it failed to propel the album up the charts, did work as a softly softly introduction to the world of The Velvet Underground. It could be accused of being a false introduction, as the rest of the album bore little resemblance to the gentle waves of Reed's subtle vocals and the chiming Celeste (a small xylophone) put down by John Cale. A close listen to the words gives an underlying sense of unease that things aren't quite right on the seemingly serene picture being painted. The album really took off with the second track, 'I'm Waiting For The Man', which gave a sense of the power of their music. As abruptly as 'I'm Waiting For The Man' had leapt out, it faded away and 'Femme Fatale' strolled into view. As Moe Tucker enthused, 'The songs Nico sang were *perfect* for her', and listening to this particular song it's hard to argue with that observation. Her air of detachment drifts along with the melody and she sounds like she really doesn't care at all. The Germanic pronunciation of words like 'clown' which comes out as 'claaahhn' is both charming and unique.

'Venus In Furs' was the first time that the album demonstrated why The Velvet Underground *really* were very different, both musically and lyrically. The opening drones of John Cale's viola still sound unique in rock music 40 years later. 'The Velvets made some beautiful music with John Cale's viola,' said The Strokes' Julian Casablancas in 2004. Moe Tucker's basic beat almost never changes through the whole song, while Sterling Morrison's guitar flutters around the viola. The tune moves along at an almost funereal pace and Reed deadpans the vocal of various sexual images. The supposed free-thinking 1960s were horrified: the song was banned from radio and the band were labelled as some kind of deviant perverts. 'I saw the book *Venus In Furs* [by Leopold Von Sacher-Masoch],' said Reed. 'I just thought it would be a great idea for a song. Now everybody thinks I invented masochism.' In the 1990s, a perfect example of how the world has changed came about when a well-known tyre company used the song for a primetime television commercial. 'I love the "Banana" album so much,' said Sterling Morrison. 'It's so innocent. Everybody was saying this is the vision of all-time evil and I always said well, we're not going to lie. It's pretty. "Venus in Furs" is a beautiful song. It was the closest we ever came in my mind to being exactly what I thought we could be. Always on other songs I'm hearing what I'm hearing, but I'm also hearing what I wish I were hearing.'

'Run Run Run', backed by what could be described as a native-American war-beat, bounced along telling, of the perils of trying to score drugs in Union Square. Each short verse concerns a different fictional character (Mary, Margarita, Sarah and Harry). 'All Tomorrow's Parties' closed side one with another Nico vocal. It builds slowly from Moe Tucker's beat, which conjures an image of her pounding away on a slave galleon in the middle ages; John Cale's wild-man piano and then Nico's intimidating vocal. Two versions of the song exist: one with Nico singing straight and the other with her voice double tracked to give more of an eerie feel to it.

'Heroin' opened side two, gaining momentum as the song speeds up, as does 'There She Goes' during the bridge. These songs demonstrated the metronome-like ability of the band to play as a unit. The latter borrowed the intro riff from Marvin Gaye's 'Hitch Hike'. 'We could, and did, play well together,' says

Sterling Morrison. 'Metronomically, we were a pretty accurate band. If we were speeding up and slowing down, it was by design. If you listen to the solo break on "There She Goes Again" it slows down. Slower and slower and slower, and then when it comes back into the "Bye-bye-byes". It's double the original tempo, a tremendous leap to twice the speed. We always tinkered with that.'

'I'll Be Your Mirror' was another delicate song sung and inspired by Nico. Lou Reed took a comment she made and wrote a song about it. Later he pointed out that the song is not just about reflecting back what you want to see, but what you *should* see.

'The Black Angel's Death Song' highlighted the more experimental leanings of the band. Distilled from a squealing Cale viola riff, Reed quickly spits out his vocal, with Cale hissing in the background. The closing 'European Son' was subtitled as being dedicated to Delmore Schwartz. While amazing for its time, it's not so outrageous today. The song begins as a guitar-driven rock track and it hops along until at the one-minute mark all hell breaks loose. The screeching chair and breaking glass are a prelude to everyone going off in their own noise-making direction for the next seven minutes. 'No one knows why that is,' said Sterling Morrison (of the Schwartz dedication). 'Everyone thinks it's because the song is thematically appropriate: "You killed your European son/You split on those under 21". Incidentally that may be true because Delmore was the son of Jewish émigrés and a great poet, who was never accepted. But the real reason is that it has only two stanzas of lyrics and a long instrumental break. Delmore thought rock-and-roll lyrics were the worst things he'd ever heard in his life; he despised songs with words. As this was our big instrumental outing on the album we dedicated it to him.'

The loss of momentum caused by delays in producing the album and the withdrawal from the shops because of Eric Emerson were compounded when the print media decided to refuse adverts for the album, based on the perceived wicked inclusion of songs about sex and drugs. 'We were surprised at how vast the reaction was against us,' admitted Lou Reed. 'I thought we were doing something ambitious and I was very taken aback by it. I used to hear people say we were doing porn rock.' Many East Coast radio stations also refused to play it, though it did get some airplay on the West Coast. The few reviews that made it to press were mixed and the LP got to number 171 in the album charts. Later estimates that the album sold 30,000 copies in the first five years seem overly optimistic.

'The Velvet Underground produces a type of music that is distinctly different from American popular music,' wrote Timothy Jacobs in *Vibrations*. 'A good first album,' he concluded, 'though in the future we hope that other efforts will not be quite as negative.'

Reed was indignant. 'We're attacked constantly,' he claimed. 'No one ever writes anything nice about us, or even looks at it very seriously, which is fine. You get tired of being called obscene. Our favourite quote was "The flowers of evil are in bloom. Someone has to stamp them out before they spread."'

In the face of this reaction, MGM were like a rabbit in the headlights: they just didn't know what to do. They didn't distribute the album as well as they might have done, thinking that the Andy Warhol name would be all the publicity it needed. 'It's still a mystery why MGM signed us if they didn't know how to deal with us,' said Moe Tucker.

The lack of hometown support in New York hit the band particularly hard. 'A rational response would have been to rent a hall in New York and play there every night,' said Sterling Morrison. 'Instead we said, "Fuck 'em. If they're not going to play us on the radio, we're not going to play here."' And they didn't. Between May 1967 and the summer of 1970 they would play only once (and that was only for 10 minutes at a fundraiser in November 1967) in New York City. 'The Fugs, The Holy Modal Rounders and The Velvet Underground were the only authentic Lower East Side bands,' said Sterling Morrison. 'We were real bands playing for real people in a real scene. We helped each other out if we could, and generally hung out at the same places.'

Meanwhile, Nico had stepped to one side again and was conducting her own sessions for her debut album, *Chelsea Girls*. These took place in April and May, with significant help from Cale, Reed and Morrison. At the Mayfair Sound Studios in New York on a single day in April, she recorded with Jackson Browne, using the songs she had been given by Browne, Dylan and Hardin, and the Velvets recorded their own five songs with her. Tom Wilson produced the sessions and was an enthusiastic supporter. With Larry Fallon[3] arranging string sections all over the album, it stands a baroque collection. The title track, 'Chelsea Girls' (a Reed/Morrison composition), and Reed's 'Wrap Your Troubles in Dreams' are two highlights of the collection. MGM thought they had a solo star on their hands, especially compared to the problems that the Velvets' debut album was having. *Chelsea Girls* was something they could relate to – a beautiful blonde singing simple songs. But like the Velvets' album, it too failed to catch fire. 'I wish they'd just have allowed Cale to arrange it and let me do some more stuff on it,' said Lou Reed. 'Everything on it, those strings, that flute, should have defeated it. But with the lyrics and Nico's voice, it somehow managed to survive.'

The summer of 1967 has become known as the Summer of Love, but there wasn't much love in The Velvet Underground camp. In what would be the final 'proper' New York show for three years, they played in a low-ceilinged basement club called Steve Paul's Scene in May. The walls had alcoves in them and each band member stood in one to play. 'It was getting so esoteric, it was nuts,' recalls John Cale. 'The Mafia was beating people up,' said Sterling Morrison. 'They were having these incredible fights, thugs coming in. So Steve Paul just shut it down. That was going on at Arthur's, too.'

The lack of commercial success with the album meant that Warhol lost some of his interest in the band and turned back to films. He was aiming to show his *Chelsea Girls*[4] movie at the Cannes Film Festival (won by Michelangelo Antonioni's *Blow Up*) and though he took a large group of people with him, including Nico, he tellingly left The Velvet Underground behind. Warhol was a mass-production commercial artist first and foremost. He'd previously taken out small newspaper advertisements saying that he'd endorse almost any product if the price was right. The Velvets weren't looking likely to make any money and so he was ready to move on.

When the Warhol troupe returned from Europe, The Velvet Underground had travelled up to Boston to play at the Boston Tea Party club. The Tea Party was starting to become one of the East Coast's premier rock venues and it was to be the spiritual home of the Velvets during their self-imposed exile from the Big Apple.

The club's entrance displayed panels of the names of 'those who had given light to the world' – Prometheus, Edison and others – and inside it had one of the best light shows around, something which obviously appealed to the Velvets. 'Boston was the whole thing as far as we were concerned,' said Lou Reed. 'It was the first time that we didn't have all these things thrown at us: the leather freaks, the druggies, the this and that. It was the first time that somebody just listened to the music. Which blew our minds.'

Nico had a show in New York and was torn between staying for her own show or joining up with the band. Eventually she set off for Boston, but was too late. The show had already started when she arrived and Lou Reed refused to allow her on stage. Afterwards her role in the band was discussed and it was thought better that she left. 'Everybody wanted to be the star,' said Nico. 'Of course Lou always was. But the newspapers came to me all the time. That's how I got fired – he couldn't take that anymore. He fired me.'

'I put it down to the fact that they had fallen out as lovers,' recalls John Cale. 'But this was symbolic of cutting the umbilical cord with Warhol.'

Meanwhile, Reed was at a crossroads with Andy Warhol. Soon after Nico left, he arranged a meeting with his manager. At the meeting, Warhol explained that he could only get the band opportunities to play at universities and art shows, and if they wanted to get into the mainstream they'd have to do it alone, and so Reed said he wanted out of the contract. Warhol agreed to release the band from its obligations but still expected to get his agreed 25 per cent of their earnings from the debut album. 'Warhol was furious,' Reed later recalled. 'I'd never seen Andy angry, but I did that day. He was really mad: he turned bright red and called me a rat. That was the worst thing he could think of.' The rest of the band weren't so sure about the wisdom of severing links with their instant publicity machine. 'A smart move, I don't think,' snapped John Cale. The era of the EPI was officially over.

'I couldn't believe it,' continued Cale. 'The only way I can look at it is that to be prepared for success, you first of all have to have a stable personality, which Lou didn't. Neither did I, to be fair. And so we were never ready for success.'

'Lou was starting to act funny,' he added. 'He brought in this guy called Sesnick, who I thought was a real snake, to be our manager, and all this intrigue started to take place. Lou was calling us "his band" while Sesnick was trying to get him to go solo. Maybe it was the drugs he was doing at the time – they certainly didn't help.'

Over the summer Reed increasingly experimented with psychedelics. With Steve Sesnick (who also co-owned the Boston Tea Party) installed as their manager, the Velvets set off on a summer tour but it was sorely missing Warhol's promotional genius and the shows were sparsely attended.

The band used these summer dates to work up arrangements for a new set of songs. 'White Light/White Heat', 'I Heard Her Call My Name' and a lengthy jam-type song called 'Searchin' (later re-titled 'Sister Ray') were all debuted, while 'Here She Comes Now' was resurrected out of the discarded demos made at the start of the year. By September they were ready to go back into the studio and work on their next album.

Chapter 8
1968
White Heat

'White Light/White Heat was all energy, the result of our experiences as a road band. We'd actually worked very hard on the arrangements for the first album. When we went in to do White Light/White Heat, no one had any patience any more to work on the arrangements, and it shows. We were rabid.'

John Cale

In September 1967, the set-up for the Velvet's second album *White Light/White Heat* was much more organised than for their debut. As they had a record deal, MGM helped arrange a studio, Mayfair Sound Studios in New York, and a respected producer, which again was Tom Wilson, assisted by engineer Gary Kellgran.

Wilson was perhaps a strange choice to keep the band in check and seemed more interested in having a good time at the sessions. John Cale says, 'Tom Wilson knew more Ladies of the Night than there are women on the planet. He was inspired, though, and used to joke around to keep everybody in the band light.' It didn't help his enthusiasm that the band were presenting him with music that he had a hard time relating to. His background of jazz and folk rock was far removed from the manic abrasiveness of the feedback-drenched songs, which often featured white noise as an extra instrument. 'Who's playing bass?' Wilson would ask. 'There is no bass,' the band would reply. 'How long does this song last?' the producer queried. 'We don't know,' they said, 'It just goes on until we finish.' The outcome was that Wilson would set them up, then wander in and out, leaving them to their own devices, just as they had operated on the first album.

The freedom in the studio meant the label had no idea what was being recorded. They must have hoped for a more conservative set of songs that might even have allowed some promotional airplay. But no, they eventually got a bizarre compendium that covered drug use ('White Light/White Heat'), manslaughter ('The Gift'), horrific medical experiments ('Lady Godiva's Operation') and a 17-minute noise fest about a transvestite's sexual adventures ('Sister Ray').

While The Beach Boys and The Beatles had set up a private competition to push the conventional limits of rock via *Pet Sounds* and *Sgt. Pepper's Lonely Hearts Club Band* respectively, The Velvet Underground truly pushed all the limits. With the amps literally turned up to their limit and little separation between tracks on the tape, they took just three days to record the basis of this reverberating black album. It was the first non-melodic noise collection in popular music and while rock and roll is a limiting art form by its very nature, they ignored this. The band wrote what they were experiencing at the time: confusion, despair, horror, even the ballads were barbed. The album's extreme white noise, stripped-down electric guitars and primal beats would inspire bands for generations to come.

'White Light/White Heat', a reference to the temporary white-out blindness that certain amphetamines can cause, bursts from the speakers in a garage thrash of guitar and piano that almost needs the listener to take speed to be able to keep up. The band wanted to preserve the excitement that the songs exuded when they played live, and they managed this perfectly, right down to the chaotic ending. 'We didn't play a lot of overdubs because if we added too much on top we wouldn't be able to recreate it live at the shows,' said Moe Tucker.

Despite the album being regarded as a document of the band's raw power, Lou Reed said it didn't capture just how powerful the band really was. 'You can hear it on some bootlegs,' he said. 'That [power] never came across on record. They couldn't get the bottom end of it in those days. No engineer was going to come out and put a really good mic on a guitar like that, assuming they knew where to put it anyway. I wanted to control that noise, to get only the stuff I wanted out of it, even if it was arbitrary.'

The mood switched manically to the 'The Gift', a lethargic spoken-word story narrated by John Cale. The band had chosen the title from a Delmore Schwartz poem of the same name. Lasting almost ten minutes, the musical backing track is presented from one channel and the words from the other. Musically, the band took an instrumental jam that they played, 'Booker T' (named in tribute to the Memphis band Booker T and the MG's, who'd had a massive hit with 'Green Onions' in 1962), and adjusted its length to fit the spoken-word story. Cale read the unfortunate tale of Waldo Jeffers and his unlikely end in an emotionless monotone that managed to convey both sadness and sick comedy. At the climax of the story Lou Reed squashed a cantaloupe with a wrench, but you have to listen closely to hear the sound effect buried in the mix.

If Waldo Jeffers' demise was shocking, the story of 'Lady Godiva's Operation' was truly a Gothic horrific fable. John Cale again took over the main vocal duties, but this time he sang in a high register that gave a Gothic feel. What appears to be the story of a sex-change operation is graphically explained, but the patient starts to come round as the operation begins. The patient, strapped to the table, screams, and perhaps the doctor changes the purpose of the operation and starts making incisions else-where. Just enough is left to the imagination to make it sound even more terrifying. 'Here She Comes Now' was originally a Nico song when they played live, but here Lou Reed does a fine job with the vocals. The song evolved in the studio. Lyrically sparse but musically delicate, it builds to a satisfying crescendo.

'There's the gender confusion in the song,' explained Lou Reed. 'Fear of sleep. The perfect thing for the people we were running around with, staying up fifteen days at a time.'

Side two contained just two songs, opening with the scream-ing guitars and gang vocals of 'I Heard Her Call My Name'. Reed's out-of-control guitar was turned right up in the mix after the band had finished working on the track and he went back and remixed the tape. This caused serious argument within the Velvets and for a couple of days Sterling Morrison walked out.

'We didn't want to lay down separate tracks, we wanted to do it in the studio live with a simultaneous voice, but the problem was that the current state of studio art wouldn't let us do it,' recalls Morrison. 'There was fantastic [sound] leakage because everyone was playing so loud and we had so much electronic junk with us in the studio, all these fuzzers and compressors. Gary Kellgran, who is ultra-competent, told us repeatedly, "All the needles are on red." And we reacted as we always reacted, "Look, we don't know what goes on in there

and we don't want to hear about it. Just do the best you can."
And so the album is all fuzzy, there's all that white noise.'

It was one of the rare occasions when the usual stabilising
influence of Moe Tucker was irked. 'When he [Reed] remixed
that, he turned the guitar solo way up and because he did that,
the rhythm section was drowned out and the solo just became
this noise,' she said. 'It was a stunning solo when you could hear
the rhythm going on, not just Lou blasting away, and still when
I hear it, it breaks my heart. In my view it's totally ruined, a real
bone of contention.'

Everything about the album-ending 'Sister Ray' was mind-
blowing. First, it lasted 17 minutes, and though other bands like
The Doors (with 'When The Music's Over' clocking in at almost
11 minutes) had recently released lengthy album tracks, this
really tested the listener's dedication. Then there's no bass, it's
just drums, two guitars and an organ. Technically it's a sonic
mess, lo-fi way before the phrase was coined. Reed's vocals
(which aren't heard until the six-minute introduction is complete)
come in and out of the mix, and tell crazy stories of counter-
culture characters. Phrases like 'Sucking on my ding-dong'
emerge from the mix and then slip back into fogs of feedback
and battles between the organ and twin guitars.

They tried several takes of the song, but each time they all
wanted to take things in a different direction. So the idea
emerged that they would all play in one take and everyone could
do exactly as they wanted and that would be the final song.
Luckily some semblance of order is maintained by Moe Tucker's
metronomic beat, which allows the improvisations to find a
base, but even she abandons her station after about a quarter of
an hour. At the point where Reed sings 'Who's Knockin', Tucker
was going to tap the rim of one of her drums. Wilson forgot to

turn on the mic at the right moment so it sounds like she's stopped playing. Homosexuality, drugs and murder are mentioned but it's hard to follow the narrative exactly. Morrison and Reed take turns to give virtuoso guitar performances and Cale's organ matches them, step-for-step. 'There is a musical struggle,' explains Sterling Morrison. 'Everyone's trying to do what they want to do every second, and nobody's backing off. I think it's great the way the organ comes in. Cale starts to try and play a solo. He's totally buried and there's a sort of surge, and then he's pulling out all the stops until he just rises out of the pack. He was able to get louder than Lou and I were. The drums are almost totally drowned out. We were doing the whole heavy-metal trip back then. If "Sister Ray" isn't an example of heavy metal, I don't know what is.'

'I like to think of Sister Ray as a transvestite smack dealer,' said Lou Reed. 'The situation is a bunch of drag queens taking some sailors home with them, and shooting up on smack and having this orgy when the police appear.' Everyone agreed that this structured mayhem was the record closest to the sound of the early Velvet Underground ever committed to tape. And what glorious mayhem it was.

The packaging of the LP could hardly have been more in contrast to the debut album. The black cover actually had a black skull printed on it, also in black, to make it almost impossible to see. It was a photograph of a tattoo on Billy Name's arm (Andy Warhol's idea that Name had carried out). This nihilistic look was in stark contrast to the other album covers of the day, which invariably seemed to feature brightly coloured graphics and colour photographs of the smiling artists. In 1971, a UK version was issued that had a completely different cover – a black-and-white photograph of toy soldiers.

The engineers at MGM were mystified when they were given the tapes of feedback and noise to master. The album sounded like it hadn't been produced at all and it wasn't until CD reissues in the late 1990s that any listenable versions of it were available. At the time, it failed to even reach the miserable chart placing of *The Velvet Underground & Nico*.[1]

After finishing the album, the band took a break. *White Light/White Heat* was not going to be released until the following January, and after almost two years of constant work and touring they needed a rest. Around this time John Cale was seeing the young fashion designer Betsey Johnson and the couple moved into the Chelsea hotel together. Cale soon went down with hepatitis after sharing one too many drug needles. He and Johnson had planned to be married, but it was postponed when Cale turned yellow and he had to spend a couple of months recovering in hospital. 'I worried whether John was going to be alive every day,' admitted Johnson, 'even though I didn't want to know what he was doing to himself.' By then Sterling Morrison had also met his future wife, Martha Dargan, and moved in with her. The days of the three male members of The Velvet Underground living together and working on songs every day at the loft were over.

It's not surprising that the staff at Verve didn't know what to make of The Velvet Underground, how to handle them or how to help them. The label had been founded by Norman Granz, a jazz pioneer who helped get jazz shows played in concert halls and played on the radio. After working with Mercury Records in the late 1940s he formed Verve in 1956 as a specialist label to handle jazz recordings. The likes of Duke Ellingon, Charlie Parker and Dizzy Gillespie all recorded for Verve. Then in the

1960s he sold the label and its catalogue to MGM, who wanted to expand its appeal to other musical genres.

Lack of understanding by the label meant that when *White Light/White Heat* was released and sold in such low numbers, the band wouldn't be seeing royalties any time soon and so they had to set off on the road again. 'There was an incoherence of where we should go,' recalls John Cale. 'Suddenly the bands that opened for us [the previous year] were having success and we couldn't get booked. There was a slow erosion of our musical camaraderie.'

Despite having recorded two albums, been on numerous tours and having had the support of Andy Warhol, the Velvets were still far from being a commercial success. Their music being out of step with the times was the main reason, having a manager and label that didn't know where/how to market them or even get them on the radio was another, but even if they had known then how they would have been up against it due to the band's sex-and-drugs image, a big barrier to getting onto mainstream radio in the 1960s. Escalating problems within the band just made things even worse. They were the disaffected and the downtrodden, the outsiders and the misfits, and when they did manage to seep through to the audiences who might be receptive to their music and aesthetic, it was too late: the band was over, but the myth would then start to grow.

Cale was becoming disillusioned that the original premise of the band, chaos and orchestration was being replaced by structure and lyrics. In short, he didn't like it that they were becoming a pop group. Despite these growing differences, they played show after show. Regular haunts in Boston, Chicago and Cleveland were visited again and again.

'The unanimous opinion was that we were ten times better live than on records,' said Sterling Morrison. 'We never played a song the same way twice: we never wanted to, maybe never could. And Lou changed lyrics all the time. One of his great talents is that he can spontaneously generate lyrics on stage, just like the old blues singers. Lou can go on forever rhyming. We had plenty of opportunity on stage to do whatever we wanted; we could croak our harmonies any way we pleased. John and I did a lot of back-up vocals, that was a riot in itself. Starting "White Light", we'd sing together. One night John just kept silent, leaving me to squawk the lyrics. I thought, "All right, I'll fix that son-of-a-bitch!" The next time we did the song, I kept my mouth shut. That kind of stunt went on all the time.'

In April, Cale married Betsey Johnson and the marriage drove a further wedge between himself and Reed. The Velvets had played in Johnson's trendy clothes store *Paraphernalia* and she had made some of Cale's classy-looking outfits. *Paraphernalia* specialised in 'experimental' clothes that moved quickly with the times. What would you wear on the Moon? was the question asked. The shop aimed to provide some answers. 'Someone showed me a photo I'd never seen of The Velvet Underground at the opening of *Paraphernalia*,' recalled John Cale. 'I knew the projectors were connected, but where were we plugged in? Where was the PA? You can see me staring quizzically. I followed the wires and what I found was that all our vocal mics and all our guitars were plugged into one Silvertone amp. We must have sounded like shit.'

Johnson was a strong woman, who Cale could turn to. Reed felt threatened by her in the context of the group's dynamic. 'There was little to disguise the fact that Lou was wary, if not paranoid of strangers,' said Cale. This in turn gave Sesnick more ammunition to further his own cause within the developing power struggle, to strengthen his hold on the band. The diverging visionaries of Cale and Reed were now at breaking point, but they still managed to work together.

The Velvet Underground made two live TV appearances during their original life span, both on Cleveland's *Upbeat* local TV show. The first appearance on 8 January 1967 featured the then-unreleased song 'Guess I'm Falling In Love'. Marvin Gaye and Tammi Terrell also appeared on the show. Their second appearance saw them rip through a feedback-drenched version of 'Run Run Run' on 11 May 1968. As they ran past the end of their allowed time, the song continued as the advertisement break kicked in.

Sesnick arranged for the band to spend the summer on the West Coast in an effort to raise their profile there. New York was a dead loss and though they'd played Boston and the Midwest to death, they weren't big markets like Los Angeles and San Francisco were. The Shrine Hall in the former and the Avalon Ballroom in the latter were played (they avoided the Fillmore), and trips further afield included San Diego and Vancouver.

It was while they were out on the West Coast that the Velvets received some chilling news. They were staying at the Beverly Wilshire hotel in Los Angeles, and Reed and Sesnick got in an elevator to go down for breakfast. As was the custom, the hotel had left a pile of the morning's newspapers in the lift for guests to take. Reed glanced down at the headline and his heart skipped a beat: Andy Warhol had been shot in New York. Unfortunately it was one of a number of high-profile assassination attempts during the decade: Jack Kennedy, Martin Luther King, and just days after Warhol was shot, Bobby Kennedy was shot and murdered in Los Angeles. The difference with Warhol was that he managed to survive. The assailant, Valerie Solanas, had been an actress in some of his films, but when Warhol lost a script that she'd written she turned on him. It was touch and go whether he would survive the point-blank shooting, but after long hours of surgery he pulled through. Solanas served just three years in jail for the attack. When Reed heard the news, he was initially scared to call Warhol, fearful that his former manager might reject him. When he eventually called, Warhol asked him why he hadn't come to visit him. Reed felt terrible and their relationship never quite recovered.

Towards the end of September 1968, the band played a couple of shows in Boston. They would prove to be John Cale's last appearance with the band. Relations between Cale and Reed were at a low and had been for most of the summer. Cale wanted big grand songs with experimental orchestration, while Reed preferred pretty songs with strong lyrical and pop content. Cale had also been spending money on extravagant electronic schemes. One involved attaching two guitars and playing them as a single instrument; another was a dream of a sub-sonic sounding drum that you could feel but couldn't hear. Moe Tucker recalls the problems were simple to understand, though: 'It has a lot to do with ego problems. If Lou said to me, "Moe, try some cymbals on this one, I want to hear what it sounds like," fine, that didn't bother me. But for Lou to say, "Sterl, try this," it didn't sit quite so well.'

Reed called a band meeting at the Riviera Cafe in the West Village. Moe Tucker and Sterling Morrison were intrigued by the purpose of the meeting: they didn't usually have band meetings as such and wondered what he wanted to talk about. They arrived early and took up a table. Then Reed arrived, but there was no sign of John Cale. 'John's not coming,' explained Reed. 'He's out of the band.' Tucker and Morrison were shocked, but the shock soon turned to anger. Fists were banged on tabletops and accusations thrown. Morrison argued that they were a band and they couldn't just kick someone out. 'Okay, you don't buy it?' countered Reed, 'Then that's it, the band is over.'

Morrison and Tucker wanted the band to continue, but without Reed's songwriting it seemed impossible and so they reluctantly agreed to his requests. 'I'm sure I knew there were tensions but I didn't think it was as bad as that,' recalls Tucker. 'I was only around at weekends and so I wasn't privy to the ins and outs of the relationship.'

'Now I could say that it was more important to keep the band together than to worry about Cale, but that wasn't really what decided me. I just wanted to keep on doing it,' said Morrison. 'So finally I weighed my self-interest against Cale's interests and sold him out. I told Lou I'd swallow it, but I didn't really like it.' For Moe Tucker it was the same situation.

'There seemed to be nothing I could do to keep John in the band,' continued Morrison. 'One thing that really rankled was John insisting on building this bass amp of his with band money. Something to do with acoustic suspension speakers producing this great wall of sound. Thousands were spent on these god-damn things, and then they didn't work. Meanwhile, we were on endorsement to Acoustic Amplifiers, who made this fabulous bass amp, the Acoustic 360. John refused even to accept a free one from the factory. Later on, John found out that if only he'd had a pre-amp, it would have worked. All this money for what I called the "Tower Of Babble". There was a general dissatisfaction with his free-spiriting and free-spending. It really did piss everybody off. What the hell was he up to? But it was an ugly business, stupid and counter-productive. Our struggles to succeed on our own terms, once directed at audiences, record execs, radio stations and what not, perhaps turned inward towards the group, with unfortunate consequences.'

The icing on the cake was that Reed couldn't bring himself to tell Cale face to face, so he got Morrison to carry the bad news instead. Betsey Johnson wasn't surprised, though: 'It seemed real logical to me,' she said. 'I just really supported him and thought that he ought to do his own music.'

'The music had become secondary,' said Cale. 'There was too much acrimony and social antics going on. Steve Sesnick built up a barrier between Lou and the rest of the band. Lou and I were very close and running the band, and gradually Steve came along and said, "Lou's the songwriter, he's the star", and I decided I was going to find another career. I don't think I'm blameless about what happened, but Lou never confronted me, saying, I don't want you around anymore. It was all done by sleight of hand, which left Sterling and Moe in a very tortured position. Whenever a new song came around, it was like picking at sores. It was very badly handled and exacerbated constantly by Steve Sesnick. Even Lou sees that now.'

Reed later defended his actions by shifting the blame squarely onto Sesnick's shoulders. 'I think it was foul and disgusting management,' he claimed. But Sterling Morrison cut to the heart of the problem: the relationship between Reed and Cale had started to schism. They were developing into very different artists and men. 'John was getting very flamboyant,' he said. 'His girlfriend [Betsey Johnson] was dressing him and he was really shaping up as a performer, playing very energetically. Then Lou just got uptight. There was some kind of collision.'

Morrison wasn't quick to let Reed off the hook, though. 'I love Lou, but he has what must be a fragmented personality, so you're never too sure under any conditions what you're going to have to deal with,' he said. 'Will he be boyishly charming? Naïve? Lou is very charming when he wants to be. Or will he be vicious? And if he is, then you have to figure out what's stoking the fire. What drug is he on, or what mad diet? He had all sorts of strange dietary theories. He'd eat nothing, live on wheat husks, I don't know. He was always trying to move mentally and spiritually to some place where no one had ever gotten before.'

Whether conciliatory, or simply resigned, Cale took it all in his stride. 'I learned a lot from Lou,' he said. 'From the first time I met him, I thought he was an interesting character. He showed me a lot of sides of New York, what life was like here. I was green when I came here, very wet behind the ears, very clerical. I found someone who understood the place very well and knew how to negotiate his way through it.'

But there was no time for recriminations: the band had shows booked and though they didn't expect to find anyone who could replace Cale's unique viola playing, they did need a bassist. The gritty, experimental New York band was about to embrace a new member – a young bassist from Boston by the name of Doug Yule.

Chapter 9
1968–1969
Despite All the Amputations

'The main reason for Doug doing the vocals is that Lou's voice wasn't up to it when we were in the studio. Lou never had a durable voice, which is one of the reason we tried not to play too often. Since we wanted to get the album done, and since Doug could sing, he got the nod.'

Sterling Morrison

Just as 21-year-old Doug Yule was about to take a shower in his Boston apartment, the phone rang. He said hello and listened to what the caller had to say. 'Yes,' he replied, 'Of course . . . you mean this weekend . . . er, yes . . . okay . . . tonight? I guess so . . . okay . . . right . . . yes, bye.' As he put the phone down his mind was racing, his head spinning. It was a little after 6p.m., but this one phone call was about to change his life. After all, it's not every day you get a call out of the blue asking you to join The Velvet Underground.

He packed a small bag and called a friend, who as luck would have it, was right that moment preparing to drive down to New York City, which is where he needed to be that night. Forgetting all about the shower, he jumped in the car and set off for the Big Apple and the life of a rock musician.

Within a year the whole atmosphere surrounding The Velvet Underground had changed. Starting with the jettisoning of Nico, then Andy Warhol's sacking and the severance of all links to The Factory, its use as a rehearsal space and cast of characters; the introduction of Steve Sesnick as manager and finally the split with John Cale. This was now a very different band both physically and aesthetically. The loss of John Cale left a big hole in the Velvets sound and so they would have to head off in other musical directions. Which, of course, was exactly what Lou Reed had wanted.

Like Lou Reed, Sterling Morrison and Moe Tucker, John Cale's replacement Doug Yule grew up on Long Island. Born on 25 February 1947, he was five years younger than Reed and Morrison, a lot less experienced and still quite impressionable. He was part of a large family, with five sisters and a younger brother.

Yule had been surrounded by music from an early age. He started piano lessons in the fourth grade and his father, Alan, had played trumpet in a swing band. His mother, Dorothy was a secretary at the church where Doug would get lessons from the organist. His brother started playing drums in the fourth grade and all five sisters sang in the church choir. As well as tinkering around on the piano at home, he had baritone horn and tuba lessons while also taking his place in the church choir. All of this musical hyperactivity meant that he'd had an all-round, balanced, musical education before he'd even discovered rock and roll. 'This gave me a good sense for the lower end of music and in fact is probably why I play a little differently than most rock and roll bass players,' said Yule of his wide musical education. 'I lean towards a more melodic view with a tendency to counterpoint. It's a lot like the way Sterling [Morrison] played the guitar, but in a different register.'

'The first single I can remember owning was Freddie Cannon's "Sea Cruise,"' he recalls. 'My older sister Ellen listened to a lot of rock and roll, and I heard it too. The first radio program I remember was Martin Block's "Make Believe Ballroom". My father listened to the radio at night and Wednesday night was "World of Jazz" – lots of 1930s' and 1940s' swing. I've never been much of a record buyer, people would lend me things, and even today my record and CD collection is really tiny. There's always been so much music going on in my head that I didn't feel the need to listen to it all the time.'

Yule first played up a guitar at the age of 13, when his cousin showed him a few chords. Being a natural when it came to picking up musical instruments, this was all he needed and so off he went. 'I began listening to folk music in the early 60s,' he explains. 'Someone gave me a tenor banjo in High School and I converted it to a five-string after the neck was severed in a bicycle accident. Then I played bluegrass for several years during the mid-1960s. My first band was modelled on the Kingston Trio.[1] I got into the blues in the last year of High School and formed a band but we never performed.'

Yule had taken part in some High School and church drama classes, and had great ambitions to become an actor. He hung out with a group of actors whom he describes as 'a strange group', but then he discovered he was more interested in music when he got to Boston in the autumn of 1965. He enrolled at Boston University's Theater Department to major in acting, but it didn't go as he'd planned. 'I was a terrible actor,' he admits. 'To be a good actor you have to be in touch with some basic emotions and be able to actually feel them, but in the family I grew up in, we didn't have feelings and we didn't discuss them, and we didn't even know that we had them and so I made a terrible actor.'

He did use the academic year in Boston to make some friends and play in a series of bands, though. The first of these started unwittingly when he signed up to be in a movie clip for The Barbarians, a local garage-rock band. They were supposedly making a promotional film for their single 'Are You A Boy, Or Are You A Girl?'. After seeing an advert for 'longhaired' extras, Yule turned up at the club but the band never showed. Yule and some others who had made the effort killed some time while waiting for The Barbarians by jumping on stage and jamming with the band's equipment. It went well and on the spot they decided they should form a band of their own. 'We fooled around with The Barbarians' instruments and formed The Nickels,' said Yule. 'Later we became Our Boys when we got a new manager at the end of the first year of college.'

In the early summer of 1966 they started playing a few shows as a covers' band. One of their first shows was at a former strip club called the Brown Derby. The audience was a mixture of college friends and regulars at the bar, who seemed to be waiting for the girls to come out on stage, unaware that the stripping part of the entertainment no longer happened. Yule initially played guitar but when a new guitarist joined the band he used his versatility to switch to keyboards. He sang mostly harmonies in these early bands. When 'Give Me Some Loving' by The Spencer Davis Group reached the chart they immediately worked out how to play it, because that was what the customers in the bars would want to hear. Several line-up changes were made before a complicated situation brought the band to a premature end. 'The lead singer shacked up with the manager's wife in the drummer's apartment,' explains Yule. 'He locked the door and wouldn't open it. That was the end of the group.'

Yule was keen to keep playing, and soon hooked up with another covers' band called The Argonauts (later, The Argos), again on keyboards. The Argonauts did have some original material too, but they pretty much had to continue playing the covers in order to keep the paying audiences, and thus the club managers, happy while they could for $100 a night. The line-up of Yule, Russell Marcus (bass), Bob Gardner (drums) and Paul MacDonald (guitar and vocals) wore matching suits and played hotels around the Boston area. As the summer wore on and the new college year approached, Yule decided that acting classes weren't for him. Instead he chose to take off to California with his cousins to try and start a music career there. As he describes it, he quit school by 'the long-distance method'. California didn't work out either, and then just as he was about to head home he received his draft papers.

The war in Vietnam was a conflict many Americans neither wanted nor understood. Often violent protests scarred the country for years, as the nation's youth rebelled. One of the worst tragedies occurred at Kent State University when four students were shot and killed during an anti-war protest. By no means a political band, the Velvets made one of their very few social references in the song 'I'm Sticking With You' later in 1968. The couplet of 'Moon people going to the stratosphere/Soldiers fighting with the cong,' was as far as it went.

To deal with the draft board, Yule had to come back to New York from California and it was a scary time. 'I successfully managed to convince the Army not to take me into the War,' he explained. 'I went to a forensic psychologist who was actively against the war and who, within the letter of the law, found that I was basically eligible for a deferment and wrote a letter to that effect, which I took to the draft board.' According to the Selective Service laws at the time if you were under psychiatric treatment you were not eligible and had to be reviewed in a year. He seems to have had a lucky escape. 'Six months later they were tearing up letters from the same doctor,' he said, 'even though he was still within the Law. But the Army can pretty much do what they like.' For an unknown reason his review never came up and he managed to avoid being called up.

Breathing a big sigh of relief that he was still a civilian, Yule headed back up to Boston and right away set about looking for another band. A brief return to The Argos ended when he got the chance to become a member of an established band, The Glass Menagerie. He was offered the chance because he was renting an apartment on River Street from the band's manager, Hans Onsager, who at that time was starting as The Velvet Underground's road manager as well, taking over from David Cezanne.

Unlike Yule's previous musical exploits, The Glass Menagerie were a psychedelic band, derivative of the time they played in. Other members of the group were a female vocalist, Willie Alexander (drums), Walter Powers (bass) and Michael Tschudin (on keyboards). Yule joined as a guitarist and played with the band through 1968. He picked up the tunes, which were all originals, very quickly. 'It was a point of pride back then whether you were in a cover band or an original band,' said Yule. 'It wasn't a very good original band, but we made demo tapes.'

At River Street, Onsager had a rehearsal room and office downstairs, and the apartment upstairs. The apartment that Yule rented a room in was a six-bedroom affair. Hans Onsager would sometimes let The Velvet Underground and Steve Sesnick use it if they were in town and the label wasn't paying for a hotel. Because of his work with The Glass Menagerie, Yule would practise his guitar constantly, sometimes playing for seven hours a day. He and the Velvets got to be on 'hello' terms when they stayed at Onsager's apartment, and between visits Sterling Morrison noticed how much Yule had improved. He told Lou Reed about it.

Yule saw the Velvets play just once at a frat party in Harvard. Coincidentally John Cale didn't play at the show seen by Yule because he was ill. The show caught Yule's imagination on several levels: the band's music, on-stage presentation and clothes were all a revelation to him. 'Lou was in black leather,' recalls he. 'Nobody was wearing black leather in those days in Boston. Black leather pants, black leather jacket, the whole thing . . . I was very impressed with the show, more for the possibilities it suggested to me than for anything else. It had a theatricality about it that pushed me in a direction that today would be called performance art. I worked up a set in my head and made copious notes about it. The set began with a big, white ceramic urn suspended in mid-air in front of a black curtain. Without warning it falls to the floor and smashes, at the same time a guitar begins the opening tune with a power chord. It was just one of those things that you see it and it kind of opens your head up, and you say, "Oh wow, I could see a million things that I could do here!"'

Why, and how Doug Yule was asked to join The Velvet Underground is still somewhat puzzling. They needed a bass player and he didn't play bass; he was 21 years old, four or five years younger than the others, and he had no experience of playing with a large-scale band that did tours and recorded albums.

Steve Sesnick called Yule and just asked him straight out: 'How would you like to join The Velvet Underground?''I figured, here it is,' said Yule. 'Here's the elevator up. I'd finally hit it, because to me, this was a big band. They were gaining popularity.' Yule is convinced that they asked him because he was a Pisces. Tucker and Morrison were Virgos, while Reed was a Pisces as had been Cale, and they wanted to keep the 'balance'. After all, this was the 1960s. Later, Yule also realised that it was a step towards Steve Sesnick's plan of gaining tighter control over the band. Sesnick figured that though Yule was certainly talented enough, he was also naïve and could be controlled pretty easily, which to a certain extent was true. 'Sesnick knew that because I was so much younger than everyone else, I'd be easy to handle. He wanted to maintain his control and the Cale-Reed rift had been a threat to that,' said Yule. 'Sterling didn't exactly recommend me for the band, he noted that I was learning how to play and a bunch of seemingly insignificant little things made it easier for them to say, "Well, come on down to New York."'

'It's not surprising when you're 20 that the world comes calling for you,' laughs Yule. 'If that happened to me now I'd just be floored.' He went straight over to Max's Kansas City bar/restaurant, where Sesnick and Reed were having a few late-night drinks. As if his sprint down from Boston hadn't already confirmed it, Yule agreed right there and then to join.

The band had an engagement in Cleveland the following weekend and as this was Thursday night, Yule had very little time to learn the songs. It was especially difficult as he was required to play bass, not his usual instrument. He spent the night at Reed's loft near Madison Square Garden. 'Lou sat in his loft and went through song by song on an electric guitar so I had no preconceived notions, I was just winging it,' recalled Yule. 'I couldn't replace John Cale. I couldn't play viola and his bass playing isn't his strongest point. I got a feel for the material, it wasn't that complicated. From early on, I was singing. Right from the first show I was singing harmonies.' The pair talked all through the night and for the next two days Yule just learned the songs from Reed. As he'd never heard any of The Velvet Underground's albums he was free to interpret Reed's instructions as he saw fit without having to try and mimic Cale's recorded bass lines.

'If you understand Sterling it becomes pretty clear why they asked me to play bass,' explains Yule. 'Sterling had to play bass half the time and Cale had played half the time, and Sterling didn't really want to play bass. I don't think he should have been playing bass – he was too good a guitar player.'

On Friday, 4 October they flew out to Cleveland to meet Morrison and Tucker, and on the afternoon of the show the quartet practised together for the first time at La Cave. It was a similar situation to when Moe Tucker had joined the band in 1965. La Cave was basically a wide, dark, low-ceilinged basement with a hippy dressing room decorated with Persian rugs and second-hand furniture. 'We played two nights there,' said Yule. 'We stayed in a Howard Johnsons that hadn't converted from air conditioning to heating yet and they had a sudden cold snap. I was walking around wrapped in a blanket.'

But he was a fast learner and the shows went well. He got through the first show by closely watching Reed for signals of when to come in and out. The band were well received and no one seemed to notice that John Cale was missing. 'Lou made a set list just before each set but it was normal to diverge as he felt the need,' said Yule. 'He was in charge on stage and we followed his lead. Occasionally he'd start a song we didn't know and we'd just follow along. The mainstream just wasn't interested. You've got to remember that at that time, when you released an album, you were going for AM radio airplay. It was a very formulaic situation we had to fit into. When Dylan hit with "Like A Rolling Stone", people were just amazed: "Wow, this is the longest song that's ever been on the radio!" It was very strict, there were a lot of limitations on what you could do. We didn't fit in there.'

After the early October dates in Cleveland, Yule undertook his first West Coast tour with the band. 'It was lots of fun,' he said. 'We played the Whisky [Los Angeles] and the Avalon [San Francisco]. I was basically running to keep up. They had been doing this for a while but for me, it was all new.' Yule had been used to a totally different touring atmosphere. Before he'd often had to drive himself to the venue, haul his own equipment inside, set it up and then play. Then he'd dismantle it, load it up and go home again, usually arriving back in the early hours of the next morning. 'With the Velvets there were roadies right from the start,' he explained. 'Someone else was always moving the equipment. Sesnick was a real hustler and he managed to get the airlines to fly these amps around. People confused him with Selznik [the Hollywood producer] and he encouraged that. They'd confuse the names and say, "Oh, are you related to David O. Selznik?" And he'd say, "Oh yeah". On one of these tours we stayed at the St. Francis in San Francisco, which is one of the oldest hotels in San Francisco. Really old money, and they don't like men with shoulder-length hair walking around in the lobby in flowered shirts. They didn't want us there, but he finagled it with his little song and dance.'

During these dates Reed was presenting the band with new songs at sound checks and interweaving them into the sets each night. The new material was very different to The Velvet Underground's previous work. Reed was still following Andy Warhol's advice of rehearsing on stage, or occasionally on the afternoon of a show. 'Lou would say, "I have a new song,"' recalls Yule. 'He'd start playing it. When I was there it was often me and him doing that before everyone else was there. But other times it would be everyone together, and we'd start fooling around with it and work it out. It would evolve over the next few nights. Most of the stuff that was recorded was worked out on stage. We'd rehearse it performing and then it would evolve, and then we'd record it. Most of the songs found their way out, one way or another. There was marginal stuff that we would fool around with, half-songs, which turned up later. I remember doing "Candy Says" live, that's the softest thing on the [third] album, and we recorded it exactly how we played it.' A review of one of these shows read: 'The distressing fact is that John is no longer with the Velvet . . . Actually it's not distressing at all, they're sounding better than I can remember them for a long time.'

After the West Coast shows the band stayed on in Los Angeles to record their third album. It was Yule's first experience of a recording studio. Living in Los Angeles, working on an album in a bona fide band, this was what he'd aspired to when he dropped out of college two years earlier. Life seemed good. 'Doug was very easy to get along with,' said Moe Tucker. 'He's a very nice guy and a very good musician. We all got along well. Of course it was strange not having John around but Doug had been in the band a while before we recorded that album so we were all used to each other.' Tucker wasn't so keen on recording in Los Angeles. In direct opposition to Andy Warhol's earlier comment, she said: 'I hated Los Angeles, it seemed so plastic.'

Steve Sesnick had only managed to finalise studio time for the third album at short notice, so mentally the band had little opportunity to prepare. Most of the material was well-practised because of them playing much of it during the preceding shows. They planned to just play the songs live in the studio, with everyone planning together at the same time. It wasn't expected to be very complicated and it turned out that way.

The band moved into bungalows at the famous Chateau Marmont hotel,[2] and after a long day in the studio they'd hang out, have a drink and a smoke and listen back to the day's work on a cheap tape deck that they had bought. 'Everything was new to me,' recalls Doug Yule. 'The lifestyle, the people, the situations . . . It was a little like being a prince. I was 21 years old and just having a ball; I was doing what I always wanted to do. We played at the Whisky [a famous club] and Jimi Hendrix came to see us, so that was a thrill.' Though it wasn't that apparent on the material that they were recording, Jimi Hendrix had a big influence on Lou Reed's playing. 'The most striking thing beside his truly incredible guitar virtuosity was his savage, if playful, rape of his instrument,' said Reed. 'It would squeal and whine, going off into a crescendo of leaps and yells that only chance could program. Anyone who does that night, after night, must go mad.'

Chapter 10

1968–1969

The Story of My Life

'We always wanted to be commercially successful, but on our own terms. We wanted to do the music we were doing, and we hoped that tastes would change, or that we could change tastes.'

Sterling Morrison

Steve Sesnick had arranged for the band to use Sunset and Highland Sound Studios (previously TTG) in Hollywood during November and December. Val Valentin was MGM's choice of producer. Valentin had a varied background as engineer and producer before working with The Velvet Underground. He'd worked with the likes of The Lovin' Spoonful, Frank Sinatra, Count Basie and Ella Fitzgerald. His first avant-rock work had been with Frank Zappa on *Freak Out*.

The task was straightforward enough and the material was very different to the frenetic songs of *White Light/White Heat*. Much of the it was acoustic based, with regular arrangements, no viola and no screaming feedback. Over half the songs were gentle ballads and the material was some of the most delicate the band had conceived to date. All songs were solo Lou Reed compositions and the lack of friction with John Cale was both a loss and a gain, allowing the mellow-sounding atmosphere of the album to filter through.

Sterling Morrison wasn't in the mood to cause any friction either. 'I didn't argue hotly about this or that feature in the album,' he said. 'My contribution was as much as ever, maybe even more, but I didn't try to get my own way all of the time. Perhaps the Cale business left me all argued out, or maybe I just didn't feel that strongly about the material, one way or the other.'

'It took a couple of weeks for the basic tracks,' adds Doug Yule. 'It was a studio live album, with overdubbed vocals played the same as we had on the road; it was very representative of the band at that time. Sesnick was in the control room when we were recording: he had an opinion on everything and his thrust was mainly to get it done and keep everyone on track.'

Lou Reed wanted Yule to be fully involved during the sessions and pushed him into the spotlight as much as possible. 'It was quite a surprise when Lou said, "Why don't you sing?" as I'd never recorded a vocal before,' Yule revealed. 'When we recorded the basic musical tracks I wasn't going to sing and then when we came to record the vocals he said, "Doug, why don't you go try it?" We ran through all the musical tracks while the studio was set up, with Lou putting down reference vocals.'

The recording came easily and the four players bounced ideas around in the studio. Reed was happy to let Yule sing and encouraged him to occasionally take lead vocals. Yule's approach was more in keeping with Reed's pop vision for the band as opposed to the avant-garde experimental slant that Cale had always been pushing. 'Rhythm and feeling, and harmony and melody' are the main factors behind Yule's recording approach: 'I play the violin,' he said, 'but when I play the violin, I'm not interested in pushing the envelope with it. I'm more interested in making something that's pleasing to my ear. I think John [Cale] is a more expansive person than I am, he's got more curiosity.'

'We were recording at night,' said Yule. 'We'd wake up, get some food, watch TV, take it easy, play some music, listen to the outtakes from the night before which were on disc, not tape and then head over to the studio late afternoon. We weren't on that tight a schedule – we'd work until it became unproductive and then head home.'

The happy atmosphere at the sessions helped the laid-back songs blossom, and vice versa. Stories of the album being more low-key because of the band's effects, pedals and fuzz-boxes being stolen are false, according to Yule. 'I only heard the story about the effects boxes being stolen within the last five or ten years,' he said. 'When we were playing dates in 1968, no one was using boxes except the occasional fuzz tone for Lou. We didn't have any effects on stage: we walked on, plugged into the amps and that was it; we didn't have pedals. From what I understand, although I don't know for a fact, I was told that Lou had built into his Country Gentleman guitar bunches of repeaters and stuff like that. I have only his word on that, I never actually saw the instrument. He was playing it the first time I ever saw him, but I couldn't swear to you what it had – I didn't know enough to pick it apart.'

The topics covered on the new songs also showed a marked departure for the band. Overt sexual references, horrific short stories and drug songs were mostly absent. 'I've gotten to where I like the pretty stuff better than drive and distortion,' Reed commented at the time. 'You can be more subtle, really say something and sort of soothe.' Instead the songs concerned love, religion and the loneliness of wasted lives. It was the antithesis of *White Light/White Heat*. Many songs used the character of 'Candy' as a central figure. Candy was a not very well-disguised take on Candy Darling, a transvestite Warhol Superstar (real name James Slattery), who was undergoing a sex-change operation and would later famously feature in the lyric to 'Walk On The Wild Side'.

Eponymously titled, or known simply as the 'grey album', the record opened with the most obvious Slattery-themed song, 'Candy Says'. It really set the mellow tone and four of the five songs on side one were ostensibly quiet ones. Singing of Candy hating his/her body the tune is almost angelic, with softly strummed guitars almost sounding like harps. Reed's lyrics and Yule's compassionate reading of them give the song a real air of love for the character who is obviously in emotional pain. 'Lou asked me to sing "Candy Says" and at first, I didn't want to,' said Yule. 'But then I did, and it was fun. He was [used to] singing every song and he wanted to get away from that.'

'What Goes On' was the anomaly of side one: it was the only rocker. Underpinned by a Gothic-sounding organ and twitchy beat, the song really bounds along. Reed used 'Lady be good' in the opening line as a tribute to one of his favourite George Gershwin songs, which went by the same name. 'I remember working on "What Goes On", on the solo,' said Doug Yule. 'Lou cranked his guitar up all the way and played a solo. It was good and we said, "Wanna try another?" We'd got a few more tracks and we put down three solos. He came back in and listened, and the engineer said, "Well, if you do another one, we'll have to kill one because we don't have any more open tracks." This is in the days when you didn't have unlimited tracks. So I said, "Why don't you play one more, and we'll play them all at once." And it worked. It sounds like bagpipes.'

Usually the guitar solos were shared out between Reed and Sterling Morrison. 'Sterling always wound up with the more organised breaks while Lou favoured the longer, louder, raunchier ones,' recalls Yule. 'He had a brilliant sense of melody but an imperfect instrument. Sterling seemed to be just the opposite, more a process of technique that lacked a soaring vision and relied on the acquired skill of filling in the final pieces of a puzzle without overdoing it.' 'Some Kinda Love' featured what Reed described as some of Morrison's best guitar work. It was a subtle song concerning the ambiguous nature of all the different kinds of love. Reading between the lines, this could be heterosexual, homosexual, bisexual and even, in the context of other songs on the album, religious love.

'Pale Blue Eyes' could have fitted nicely alongside some of Nico's songs on the Velvets' debut album, but it wasn't out of place here alongside the quieter moments. The type of love in this particular song was adultery, to go along with the various other kinds addressed on the record. Reed also sang that it was a sin, marking another religious reference. 'Cale's departure allowed Lou Reed's sensitive, meaningful side to hold sway,' explains Sterling Morrison. 'Why do you think "Pale Blue Eyes" happened on the third album? My position on the album was one of acquiescence.'

'Jesus' was the first directly religious song that The Velvet Underground put to tape. It was presented as a country-tinged song: Reed asks for divine inspiration and strength as he's 'fallen out of grace'.

'The bass part for "Jesus" was great,' said Yule. 'It's a finger-picked bass line. It's something that I do, which I don't hear many bass players do. I play bass from a very different attitude. It has to do more with counter melodies in a bass structure against upper melodies, so I don't play bass the way most people play bass. I can't. I don't think the bass is a rhythm instrument, which is how it's used, for the most part, in rock'n'roll. I use it as part of a larger harmonic structure. When I play bass, I don't play notes and rhythms, I play parts. The thing for "Jesus" actually becomes the main melody at one point.' As Lester Bangs later pointed out, the Velvets had gone from heroin to Jesus in just two years.

'Beginning To See The Light' continued the religious theme, with a perky rocker to open side two. 'I'm Set Free' was sung powerfully by Doug Yule, but was Reed writing about getting John Cale out of the band? Like the previous song, the lyrics concern finding redemption and getting the chance of a fresh start. The song is given an impressively large-sounding arrangement.

'That's The Story Of My Life' was a jaunty little song with a four-line repeating lyric. On the other hand, 'The Murder Mystery' is a throwback to the days of *White Light/White Heat*. It's an incomprehensible mix that spoils the effect, which should have consisted of two voices telling stories at different speeds, one from each speaker. All four band members provided vocals for the song, which leaves the listener dizzy and disorientated. Reed considered it a failed experiment because neither monologue could be clearly heard. He wanted one vocal to be saying the opposite of the other so the listener might be sad and laughing at the same time.

'Afterhours' gave Moe Tucker the chance to take lead vocals for the first time on a Velvet Underground song. Reed wanted her to tackle the topics of late-night drinking and taking solace in alcohol because he thought listeners wouldn't think he could sing the words and be sincere about them. Tucker was reluctant to take on the vocal duties, but eventually Reed persuaded her to have a go. 'When we were in the studio I had to finally make everyone leave,' she laughs. 'Sterling was laughing at me and teasing while I was trying to do it as good as I could. I was nervous because I didn't want to mess it up and I didn't want to be wasting time, so I kicked everyone out. So, Lou and I and the engineer did it – it took a couple of takes, I don't remember exactly. I like it now.' As it turned out, she was perfect for the song and its delicate acoustic strum was a fitting end to what was for The Velvet Underground an unusual album.

Years later, Lou Reed explained that he'd planned for all the songs to carry on a narrative through the album. He said that Candy asked questions in the opener, a 'guy' responds by saying what's going on, then they talk about love and then adultery, and then 'real' love, at which point he says he's beginning to see the light and asks how does it feel to be loved?

Once the album was finished and mixed by Val Valentin, Reed returned to the tapes and remixed them himself. The resultant mix was somewhat flat sounding and is referred to as the 'closet mix' because it sounds like it was recorded in a cupboard, an accusation levelled by Sterling Morrison.

'I thought it sounded like it was recorded in a closet,' said Morrison. 'Why did he do it? I don't know specifically. To judge from the result, to bring the voices up and put the instruments down. I guess he felt the real essence of the tracks was the lyrics. Whereas one thing I always liked about Rolling Stones' records was the voice was always back in the mix.'

The original US vinyl version of the album used the 'closet' mix, while later CDs employed the Val Valentin version.[1] For the cover they used a Billy Name (with whom Reed was having an on-off relationship) photograph of the band, which was taken at The Factory. Reed was holding up a copy of *Harper's Bizarre* magazine, which had to have its cover airbrushed out.

140

Though the album was issued on the main MGM label in March 1969, rather than on the Verve imprint, it still suffered from poor distribution and promotion. Steve Sesnick was looking ahead and thinking that it might be time to change labels if the album didn't sell well. 'We were getting bigger and bigger, while they [MGM/Verve] were getting more chaotic with the loss of presidents,' he told Victor Bokris. 'I was dealing with a different president every month. Either they were really going to do it for us, or we would be with another company.'

'I can specifically remember playing in St Louis long enough after the third album that it should have been in the stores, especially if we were going to play there,' recalls Moe Tucker. 'We had never played there before, and we expected 30 people to show up and we really packed the place. It was one of those open ballrooms and a couple of thousand people showed up. The guy who owned the club was ecstatic.'

Reviewers certainly felt that this was the album that would get the band into the mainstream. 'The group creates a sensuous sound, and the LP could pick up considerable sales,' claimed *Cashbox*. 'By virtue of their name The Velvet Underground sound as if they're about to break through to a large audience,' concurred *Record World*. The biggest critical coup was getting an excellent write-up in *Rolling Stone*, their first: '[the album] will go a long way toward convincing the unbelievers that The Velvet Underground can write and play any kind of music they want to with equal brilliance.' And the reviewer? None other than the legendary Lester Bangs.

Chapter 11

1969

On the Road

'We had sound checks but there wasn't much to check. We only had about three microphones and we'd make sure the vocals were high enough, that was about it.'

Maureen Tucker

hile The Velvet Underground were in California, two of the band's cast-offs, John Cale and Nico, were working together again in Los Angeles. With no one handing her songs to sing anymore, Nico had spent her time writing her own material, while Cale admitted that after leaving the Velvets he had floundered for a while. When the chance came for him to work with Nico he grasped at the stability it provided. Nico had spent some time with The Doors' Jim Morrison and he encouraged her to write her own songs. They'd initially met at the Castle during the Velvets' first trip to Los Angeles in 1966 and they'd had the occasional rendezvous ever since. On one occasion they ended up fighting in a fountain, and on another Morrison tried to get Nico to run naked with him along a ledge of the roof of a tall building. She declined.

Along with A&R man Danny Fields, Jim Morrison suggested that she should try to get a record deal with Elektra, the same label that had signed The Doors.

Nico managed to get Elektra founder and owner Jac Holzman to listen to what she had. Elektra was one of the real record label success stories of the 1960s. Jac Holzman formed the company in 1950 and acted as president until 1973. Initially a folk label, they signed The Doors in 1965 and provided a home for the MC5, the Stooges and The Incredible String Band. 'She came up to Elektra with her harmonium and performed some of [her songs] for Jac in his office,' recalls Danny Fields. 'And he said, "Fine, as long as it doesn't cost a lot of money. Let's do a record."'

The resultant album was a shock to anyone who had heard her previous work, either with The Velvet Underground or on *Chelsea Girls*. Given the opportunity to record her own songs, the world got a chance to hear the music that was inside her head. And what strange music it was. Gone were the folksy melodies and arrangements, and in their place were cold, harsh drones and ghostly medieval chants drifting around. The blonde goddess had vanished and she'd metamorphosed into a Gothic horror princess. The songs were unlike anything being recorded in the late 1960s: they sounded like something that had been dug up from centuries ago.

The haunting songs were arranged by John Cale. Elektra were too nervous to let him produce the album as well (that task was given to Frazier Mohawk, real name Barry Friedman), and his stamp is all over the record, playing bass, piano, viola, glockenspiel and harmonica. The sessions took place at Elektra's own La Cienga studio in double-quick time. Unfortunately, Nico's harmonium-driven songs had little effect on the record-buying public and *The Marble Index* (she took the title from Wordsworth) disappeared from view and went out of print until the CD version came out in 1991.

By 1969 the early promise that The Velvet Underground showed of being something fresh and new, something that hadn't been seen or heard before, was now a distant memory. They still played the early songs of course, but the energy and verve was missing, the edge dulled. There were no whip dancers or crazy lighting effects. They were the same as almost all the other bands of the day: they toured clubs and played rock and roll; they were very good at it but then again so too were scores of other bands. They didn't stand alone anymore. 'The Band was never the same for me after John left,' said Sterling Morrison. 'He was not easy to replace. Doug Yule was a good bass player, but we moved more towards unanimity of opinion and I don't think that's a good thing. I always thought that what made us real good were tensions and oppositions.'

Though the Velvets weren't selling significantly large numbers of albums, they did have a steady following and Steve Sesnick's guile in making sure the band travelled first class proved to be invaluable. In doing this he arranged for the label to cover the cost of expensive hotels, first-class flights and decent expense accounts for food. This would be an important perk because they would be spending most of their time on the road for the foreseeable future. The touring meant the band had more money coming in, so they wouldn't have to live on meagre royalty cheques alone, but the expenses would be set against their earnings. 'If I'd known how much we were spending, I would have said, let's go to a cheaper hotel,' said Moe Tucker. 'It was nice to stay at the Beverly Wilshire, but later they said you owe us x thousand dollars for the stay.'

'There was a time when we just travelled weekends,' recalled Doug Yule. 'The limousine would come pick you up at your apartment, take you to the airport; you'd fly somewhere for the weekend and play a couple of nights and then come back.' The band were part of a constantly touring circus of bands criss-crossing the country. They played with The Holy Modal Rounders, The Fugs, The Grateful Dead, The MC5 and The Byrds, among others.

Initially the travelling that the Doug Yule-era band did was always on a first-class ticket. Yule recalls that Sesnick would bill all of the travelling expenses directly through to MGM, but after a while they started to askg questions. The bills were mounting up and not being counter-balanced by record sales, so eventually the label put a stop to it.

The contract that Yule had eventually signed had no stipulation of what his financial payments should be. 'I never got a pay cheque,' he explains. 'No one ever said, "Here's the accounting for the group." I had an apartment in New York and when my rent was due, I'd tell Sesnick and he'd write a cheque for the rent. I bought my first stereo when I was there, and I told him and he said, "Okay", and he gave me some money and off I went. I can't speak for anyone else, but I never got paid. I was given some money for daily expenses on the road but Sesnick was completely in control of the purse strings.' To his credit, Sesnick was always optimistic, energetic and convinced he was managing the next Beatles.

As time went on, the dynamics within the band morphed constantly, and increasingly unhappily. Initially Lou Reed really took Doug Yule under his wing and the pair became quite close. Reed encouraged Yule to sing more material, but not too much. He was happy to let the young bassist take the spotlight for a while because he was starting to feel the pressure of having to bear the brunt of it all the time. But also he didn't want to give it up completely. He let Yule have some of the glory, but it had to be on his own terms.

Still bitter about the way John Cale was ousted, Sterling Morrison withdrew himself from any high-jinx within the band. He wasn't particularly cold towards Yule, but as Yule and Reed grew closer, Morrison felt himself being pushed out. 'Sterling gave the impression he never liked anybody a lot of the time,' recalls Yule. 'He was kind of gruff and critical. I think he wanted to be recognised and have people say, "Sterling, you're wonderful. We love you." Which is what most people want.' Meanwhile Moe Tucker just let them all get on with it and concentrated on playing her drums.

Touring with other 'name' bands did throw up some interesting situations. One time Sterling Morrison was given an LSD hit when members of The Grateful Dead smeared the acid on the tabs of Coke cans backstage. The Dead and the Velvets took it in turns to play first and second, so neither could claim to be the headliner or the support. On the first occasion The Dead opened they played, as they often did, for the best part of two hours, which cut into the time allowed for The Velvet Underground. Retaliation came the following night when the Velvets played first. They opened with a version of 'Sister Ray' that continued for over an hour and then they completed the rest of their set.

The occasional trips out to Chicago and Detroit were always backed up by numerous shows at La Cave in Cleveland and the Boston Tea Party. One show at the Tea Party was opened by the MC5. 'We might have had 600 or 700 in there,' recalled MC5 leader Wayne Kramer. 'It was our first time in Boston and we were getting a big push because we'd just signed with Elektra. I remember they [the Velvets] went over very well, but it was two different things. We were trying to be this show band and we had these spangly clothes and sequins, and they were very plain-looking.' The MC5 were in full anti-establishment mode and did their best to incite the crowd. 'John Sinclair was ranting, yelling "Revolution now!", "Tear down the walls!", "Kill the pigs!"' recalls Doug Yule. When The Velvet Underground took to the stage the crowd was worked up and ready to explode. 'It was really unsettling,' he continues. 'We were standing on the edge of a riot, waiting to see if it was going to happen. Everyone was kind of nervous. Charles, who did the introductions at the Tea Party, walked out and said, "Here they are, you know them, The Velvet Underground." Lou walks up to the microphone, looks out at the audience and says, "I just want you to know, before we begin, that I don't agree with anything that's been said." And the crowd cheered and that was it: it was defused. He attacked things head on, he went straight in, straight for the jugular.'

During these shows Moe Tucker was receiving a lot of good attention about how her drumming was the power behind the band. One review read: 'Its source is the train-like rhythms of Maureen Tucker, their curly red-haired drummer. Hunched over her drums, flailing the skins like some madwoman, she was quite an impressive sight. Tucker is not a very good drummer by any means, but her primitive, nerve-throb style and her seemingly endless fount of energy make her ideal for the Underground. I was so fascinated by Tucker's movements as she tortured her drums that I only got around to noticing Lou Reed towards the middle of the lengthy "Sister Ray". The whole time Maureen Tucker was smashing away at the skins, Reed just floated aloof through everything.'

The first time the band played at Washington University (which, confusingly was located in St Louis, Missouri) in May 1969, they caught the eye of a young law student named Robert Quine.[1] The day before, Quine had bought a tape recorder and he took it along to the show. 'The sound was sort of muddy,' said Quine. 'It was a basketball gym, and it was pretty echoey.' This was the first of many recordings that Quine made of The Velvet Underground, some of which were officially released over 30 years later. One of the most famous of these was at a San Francisco club called the Matrix. Different members of the band (everyone except Moe Tucker) had often played while under the influence of various narcotics: LSD, speed and pot. In San Francisco they played two sets a night. During the first they were all pretty sober, apart from the odd beer, but in the intermission they passed a joint around and the effects were there for everyone to hear throughout the second set. 'I kid you not,' said Doug Yule. 'We were tuning for 15 minutes. And it wasn't working. This was before the little tuning machines came out, so you had to actually tune and we tuned forever, and then we'd play a song. Then we'd tune for another five minutes.' And so it went.

In order to prepare material for their planned fourth MGM album, Steve Sesnick booked a series of studio dates at the Record Plant in New York between May and October 1969. These sessions were again recorded by Val Valentin.

They were adding songs to their live set as Lou Reed wrote them, so it made sense to get them on tape as soon as they'd been brushed into shape on the road. The fact that the sessions were widely spread out alleviated any pressure the band might have felt and they could kick back and enjoy the session, as and when they rolled around. Usually only one or two songs were attempted at any single session but soon a sizable body of work was built up. The sessions also marked the second meeting between the band and Jimi Hendrix, who was also working at the studio over the summer.

The first session took place on 9 May. 'Foggy Notion' and 'Coney Island Steeplechase' were recorded that day. The former was almost seven minutes long, but was possibly the most commercial of the Record Plant songs. Its irresistible beat and catchy melody would have made it a contender as a single. Different parts of the song evoke different memories of rock and roll's past, from the 1950s through the 1960s. 'Coney Island Steeplechase' has a driving beat, over which Reed sings through a vocal distortion device.

Four days later they returned to record another two songs, 'Andy's Chest', a 1950s sock-hop sounding rock and roll pastiche (which would turn up on Reed's solo album *Transformer* in 1972), and the child-like nursery rhyme of 'I'm Sticking With You', which was sung by Moe Tucker with help on the chorus from Reed. In full flow they were back a day later with 'She's My Best Friend'. This was a well-produced track that evoked mid-1960s' Beatles and another song that Reed would use on a solo album much later (*Coney Island Baby* in 1976).

'I Can't Stand It' contained a Hank Marvin guitar sound, while Reed looked back to his Syracuse days as he proclaimed, 'If Shelly would just come back it would be alright.' Other songs included 'Ferryboat Bill', a bizarre fairground miasma of organ and cymbals, the original version of 'Rock And Roll', which sounded relatively pedestrian compared to the later *Loaded* version, and 'Ride Into The Sun', a clanging masterclass of melodic guitar playing. Four sessions in eight days between 24 September and 1 October finished the recording sessions for the year. 'I'm Gonna Move Right In' was a lengthy (6.5-minute) instrumental jam, which allowed the guitarists to show off, 'We're Gonna Have A Real Good Time Together' was a brisk, Buddy Holly-esque ramble and 'Lisa Says' was a slow ballad, reminiscent of 'Femme Fatale'. One other track recorded over the summer, but not at the Record Plant, was 'One Of These Days'. This was used as a guinea-pig track at an office on 57th Street that MGM had set up as a temporary studio. 'We wanted to see whether or not it could be used for music,' says Sterling Morrison. The track itself was a success. With Beatle-esque vocals and a country guitar riff, it was unlike other Velvets' songs and would have been a welcome addition to *Loaded*.

Partway through these recordings it became evident that the band might not be on MGM for too much longer. Rather than submit a bunch of second-rate songs for their final album on the label, they intended to use the best material they had available. There was always a slight chance that they might be able to strike a bargain and take the songs with them to a new label. As it was, the songs were held by MGM for the next decade and a half before they were officially released.

In between the sessions the Velvets played as often as they could to keep some money coming in. They tried playing at some new venues in some cities, a good example of this was at the Second Fret in Philadelphia. Actually, it was a very small folk club and not really a prime venue for a rock show. The stage was only about a foot off the floor and the floor area only about six metres wide and twenty-five metres deep. During most of 1969 the band were recorded either officially or unofficially. One of the most important chroniclers of The Velvet Underground's live history was Robert Quine, who had first taped them back in St Louis. During the autumn of 1969 he was living on the

West Coast and saw them numerous times. He took his tape recorder to just about every show and taped it for posterity. 'Fame-wise, they were hardly on a Stones' or Beatles' level,' said Quine. 'That's unfortunate, but it made it not so difficult to meet them and hang around with them. They were relatively happy, getting along well. And Lou Reed was going through an especially creative period. He was writing a lot of new songs, including "Sweet Jane", "New Age" and "Ride Into the Sun". Each night he'd improvise new lyrics on the spot and best of all, I got to spend a lot of time talking about music. Between sets, I'd hang around with them in the dressing room, sometimes playing them cassettes of stuff they'd done that night. It was a real privilege and something I'll never forget.'

Some of Quine's tapes have since been given official releases (*Live 1969* and *The Bootleg Series, Vol. 1*) and they prove invaluable when looking back at Doug Yule-era Velvets' shows. In late 1969 'I'm Waiting For The Man' had been reworked to give it a slinky, sexy groove, while the live version of 'I Can't Stand It' sounds like it's about to break into The Beatles' 'Get Back' at any moment. Moe Tucker would step forward to sing a mini two-song section in the middle of the sets ('I'm Sticking With You' and 'After Hours'). Otherwise unreleased songs like the pure 1950s' dance routine of 'It's Just Too Much', the largely instrumental improvisations of 'Follow The Leader' and 'Over You' all featured in the shows too.

The venues used to record these shows were typical of the ones that the Velvets played in 1968–1970. The Family Dog was out at the beach and took a long drive to get there; The Avalon was a bigger venue and could hold a few thousand people compared to the more typical 500 to 1,000 and The Matrix was a little club in San Francisco.

The reaction of the crowd on the early tapes is mainly indifferent. Quine recalled that sometimes the earliest set of the night would begin with less than half a dozen people in the club. Under those circumstances, the band saw Quine standing there, night after night. As the band spent longer in any venue (they played for a couple of weeks at some places), gradually they built up bigger and more appreciative audiences.

Being so far from home for such long periods was starting to wear the band down, though. 'By the end of 1969 we were feeling pretty low,' recalled Moe Tucker. 'I can remember being in Seattle, Vancouver, Portland, Chicago and having like, two dollars a day to eat on. What pissed me off the most was if we had released the albums, and MGM had pushed them and played them on the radio and no one liked it, it would be one thing, but whenever we played live we always, always did well. So I knew if the record was out there it would sell and that was discouraging to me, to be at the mercy of these people who just didn't have any sense.'

The band were getting to the end of their tether as the decade ended. After four years of touring and recording, they were still pretty much playing the same-sized venues that they had started out in, they never saw a royalty cheque and were suspicious of Steve Sesnick's book-keeping abilities. On one occasion, Sterling Morrison stormed into Sesnick's apartment on 62nd Street and demanded to see the books. The band thought that by his address he seemed to be living better than they were, but when Morrison arrived he noticed that Sesnick had a nice apartment, but he couldn't afford to put any furniture in it. Moe Tucker recalls that she was being paid less than $200 a month. 'I used to go and get a temporary job for a week when I was home,' she said. 'I didn't need as much money as the others did for their apartments. I lived at home, rent-free.' If things were to continue, 1970 would have to bring some pretty drastic changes with it.

Chapter 12

1970

In the Country Much Too Long

'Many people said Lou was The Velvet Underground, and in the sense that it was his brainchild, he was. He was the main force behind it, but it was a band and like any band, its totality is made up of all its members, not just one person with side musicians.'

Doug Yule

For Sterling Morrison, the summer of 1970 was an especially busy one. He was playing two sets a night with The Velvet Underground at Max's Kansas City and he was also working on the Velvets' new album at the Atlantic studios during the day. If those two pursuits didn't keep him busy enough, he was also studying hard to complete his degree from City College.

It's been said that Morrison was a little more detached than usual on these sessions, and he probably was. During breaks in recording he'd sit quietly reading in a corner; between sets at Max's he'd do the same, or hunker down over a hamburger with a clutch of his notes. He read over 20 plays that summer. The late afternoon before he went into the studio was his favourite time of day. He'd cycle into Central Park to read his latest assignment. He'd enjoy the sun and then watch it sink behind Lincoln Center. Then he'd pack his bag and leisurely cycle over to the studio.

Although Atlantic Records supremo Ahmet Ertegun had turned down the tapes of *The Velvet Underground & Nico*, he had kept tabs on their progress and was impressed with the album. Sesnick had been courting him via letter and long-distance telephone calls for some time. Ertegun felt that if the Velvets were encouraged to write slightly more mainstream rock songs, they could break through to commercial success. By the start of 1970 he was ready to work with the band to get them out of their MGM contract.

'MGM were ready to let us go if we wanted to because of our demands and the lack of record sales in that confusion they had over their direction,' said Steve Sesnick. 'At this point they brought in Mike Curb from California, who had some choral group and was suddenly head of MGM. We were about as far away from being able to discuss anything with him as East meets West, so the attorney I had was able to work it out with him amicably.'

MGM weren't unhappy about the Velvets' request to leave: neither party had made any money and with an album's worth of material being left behind, they had basically fulfilled the four-album deal without having the fourth LP actually issued. They were now free to sign a two-record contract with Atlantic. 'Basically MGM would have dropped us,' said Doug Yule. 'They had been charging travelling expenses to future royalties, so they said they weren't going to make any money on us. In terms of the band, it didn't really make any difference. It just meant going to a different studio to record, which was nice because Atlantic had a really nice studio in town.'

Ahmet Ertegun was glad to finally sign the band: he thought he could smooth their rougher edges and make them a decent chart proposition. He'd certainly been able to weave similar magic in the past. Turkish-born Ertegun moved to the US when his father was positioned there as the Turkish ambassador. In 1947, Ahmet convinced Vahdi Sabit, his dentist, to contribute $10,000 to a record label that he was trying to found. The company they formed was called Atlantic Records and it went on to become one of the most successful labels of the last 50 years. Atlantic were different from other independent labels in that they weren't under the usual pressure to pay back the financial investment right away. They had room to evolve at their own pace and make more artistic-minded decisions, rather than just financially driven ones. Ray Charles was one of the first to benefit from this more relaxed style. Atlantic also entered an unorthodox arrangement with Memphis label Stax. Booker T. and the MGs, Otis Redding and Sam and Dave all had hits under this contract.

Throughout the spring the Velvets toured as usual. Moe Tucker always took one dress with her and eventually, Yule figured out why. Early on a Sunday morning while everyone else slept off the excesses of the night before, she would rise, put on her dress and head out to church. Being the good Catholic that she was, she rarely missed Sunday mass and though she was at times surrounded by debauchery, she handled the various crazy scenes with aplomb. 'She wouldn't swear a lot,' recalls Yule. 'I would say she never swore, but I seem to remember some occasions. She was very proper in a lot of ways. She didn't expect anybody else to live up to her standards but she would occasionally not allow certain behaviour. You weren't supposed to get into any explicit talk about sex with Moe around. She could drink, though.'

That spring it also emerged that Tucker was pregnant. She had met the father, Steve Mikulka, while working as a computer card puncher. The band played shows in Philadelphia and Boston, but with the baby due in the summer she was forced to bow out of some of them. The main problem was that Tucker liked to play drums while standing up and being pregnant, she couldn't physically reach to play them properly. Doug Yule played drums on some songs but they would soon need a short-term replacement. The sessions for the fourth Velvet Underground album were scheduled to begin in April and then take place over the summer.

Overlapping with the sessions was a lengthy residence at Max's Kansas City on Park Avenue South in New York. The Velvets were no longer an avant-garde group, but more of a bar or club band. They spent the summer from late June to September playing two or three sets a night, five nights a week.

Max's Kansas City was one of New York's most important music and cultural venues. Just off Union Square, Mickey Ruskin managed to create an atmosphere at his bar/restaurant that attracted the hippest clientele from the worlds of music, art, film and literature. The rich and famous ate, drank and networked through the various rooms while The Velvet Underground, Bob Marley or Bruce Springsteen played, and future Blondie lead singer Debbie Harry waited tables. In the old days the Warhol crowd might have held court around a table in the back room, but this was a new decade and the old days were gone.

The small upstairs room that the Velvets played in was soon packed out every night and they were treated like returning heroes, even if it was on a small scale. Under red lights (it was normally used as a disco), the first set of the night would usually begin at about 11.30 and would include material from across their three albums, plus selections that were due for the fourth album. They were the first New York shows since 1968. Lou Reed had to confront his past every night. 'It was uncomfortable for Lou to play in front of his past,' said Doug Yule. 'He had made a lot of compromises with a lot of very interesting people in New York. I know when we later played at Max's, a lot of that came back to haunt him. People started showing up that he didn't want to talk to; it really bugged him.'

During the summer Sterling Morrison was keeping himself extra-busy. The band were going to be playing regular shows and trying to fit recording sessions for the fourth album around them. On top of this Morrison had enrolled at City College to take a summer course of 'Modern Drama and the Victorian Novel'. The reason for his study was to complete the BA he'd left unfinished six years earlier so that he could apply for graduate courses at various universities. He realised that he wouldn't be making a decent long-term living from The Velvet Underground and was already making other plans.

With his sojourns to the park, Morrison was withdrawing from the camaraderie of the band and his relationship with Reed was especially frosty. They only spoke when it was absolutely necessary and when Reed later needed support, it wasn't forthcoming from Morrison. Tucker was away on pregnancy leave and Yule was being told by Sesnick that he should be the star of the show.

'Maybe I never forgave [Lou] for wanting Cale out of the band,' said Morrison. 'I was so mad at him, for real or imaginary offences, and I just didn't want to talk. You know that poem

"The Poison Tree" by Blake? "I was angry with my friend/I told it not" I was zero psychological assistance to Lou.'

Morrison read 30 plays that summer, and when he got to Max's, he'd spend every spare minute poring over the texts. He left his guitar locked up at the club so he could arrive, read, play and leave with the minimum of fuss and contact with the others. 'There was some "static" going on while they recorded *Loaded*,' said Martha Dargan. 'Between songs, Sterling and I would sit in Central Park to get away from it because people were arguing. But that had been going on the whole time, the arguing. I recall one practice where they were giving each other electric shocks on purpose: I would try and be peacemaker.'

Rather than wait for Moe Tucker to have her baby and return, Steve Sesnick prompted that they should get a short-term replacement and carry on regardless. This marginalised Sterling Morrison even more because his main ally was removed from the day-to-day goings-on within the group. Yule and Reed controlled things in the studio and Morrison's input diminished almost by the day. 'Looking back now, it seems obvious that when faced with the prospect of recording without Moe, we should have simply said no,' said Yule. 'Waiting for her would have produced a more coherent, unified album and might have kept the group together longer.'

'I was insulted when they went ahead with *Loaded*,' said Tucker. 'I was disappointed because there were some songs like "Ocean" that I really wanted to play drums on. Doug and Lou have said in recent years that they should have waited for me.'

Finding Moe Tucker's replacement in the band took a twist when Doug's younger brother, Billy Yule, came in to play drums at Max's. The younger Yule was just 17 years old, still in High School and like his brother, had never heard The Velvet

Underground play before joining. The first time he did was when he was on stage with them for the first time. Sesnick initially offered him the grand total of $60 for the 10-week stint, but he eventually haggled it to about $25 a week, which included his train fares to and from Long Island, free food and beer and some cinema tickets. With Sesnick siding ever more frequently with Doug Yule, the addition of Yule's brother to the band left Reed feeling more peripheral than ever.

'It was kind of a joke: there we were in the studio and there was nobody to play drums,' laughs Doug Yule. 'So I played drums, Adrian Barber played drums and some of the songs were recorded without drums – I don't think there was a stable drummer. Billy [Yule] came in and played on a couple of them near the end after he'd been playing with us live and he was only in High School. It was tricky because here was this High School kid playing in a club that served alcohol and in New York they get antsy about that. My parents were oblivious to it all.'

Against a backdrop of simmering personal differences, Steve Sesnick's agenda of divide-and-rule, Moe Tucker's absense and constant, gruelling shows at Max's, the band nonetheless managed to pull together in the studio and produce the most underrated, yet delightful Velvet Underground album. This was precipitated by Lou Reed hitting a high point in his songwriting career, one that he has since been unable to match so consistently over the course of a single album. 'I gave them an album full of hits,' deadpanned Reed.

As had been the case with *The Velvet Underground*, Steve Sesnick gave the band little notice that the sessions were booked. Preparations were made during sound checks and shows, and then they recorded. The first sessions were booked in April, with more planned for later in the summer. 'Sterling became discouraged early on because he felt I had too much of an influence in it,' said Doug Yule. 'He basically felt cut out, which I'm sure . . . has to do with the fact that I was feeling much more confident . . . I felt more a part of the group. Also Lou leaned on me a lot in terms of musical support and for harmonies and vocal arrangements.'

The album *Loaded* (so-called because Reed felt it was loaded with hits) was recorded in a strange atmosphere where people came in, put down their part and then left. Often it was just two or maybe three people in the studio together, very different to the live band feel of the last album. 'The emphasis was on air time,' said Yule. 'Every song was looked at with the understanding that there was a need to produce some kind of mainstream hit. On the third album we had just played what we wanted, but now we brainstormed. New things were tried for the first time on the studio floor and they were usually taped. Songs were built intellectually rather than by the processes that live performances brought to bear – of instinct and trial and error. There was a sense of mission at those sessions to make a commercial record. And each song is like a different view of what a commercial song is. "Sweet Jane" is kind of a power trio song, "Head Held High" is kind of a metalish thing, "Cool It Down" is mellower, funkier. "Who Loves The Sun" is a popier thing. It was as if someone had said, "One of these songs has to be a hit. We'll do each different style, something has to take."'

Though she didn't play, Moe Tucker attended the first two sessions on 15 and 16 April at Atlantic Records in New York. The initial producer was Englishman Adrian Barber, an Atlantic staff producer. His major claims to fame were that he'd recorded The Beatles at the Star Club in Hamburg back in 1962, and had been a member of one of Merseyside's most popular early-1960s' bands, The Big Three. Brian Epstein had signed them and taken them to play in Hamburg, but it didn't work out and the band returned to England minus Barber, who became stage manager at the Star Club, where he recorded The Beatles.

Partway through the summer Barber was replaced by Geoffrey Haslam, another English Atlantic staffer. It was Barber who took over on drums and the band put down the basic tracks for eight new songs, seven of which wouldn't make it to the final album. 'Satellite Of Love', 'Oh Gin', 'Walk And Talk', 'Sad Song', 'Ride Into The Sun', 'Here Come The Waves' (later retitled 'Ocean') and 'I Love You' were all recorded in demo form and then dropped. Only 'Rock And Roll' survived from these sessions to the album. 'Satellite Of Love' was a headstrong rocker, while the bouncy 'Oh Gin' would later become 'Oh Jim'. 'Ocean', 'Ride Into The Sun', 'Walk And Talk It' and 'I Love You' were all used on Reed's debut eponymous solo album.

The drumming was handled by whoever happened to be there at the time. Barber played on the first set of demos, Doug Yule played on a few songs, Tommy Castanaro came in from Long Island for a session, and towards the end of the session Billy Yule played the new songs that he'd worked on at Max's all summer – 'Oh! Sweet Nuthin'', 'Lonesome Cowboy Bill' and 'Ocean'.

The band were recording all through the summer, with the final sessions taking place in July. As some of the early demos were dropped, they were replaced with new songs and early demos of other songs were re-arranged and being played many times at Max's Kansas City, night after night. They had never had such a wealth of material to choose from and the final 10 songs on the album were eventually whittled down from a list of 19 prospective candidates. Within this plethora of material was a song that they'd tried out for the last album: 'Sweet Jane' was revamped and became the centrepiece of the new record.

For first-time listeners, even in the light of the acoustically based *The Velvet Underground*, *Loaded* was a radical departure from the band's previous work. Right from the opening chords and the angelic vocals of Doug Yule, 'Who Loves The Sun' sets the scene that this is something different. It's The Velvet Underground's pop album. Within a minute of the first song starting, you hear that old grudges against the West Coast scene have evaporated because the harmonies on this track are derivative of The Mamas & The Papas or The Beach Boys – they're even singing about the sun! While Lou Reed was the sole composer for every song on the album, Doug Yule is all over this track. Not only does he sing, but he also plays bass and keyboards and added drums to some of the takes. The album would feature more of Yule's vocals because Reed couldn't keep his voice in tip-top condition when they were playing multiple sets in the smoky atmosphere of Max's every night, where he'd sing the majority of the band's older material and then record in the afternoon.

Yule was the drummer for 'Sweet Jane', a song that had numerous versions prepared and mixed. The original album version cut out the lovely 'wine and roses' bridge and knocked almost a minute from the playing time. It was later restored to CD issues in the 1990s. The song itself opens with an echo-delayed guitar ditty that was just a random piece of sonic doodling that second producer Geoffrey Haslam heard and suggested using as an impromptu intro, a nice little set-up for the opening guitar riff. The song takes Reed back to his short-story style songs about Jack and Jane, and their lives sitting by the radio at night.

With the placing of 'Rock & Roll' as the third song on side one, the opening of *Loaded* could be compared to some of the best opening trios of any album. The Beatles could put forward *Sgt. Pepper* and Dylan has *Blonde On Blonde*, but none of these had the perfect rock melodies of Reed's three songs. 'Rock & Roll' as a standalone is also possibly the greatest example of a rock song tackling the subject of its own art. Reed manages to write with an objectivity that moves him away from his own medium. He admits the song is autobiographical and that if he hadn't discovered rock and roll, then he 'would have had no idea that there was life on the planet.'

The honky-tonk bounce of 'Cool It Down' could have been a Mungo Jerry cover. Reed sings about Miss Linda Lee, a hooker he's waiting for on the corner because she can 'love him by the hour'. This was one of the few songs actually conceived in the studio, while 'Head Held High' was written back in Seattle. Sterling Morrison remembered that, 'Lou and I were working on the guitar break in a motel room in Seattle. The cab was out there waiting for us, honking and honking, and we're going, "Wait, wait, wait, we've almost got it. One more note!"'

'New Age' was a dramatic piece of arranging that began with a gentle, conversational opening and builds to a grand finale, declaring it's the beginning of a new age. This was another chance for Yule to show his multi-instrumentalist colours as he sang and played bass, piano, drums and organ.

Supposedly about Beat writer William Burroughs (though Reed later denied this), 'Lonesome Cowboy Bill' was an energetic rocker, powered by Billy Yule's enthusiastic drumming. 'I Found a Reason' was a sharp change of style. It harked back to Reed's earliest influence, the 1950s' New York street band vocalists. 'Oh! Sweet Nuthin'' had evolved over the summer and now it eased the listener to the end of the record with a gentle vocal and easy listening beat. The early version was an undulating organ and tremolo guitar-led song, which Reed sang in a powerful voice, unlike the lullaby that Yule used on the final album cut.

Most of the outtakes were so good they found their way onto Lou Reed solo albums over the next decade. One of the most mysterious of these was 'Ocean'. Steve Sesnick somehow convinced John Cale to stop by the studio and play keyboards, though there is confusion about which version his input was included on, as at least three separate arrangements of the song were attempted. On one version Yule arranged and conducted a string section of two cellos and an upright bass. 'I wrote out a basic chart, just following the chord changes,' said Yule. 'I scored it out and recorded it, that's the strings that you hear on there. They are very, very subtle, they are way down in the mix.'

'The original first tracks that were laid down included organ, Lou singing and playing guitar, Billy Yule playing drums,' recalls Doug Yule. 'I was playing organ on this original version. Then I overdubbed tympani and some vocals – and that's all that's on there and it's clearly me playing the organ. Now, if John came in there and did another organ part that's on top of that, I can't say.'

Though she didn't play drums on the album, Moe Tucker did stop by to add the lead vocal to the childlike 'I'm Sticking With You'. It was cut from the album, but was made famous 30 years later, when it was used for a car commercial in the UK. 'I have a distinct memory of playing that song with Moe and Lou, and me singing at the piano,' recalls Doug Yule. 'Moe was only there for the initial track of us singing live. There's a mistake, too, on the piano. I definitely remember making that mistake.'

Finally, in August the sessions were complete. The album had taken five months to record, used multiple drummers, the sessions were often fractured and the styles of the songs varied enormously. There had been personality conflicts with the band and two different producers worked on the record. Against all these odds, it was a success. 'People never got used to the idea of having these raging guitar and then these nice ballads,' said Lou Reed. 'Now it makes more sense to people. Why wouldn't you? Why wouldn't you have everything available?'

For Sterling Morrison the completed album was vindication that they could play straight ahead pop songs if they wanted to. 'To me it illustrates that we could have, all along, made truly commercial-sounding records,' he said. 'We opted not to, because the material was incompatible with standard treatments or whatever other reasons. But people would wonder, could they do it if they had to? The answer was, yes, we could. And we did.'

'Sterling would be there for a while and then take off,' recalls Doug Yule. 'I think he was feeling a little bit like an outsider at that point, it was more situational. I never thought that Sterling wasn't part of it – possibly he resented me because I was doing much more guitar work then, that may have affected him. Lou's a funny guy: he can be very hard in a lot of ways and he won't give an inch, and then all of a sudden out of the blue he'll say, "You really like to play the guitar, don't you? So you should." I wasn't demanding it at all.'

Everyone who was there agrees that, in hindsight, things would have been different if Moe had been around the studio. 'One of the things I love about Maureen is that she is without bullshit,' said Yule. 'She's right in your face and straight ahead. If she likes something, she says it. If she doesn't like something, she says it. If she thinks someone is running a programme on her, she points it out, and she's like that with everyone and she can do that with Lou. She's the only person I've ever known who can do that with Lou and she's the only person that I've seen back him down to when she was right.'

If Tucker had been playing at Max's too, she might have diffused some of the problems. As the residency continued, Reed grew more unhappy. 'I couldn't do the songs I wanted to,' he complained. 'I was under a lot of pressure to do things I didn't want to do. There was a large part of me that wanted to do something else – I didn't belong there.'

Chapter 13

1970–1971

Nothing Going Down at All

'Loaded was supposed to be harder rock than the third one,
but not as bombastic as the second one – somewhere in-between.
But it was very difficult because of Sesnick. He was trying to
make the group less dependent on me and more dependent on
Doug Yule. And there was still the terrible wound of Cale being
removed. If Sesnick hadn't been there, who knows what would
have become of the band?'

Lou Reed

For The Velvet Underground show at Max's on 23 August 1970, Brigid Polk took her tape recorder. She attended the show with writer Jim Carroll, who can be heard talking at various points between songs. At the time Polk didn't realise that it would become an important historical document in the Velvets' career.

A chatty Lou Reed announced that it was okay for the audience to dance and that the first song, 'Waiting For The Man', was a 'tender folk song from the early 50s'. The version they played bore little resemblance to the sublime take on *The Velvet*

Underground & Nico. It had completely lost the undulating drive and verve that made the original so priceless, but for your money you got extra elaborate drumming from Billy Yule and an extended Reed guitar solo at the end. 'Sweet Jane' was closer to the *Loaded* album version – after all, it had only just been recorded and used the same line-up – and they played the extended version that was originally cut and then re-instated to the album version. A good portion of the as yet unreleased album was played, with 'Lonesome Cowboy Bill' and 'New Age' performed in pretty straight takes.

On 'Beginning To See The Light', Billy Yule's overly enthusiastic drumming doesn't allow the song to breathe. He felt the need to put in as many rolls and fills as he could, and the simplicity of Moe Tucker's original beats is sorely missed. The overall vibe was of an intimate party, the band and crowd seemed laid-back almost to the point of sounding like a lounge act. 'You really had to be laid-back,' recalls Doug Yule. 'The room at Max's was about twice as big as your living room, the stage was just a little tiny corner.'

'Part of it was the time, the zeitgeist,' said Yule of the relaxed set they were performing night after night. 'Music was for grooving to and the best thing that could happen to you when you played a strange club or hall was that people started to dance. That was always good, it made you feel good. When we were at Max's, we had a few beers, got on stage and played a set. We were doing three sets a night, which is not a concert situation in the least, and this was happening five nights a week. We were a club band playing original stuff, doing all Velvets' songs. So it was kind of laid-back, just bang it out. There wasn't the same kind of pressure there is when you play a concert. This was not a 40-minute set, blowing your heads off. No, let's get mellow, we're gonna be here for a while. Just relax, otherwise you'll kill yourself.'

'Sunday Morning' was especially laid-back to the point of being pedestrian, but the slower ballad-style songs worked well, with 'Pale Blue Eyes' and 'I'll Be Your Mirror' sounding good, if different. Reed rejected all requests for 'Heroin', saying they didn't play it anymore. The show was appropriately closed with 'After Hours', Reed doing a good job of Tucker's vocals. The take was slightly rearranged, giving more of an upbeat country feel, mainly because of Billy Yule's drumming and Reed's over-the-top cabaret singer delivery.

As fate would have it, the night that Brigid Polk decided to record the band would be the night when Lou Reed walked out. Sterling Morrison got the idea that something was afoot when Reed met him before the show. 'I was sitting in a booth upstairs at Max's, eating a cheeseburger, and Lou came up and said, "Sterling, I'd like you to meet my parents." They hated the fact that Lou was playing music and hanging around with undesirables. I was always afraid of Lou's parents – the only dealing I'd had with them was that there was this constant threat of them seizing Lou and having him thrown into the nut-house. That was always over our heads. Every time Lou got hepatitis his parents were waiting to seize him and lock him up. So I was thinking, "What in the world can this portend?"'

'I hated playing at Max's because I couldn't do the songs that I wanted to do,' said Reed. 'I was under a lot of pressure to do things that I didn't want to do and finally it reached a crescendo. I never in my life thought I would not do what I believed in, and there I was not doing what I believed in, and it made me sick.'

After the 23 August show, Reed quit the band.

The first person he told was Moe Tucker. After the show she had seen him go into a dark stairway and she followed him in. She found him sat in near total darkness with his head in his hands. He seemed inconsolable. Reed told her it was over: he was leaving the band and that night had been his last show. Tucker was understandably surprised and tried to talk him out of it, whatever was wrong could surely be worked out? But no, he'd made his decision and it was final. He was going back to Long Island to live with his parents that night and he wouldn't be back.

Reed later said that out of the whole 10 weeks at Max's he only really enjoyed the final show, because he knew it was his last performance with the band and he played exactly what he wanted to.

When the current line-up of The Velvet Underground arrived at Max's Kansas City on 24 August 1970 for that evening's show, Sesnick told them the shocking news. Lou Reed was gone and he wouldn't be coming back. Though in hindsight it might seem surprising that The Velvet Underground would even consider continuing without him, at the time they had a couple of nights at Max's to fulfil. Indeed, it wasn't seen as a case of them being a really big deal band that had lost its most famous member: they were just an average scale bar and club touring outfit and they just needed a replacement to carry on with their schedule. *Loaded* was all but finished, so they would have a new album to promote and Yule was expected to carry the load of songwriting in the future. With Moe Tucker still on maternity leave, Sterling Morrison was the only original member of the band.

Reed's decision to hire Steve Sesnick as the band's manager had ultimately come back to haunt him. '[Sesnick] had placed himself in a position where he was Lou's best and only friend,' explains Doug Yule. 'Lou put a great deal of trust in him. During that summer Steve decided that Lou was no longer manageable, so he began to look to me because I was young and more easily handled. He had me believing I would be the next Paul McCartney. He told Lou he was through with him, that he didn't care about him, and it upset Lou quite a bit.' In hindsight, Yule admits that he should have contacted Reed and suggested they get together and fire Sesnick, thus continuing as The Velvet Underground without their manager.

Reed was fed up with the daily grind of touring, frustrated that he couldn't write songs while on tour and disillusioned by the lack of financial reward thus far. 'There were a lot of things going on that summer,' he said. 'Internally, within the band, the situation, the milieu and especially the management.'

In the face of losing control of his own band, Reed withdrew and took the surprising step of moving back in with his parents on Long Island. He contacted Sterling Morrison and tried to get him to leave the band and start a new venture, but the guitarist was still unhappy with the way Reed had handled John Cale and more interested in keeping some steady, paying work with the Velvets while furthering his education. So he declined the offer. 'Lou didn't want Doug or Billy involved,' said Morrison. 'It was just going to be me and Lou, and new people. And I said, 'Well, we haven't been talking really, and it'll take us two years to get back to where we are today, to repackage ourselves, and why do it?' Lou really made me a strong pitch and in retrospect, maybe I should have done it. Martha, my wife, said, "Why are you doing this to him? What does he have to do to get you to keep playing?" I said, "I guess nothing. Maybe I don't want to do it anymore."'

'I had no idea what was going on with Lou until it happened,' said Doug Yule. 'Steve Sesnick was Lou's emotional refuge and he told Lou he wasn't going to do that anymore . . . That triggered Lou to run home. That's what someone told me who was involved in the situation and so it's hearsay, but it fits in with what I felt was going on with Lou and Steve.'

Moe Tucker felt that the lack of communication between Reed and Morrison didn't help the situation. 'Neither of them talked about [it],' she said. 'I don't know if he [Reed] wanted to be on his own, or didn't want certain people around. I'm not saying "certain people" because I don't want to say their names, but because I don't know who. I was closer to Lou than Sterling was. Lou and I used to share rooms and be more social. Sterling wasn't mean or hateful but nine times out of ten he wouldn't go out and eat with us.'

The final touches to *Loaded* were made after Reed had walked out. 'Sesnick was trying to minimise Lou's contribution and maximise my contribution because he had it in his head that he would transfer The Velvet Underground onto me and he could keep it,' said Doug Yule. 'This had been his meal ticket for four or five years. I was a very arrogant ambitious young man. I was very critical of anyone else because of low self-esteem and fear that I wasn't adequate. Sesnick played on that. I just went for it hook, line and sinker. You can't con someone unless they are greedy, and I was real greedy.'

Sesnick was, of course, looking after his own best interests, but what else could he do? He had just lost his principal songwriter and he was left with a band he had to promote. Why shouldn't he talk up Doug Yule? When *Loaded* came out in October, Sesnick had done what he could to protect the remaining members of the band. Lou Reed was listed at the bottom of the credits and Moe Tucker was listed as the drummer, even though she hadn't played drums on the album at all. 'Can you imagine what it felt like to have written it, to have them say all the songs were written by everybody, and then list me last?' raged Reed.

The front cover of *Loaded* was designed by the 37-year-old Warsaw-born artist Stanislaw Zagorski. His impression of 'underground' meant 'subway', so he produced an illustration of a subway entrance with pink smoke billowing out. He'd previously designed covers for Ornette Coleman and the Modern Jazz Quartet. For some reason the Dutch version of *Loaded* had green, instead of pink, smoke on the cover.

Reed was also very unhappy with the editing and song sequence that had been chosen. 'The songs are out of order,' he snapped. 'They don't form a cohesive unit, they leap about.' He also criticised the fact that edited versions of 'Sweet Jane' and 'New Age' had been used rather than the longer versions that they'd worked on. He claimed that it was a case of the 'fools' he'd left behind ruining his great album. The truth is that while the final album may have fallen short of the band's ambitions, Reed, just like Sesnick, was simply defending his best interests. The edited versions that made the album were actually Lou Reed edits, according to Doug Yule: 'You have to understand at the time what the motivation was. Lou, and all of us were intent on one thing and that was to be successful, what you had to do to be successful in music was to have a hit, and a hit had to be up-tempo, short, and with no digressions – straight ahead basically. You wanted a hook and something to feed the hook, and that was it. "Sweet Jane" was arranged just exactly the way it is on the original *Loaded* release for that reason: to be a hit! The first time he ever conceived of the song "Satellite Of Love", he . . . was in a limousine. He, me and Sesnick were riding in a limo and he was talking about someone who had just launched a satellite. He was riffing off that idea and conceiving of this song and tying it back into songs about love. Because that's what always sells and that's literally where it came from. It was designed in his mind as a hit and that's what he was looking for, a hit.'

'Me, Lou, Steve and I think Geoff were there when we did the editing in one of those late-night things,' adds Yule. 'In retrospect it would have been better to re-record them because some of the songs have been chopped up pretty badly. The unedited versions are pretty interesting. To get a hit single it had to be less than three minutes, and it had to grab the DJ's attention in the first ten seconds. They would just pick the arm up and move on to the next thing if they weren't interested, they didn't waste time listening through everything.'

The album was issued to favourable reviews. Lenny Kaye writing in an end-of-year *Rolling Stone* claimed that it 'is merely a refinement of The Velvet Underground's music as it has grown through the course of their past three albums . . . there's so much variety on the album that you could go through any number of cuts and pick out much the same things, those extra little touches that make each one special and able to stand up in its own right.' The respected critic Robert Christgau gave the album an 'A' grade in the *Village Voice*, but by the time it was in the shops the band's lead singer and songwriter had departed. Atlantic didn't feel like pumping money after a 'headless' band, and so the album unfairly sank without trace.

It had been the first time that the Velvets had really been able to take their time over an album. They were now signed to a respected label that was fully behind them and the material was radio friendly. It should have been a sure thing, but like much of the Velvets' story, things found a way to unravel.

John Cale, Lou Reed and Moe Tucker at the Café Bizarre in late 1965. Note that Moe was only allowed to play a tambourine during these shows. *Courtesy of Redferns/Getty Images*

Stripped and painted for a filming during 1965. *Courtesy of Redferns/Getty Images*

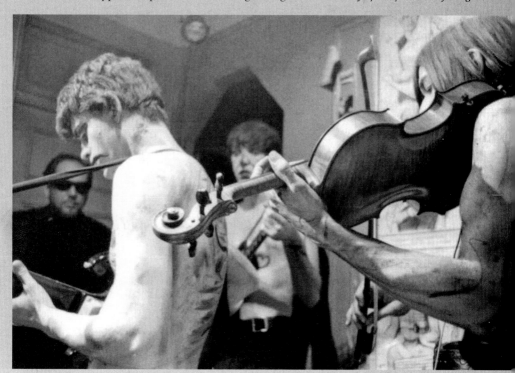

Nico and Lou Reed face
the spotlight during a
1966 Andy Warhol show.
Courtesy of Getty Images

John Cale and Edie Sedgwick share a moment, 1966.   *Courtesy of Getty Images*

Genius at work: Andy Warhol working on the peelable banana image used for the band's debut album.   *Courtesy of Camera Press*

Nico, John Cale, Lou Reed and Sterling
Morrison in the studio for the first album.
Courtesy of Corbis

The Velvet's first New York Residency
was at The Dom. *Courtesy of Getty Images*

Edie Sedgwick and Gerard Malanga provide the on-stage
dance moves while the Velvets play on. *Courtesy of Getty Images*

Reed, Cale, Morrison and Tucker at
the Delmonico Hotel, January 1966.
Courtesy of Getty Images

The psychiatrists didn't know
what hit them when Andy
Warhol presented the Velvets
and entourage at their annual
dinner in January 1966.
Courtesy of Getty Images

Nico and Lou Reed in California,
spring 1966.   *Courtesy of Lebrecht
Photo Library*

The *Exploding Plastic Inevitable* at
The Castle in Los Angeles, spring
1966. Left to right: Mary Woronov,
Gerard Malanga, John Cale, Sterling
Morrison, Moe Tucker, Lou Reed,
Nico and Andy Warhol.
Courtesy of Corbis

Left to right: Reed, Tucker, Morrison and Doug Yule on-stage at an anti-war rally in Texas, 1969. *Copyright Doug Yule, Courtesy of Salvatore Mercuri*

Doug Yule during the sessions for *Loaded* in 1970.
Photo by Henri ter Hall, Courtesy of Steve Nelson

Courtesy of Salvatore Mercuri

the woodrose ballroom presents

THE VELVET UNDERGROUND

AND FROM L.A. **country funk**
wmas 94.7 fm 1450 am
may 16 & 17 $2.50 lights by the road
RTE. 5, DEERFIELD (USE DEERFIELD-CONWAY EXIT FROM ROUTE 91) 665-8742
ADVANCE TICKETS: MELODY CORNER, KRACKERJACKS, AMERICAN REVOLUTION

Reed, Cale and Nico on-stage in January 1972.
Courtesy of Redferns/Getty Images

Sterling Morrison on-stage in
Hamburg, Germany, during
the 1993 reunion tour.
© *1993 Jutta Brandt*

Moe Tucker, Martha Morrison, John Cale and Lou Reed at the Rock and Roll Hall of Fame
induction ceremony.   *Courtesy of Corbis*

Reed eventually regained control of the songs when he sued Sesnick in 1971. The disagreement was hushed over out of court and when the dust settled, Sesnick kept control of the band's name. In return, Reed was given sole ownership of the songs on *Loaded* and *The Velvet Underground*, something which caused distress for the other band members, who felt they had been squeezed out of the new deal. 'I'm the last person to deny Lou's immense contribution and he's the best songwriter of the three of us,' said Sterling Morrison. 'But he wanted all the credit: he wanted it more than we did and he got it, to keep the peace.'

Once the season at Max's was complete the band took a break to reassess the situation and see what reaction *Loaded* would get when it was issued in September. With Doug Yule now taking over the lead vocals, and by default, the leadership of the band, they needed to re-jig the line-up. Moe Tucker was now back, with baby daughter Kerry in tow, and along with Sterling Morrison half of the original band was still present. The big question was would the absence of Reed cause an adverse public reaction? No one seemed to complain when John Cale left, but Reed had been the band's most public face. Yule changed to play guitar, so they needed a bassist and Walter Powers was brought in. He'd played with Yule in the Glass Menagerie and also in Lost and Listening. The new touring band was now complete, but what would happen in the future without a recognised songwriter? Only one weekend of shows was played before the turn of the year. They practised a new set with the new line-up.

For a while Reed completely dropped out of sight. He didn't contact anyone and most people didn't know how to contact him. 'Lou didn't know what to do for a while, so he basically had to protect himself,' said Yule. 'Lou was very reclusive, he doesn't like to be vulnerable at all.' Reed was actually considering giving up music entirely. There were unconfirmed reports related by Lester Bangs in *Creem* that Reed had suffered a nervous breakdown and gone back to work for his father's accountancy firm for a while before he regained his confidence enough to start writing again. Another rumour even claimed that he'd been killed by Steve Sesnick! None of the above was true, but it would be over a year before he made another public appearance.

For the remaining band members, talk of not continuing without Reed just didn't come up. Sesnick told them that Reed wasn't coming back almost as a passing comment, the on-stage responsibilities were reshuffled and the band carried on. Doug Yule only knew the verses to some songs so he had a certain amount of revising to do as he was now the band's only lead singer. 'Sterling and I were having fun playing and it was a good little band,' explains Moe Tucker. 'People had changed places and it wasn't The Velvet Underground anymore but what the hell, we'll keep playing. I didn't want to look for a job then so we stayed together.'

Few dates were booked in the immediate aftermath of Reed's departure. Walter Powers, who had played with Doug Yule in the Glass Menagerie, joined the band. He had a long and varied musical history. He'd given up his early piano lessons in favour of a guitar in the mid-1950s, after seeing Elvis on *The Ed Sullivan Show*, and after a brief dalliance with acoustic guitar he fell in with a like-minded Beatles- and Stones-loving gang, who formed a band called The Lost.

'Of the three guitarists, I was the least accomplished, particularly playing rock and roll,' explains Powers. 'So band leader Ted Myers asked me if I would try bass; the band would use its earnings from gigs to pay for it, and I was agreeable. I didn't really know what I was doing but I listened to other bass players and progressed; I was particularly influenced by the basslines on Motown records.' The Lost had a modicum of success, signed to Capitol and toured with The Beach Boys. When that band broke up, he joined The Glass Menagerie.

'I think I was aware through the media that Andy Warhol had a regular band called The Velvet Underground playing with his Exploding Plastic Inevitable "happening,"' recalls Powers. 'Somebody played me the "Banana" album when it came out. I didn't really respond to the music. A year or two later, I heard that Doug Yule had joined the Velvets. Subsequently, I went to see them for my first time at the Boston Tea Party. I liked their sound: it was more searingly evocative in person than I had gotten from the record.'

The band were now undergoing fairly regular personnel changes and the shows were a million miles away from the Warhol-influenced extravaganzas of their early days. During one show Walter Powers threw himself from the stage, as Doug Yule recalled: 'Walter flew off the stage like Superman and broke his eye orbit. The story he told about how they set it was awful: he had this thing up his nose so they could move the bone, it was unbelievable.' Through to the end of 1970 the new band played a handful of shows before being booked into an unlikely venue for a rock band, a ski lodge in New England, in January 1971.

The Alpine in North Conway, New Hampshire was a bar with a small stage at a ski resort. A local review said the band sounded like the Jefferson Airplane. 'Sesnick couldn't sell the band to the larger venues we used to play, so he started looking around for anything he could find,' explained Doug Yule. 'I remember playing the ski lodge in Vermont and it didn't snow, so no one was skiing, so there was no one in the bar. And on top of that, it was a circular stage and the bar was around the stage. It must have been a strip club at some point and it was the worst venue I've been in – there was nobody there, it was just horrendous.' The venue's management must have enjoyed having the band as they booked them back a few weeks later when the skiers had returned. 'We played on a stage that was as big as a dining-room table, in the corner,' recalls Yule. 'It was jammed with people attempting to dance and drink themselves into oblivion. We played the Alpine for many weeks [they returned for a second engagement in February] – in fact, we played there so long I learned how to ski. There was no record company footing the bills and Sesnick was having trouble booking the group. So he got whatever he could.' After a show in Birmingham, Michigan, Walter Powers fell down some stairs and broke his jaw, meaning he had to miss some shows and was briefly replaced by Larry Estridge. 'Larry Esteridge was a temporary thing,' said Yule. 'Sesnick brought him in, he played a short series of shows. We were touring on a bus at that point, which shows how far we'd slipped.'

A major change in personal came at the end of August 1971. The Velvets had just played a pair of shows in Houston at the Liberty Hall, a converted cinema that held fewer than 200 people. When the Velvets' party arrived at the airport to fly home on the Monday morning, nothing seemed to be amiss. They were all present and accounted for, and Sterling Morrison had his trademark large brown suitcase with him. But as they approached the check-in desk, Morrison stopped in his tracks and said, 'There's something I've got to tell you all. I'm not going back.' According to Doug Yule: 'I said to him: "Where you going now?" He said: "I'm going back to the hotel." I said, "Why did you bring your suitcase?" He said, "'I dunno." I said, "Is there anything in it?" He said, "No."'

Morrison felt so guilty about leaving the band in the lurch that he couldn't bring himself to tell them. He'd left it until the last moment at the airport so that they couldn't try and talk him out of it because they had a plane to catch. He'd been applying for a teaching post at several universities, including the University of Texas. While in Houston he had decided to drop in on them to see how his application was progressing. They said they'd been trying to contact him: they wanted him to start right away.

'I think he was just embarrassed,' said Doug Yule. 'Sterling was like that – he was very, very sensitive. He was very private in a lot of ways. So he hopped back in the car and went back to the hotel, and then went on to Austin. That's one of my favourite stories about Sterling because it says so much about his character: that he was afraid to confront the people he worked with, to tell them right up front something that he really wanted to do. He was afraid that we wouldn't support him. We didn't want him to leave, we wanted him to stay.'

'Sterling called me and said, "I have a bolt out of the blue,"' recalls Martha Dargan. 'He told me he'd left the band and he told me that he was over at UT as a teaching assistant and going to grad school. I just stood there and I looked around the kitchen, and I said, "Okay, I'll take the yellow chairs and the cutting board," and I was mentally packing already, there was no decision. I thought it would be a couple of years and it turned out to be 16. He loved Texas, and Austin was a great place then.'

Morrison was unsure about the timing of his departure as the band was preparing for their first trip to Europe, which was coming up in a few weeks' time. The next day he got a call from home: there'd been a bad fire at his house in New York and most of his possessions had been destroyed. He took this as a sign from above that it was time to move. 'Austin was a nice, out-of-the-way location,' he said. 'The music scene was zero as far as I was concerned. I thought, this is great, nobody'll be knocking at my door. For the first two years I didn't even have a phone. I didn't want any late-night offers from lunatics rocking my boat.'

'The fire was serious,' said Dargan. 'We lost everything, but a friend of ours got there and got the guitars out. Three were charred but I think one was okay.' Martha drove down to join Sterling in Texas that autumn and they decided the time was right to get married. The ceremony took place at the UT chapel on 29 December 1971. For the Morrisons it was the start of a completely new life, well away from the stress and financial worry of being in a rock band.

Chapter 14
1971–1974
Squeezed

'Squeeze was weird. I don't know what that was all about.
I was still around but for the life of me I can't remember the
explanation that someone else was playing drums. I remember
being extremely pissed off and like, "What the hell is going on!?"'

Maureen Tucker

The scene in the recording studio was a strange one. These were supposed to be the sessions for The Velvet Underground's fifth album, *Squeeze*, but none of the original band members were present. In fact, hardly anyone was present. An engineer sat patiently in the control room, while Doug Yule was left alone to pretty much record the whole thing himself. The omnipresent Steve Sesnick popped in and out, and a hired drummer called in to play on a few tracks, but basically Yule was left to his own devices.

To find Sterling Morrison's replacement the band again went back to Doug Yule's musical roots and recruited Willie Alexander. Alexander was born in Philadelphia, the son of a minister. His first musical adventures included sneaking into his father's church to play on the piano. Alexander's first professional gig had been as a country and western cocktail drummer, but he soon progressed to rock and roll.[1] He'd recently played in The Glass Menagerie with Walter Powers, who also signed up for the next series of live dates.

In the first week of October 1971 they flew to London for the first European dates of the band's career, but only Moe Tucker survived from the original band. 'When Sterling quit, Steve Sesnick had booked this European tour as the "Velvet Underground,"' recalls Moe Tucker. 'I stayed with it for two reasons: one, I wanted to see Europe and two, I thought it needed to have at least one member of The Velvet Underground if people were paying good money to see The Velvet Underground.'

Almost 20 UK dates had been booked, and a few more in Holland. 'We went to London,' recalls Walter Powers. 'We had an apartment there, sort of a base of operations. Also coming with us was Maureen's baby daughter, Kerry, plus her brother came over and stayed with us, so there was some real family around.'

'Walter and Willie were great musicians and we had a good time – I liked them a lot,' said Moe Tucker. 'My daughter was a real good baby and my younger brother who was in High School came over to babysit about three weeks into the tour, so I didn't have to drag her around the country. Before he came over I would have to take her to all of these shows and then drive home, and some of these were pretty far away. We'd get back at four in the morning and she'd just sleep all the way.'

The tour began on Bonfire Night 1971, with a show at the School of African and Oriental Studies in London. Taking the stage introduced as the Andrews Sisters, they opened with an almost a cappella version of Phil Spector's 'Chapel Of Love' before 'I'm Waiting For The Man' exploded with an organ-heavy, blues-riff reworking. Willie Alexander's 'Spare Change' was a Jerry Lee Lewis barrelhouse piano-inspired number and they received a good reception, complete with a couple of drunken-student hecklers. 'Some Kinda Love' built nicely and the band was reasonably tight despite Doug Yule saying, 'When Lou and John, or Lou and I were on stage there was a balance. With Lou gone, the balance was gone – it wasn't the same.' It wasn't the same, but it wasn't that bad either, though 'Rock and Roll' was almost unrecognisable and badly missed Reed's subtle vocal intonations. Understandably there were few songs from the first two pre-Doug Yule albums, but they did play four Willie Alexander numbers in the 13-song set ('Pretty Tree Climber' could have been a Jimi Hendrix b-side). Of the older material 'White Light/White Heat' struggled to capture the zest of the original and 'Sister Ray' noodled away but missed the musicianship and power of Reed, Morrison and Cale. Yule's composition 'Dopey Joe' and Moe Tucker singing 'After Hours' ended the show. Two weeks later, in Amsterdam, they played a similar set that was recorded by Dutch radio.

The band covered most of the university circuit through October and well into November, from Southampton in the South to Glasgow in the North. No one ever came to ask where Lou Reed was, although one fan did start talking to Doug Yule as though he was Reed. He turned out to be David Bowie! A handful of French and Dutch shows ended the tour. Just as the tour was over, Sesnick told Yule he'd arranged for him to stay behind to record an album. When Yule asked if Moe Tucker was going to play on it too, he was told no, she's going home. For Tucker she had had enough, and the last original member of

The Velvet Underground left the group. 'Of course it was not The Velvet Underground anymore,' said Tucker. 'I had never thought of myself as a musician so I decided it was time to just get a job.'

At this point in The Velvet Underground story a strange twist occurred that no one can satisfactorily explain. When Moe Tucker flew back home, Doug Yule stayed behind in London to record a new 'Velvet Underground' album, *Squeeze*, at the request of Steve Sesnick. There seems to be no documented explanation as to why Moe Tucker didn't stay to play on the album, even she can't recall the reason, and her replacement can't even remember attending the sessions.

It seems that Sesnick approached Yule with the idea of recording the new Velvet Underground album in London on his own and didn't want the others playing on it. Sesnick still owned the band's name and had negotiated a deal through Polydor. An advance had been agreed to pay for the album sessions, but Sesnick was eager to save as much on costs as possible. That meant Yule playing virtually everything and Ian Paice from Deep Purple being brought in to add drums. Yule was uncomfortable about it being under The Velvet Underground name, but he had Sesnick by his side saying it was all okay. The opportunity for him to get into a studio and record his own material was too much for Yule to resist.

'You have to understand that I was 23 years old and I had led a very sheltered life, I was not very world-wise,' explained Yule. 'I didn't have any skills in terms of confrontation. It would have been easy to go to Maureen and say, "Steve tells me I'm gonna do an album and you're not gonna do it with me. Why's that?" That would have been a perfectly logical thing for me to do, which I'd do now. I would never even conceive, if I was in a group now, of doing an album without sitting down with the whole group and saying, "Now we're gonna do an album, what do you think about that?" Anyway it happened, and I was very much caught up in my own hubris at the time. I was so full of, "Okay, here I am. I'm in England. I'm recording. I'm working with Ian Paice of Deep Purple." It was like the blind leading the blind. Me leading myself. I don't even have a copy of it. But it's kind of a nice memory for me and kind of an embarrassment at the same time. I wish I had my eyes wider open, but it was nice to get my name and my songs out there. A lot of that stuff is about Lou, anyway . . . some of it about Maureen. I'd been writing for quite a while and Steve gave me some things: "She'll Make Me Cry", he gave me the tagline and I wrote the song around it, and there were some others where he gave me a phrase and I turned it into a song. Musically I think there are some interesting ideas on the album and lyrically it has its moments, but it wasn't until I started to write narrative fiction that I learned how to write songs.'

The album was recorded at a small studio near to Piccadilly Circus and was all wrapped in only ten days. 'I recorded with Ian and then I went back and overdubbed everything,' explains Yule. 'I wasn't even there for the mix and I had nothing to do with the album sleeve. I learned later that the notes I sent back about the mixing were thrown away and never used'. He ruefully admits of his ambitious, younger self, 'When your eyes are full of stars you tend to overlook a few things.'

For his part, Ian Paice must have played on the album in a haze. 'I have no recollection of the sessions,' he claimed to *Mojo* magazine. 'I might have played on some of the tracks but definitely it doesn't sound like me.' Steve Sesnick wrote some of the lyrics for the tracks 'She'll Make You Cry' and 'Mean Old Man'.

The opening song, 'Little Jack', sounds like an outtake from David Bowie's album *The Man Who Sold The World,* which was released in the same year. The songs are competent, a collection of guitar- and piano-based pop songs that sound like they were written in the early 1970s. Links to Reed's songwriting are evident, with one song simply called 'Caroline' and another titled 'Jack & Jane', a reply to 'Rock & Roll', perhaps? Sesnick made sure the production and arrangement credits on the album read 'By The Velvets', but, of course, it didn't point out that, by now, 'The Velvets' were just Yule and himself. When the album was released in the UK in February 1973 (it was only released in the UK, Germany and Spain) it immediately sank without trace and is now a true collector's album.

'I agree that *Squeeze* was the work of a very immature songwriter,' said Yule. 'Sesnick was right beside me the whole time, offering me the chance to make a record and telling me I was going to be somebody. He was even helping me write some of the songs. So I had no doubts. I wanted to be somebody too! I personally have one or two songs on there that I'm fond of, but you know if you're a writer and write a book and it gets published in a very small market and then 15 or 20 years down the road, you look at that book and go, "Jesus, I was really, really raw at that point!" It's not something you're real proud of, but that's what you were doing at the time. It's part of your development. So, that's the way I look at it. It was what got me to the point of where I am now, in terms of learning how to write music and write words, you know. I mean, Lou is a very talented guy: he learned how to write words when he was very young and he had an innate ability to adapt music to his needs and to create songs out of the notes that were available to him. But me, I had to learn it – it took me a lot of years to learn it. So I look at *Squeeze* as being, it's like the equivalent of a tenth-grade term paper; it's a piece of work that I did. It's not my best work, but it shows a lot of where I was going.'

While Doug Yule was completing *Squeeze*, Lou Reed also arrived in London to work on his debut solo album. He'd slowly got back to work and made a series of demos on a home tape machine before flying to London in December 1971 to begin recording. After a couple of weeks in London, Reed received a surprise visit from John Cale, who asked him to join him and Nico for a one-off show in Paris at the end of the month. Reed accepted the invitation and even held some practice sessions with Cale in London before travelling to France.

The show at the Bataclan Theatre on the Rue Voltaire took place on 29 January 1972, six months after Nico's ex-lover Jim Morrison had died in the same city. On the cold January night the theatre was mobbed by Velvet Underground fans, as this was going to be the closest they ever came to seeing the principal members of the band play live, and the event was being filmed for French television. The venue was too small for the crowd, with an estimated 2,000 fans being locked out of the packed venue. The three figures on stage would have taken a little bit of recognising from a distance. Nico had her hair in its natural brunette colouring, John Cale wore a wool sweater and looked like a school teacher, while Lou Reed had clearly gained some weight and let his hair grow into a semi-afro.

The 14-song set covered songs from the Velvets' career ('I'm Waiting For The Man', 'Heroin'), Cale's new solo album ('Ghost Story'), unreleased Reed solo songs ('Wild Child', 'Berlin') and Nico sang material from her solo albums and her trio of Velvet

Underground songs ('Femme Fatale', 'I'll Be Your Mirror' and 'All Tomorrow's Parties'). Many of the songs were played with only an acoustic guitar, others also had John Cale on piano or viola. Lou Reed soaked up the atmosphere and played like a nightclub diva, sitting cross-legged and hamming it up with the audience. The night was a success, but at the end of the show the three ex-band mates went their separate ways.

At the end of the 1971 tour, when Moe Tucker retired from the music industry, she moved to Georgia and really set about bringing up a family. She eventually had five children. Doug Yule also thought it was over: no salary, no shows to play, no studio time available, it was time to move on. In early 1972, he started work as a carpenter and was arranging a move to Denver. He was just packing up a little van with his possessions when he got a call from Steve Sesnick. He'd managed to provisionally book some more dates in England under the name The Velvet Underground, would Yule like to lead a band over there? Doug Yule takes up the story 'I said, 'Sure I'd love to. I don't want to be a carpenter, I want to be a musician! Nobody said a word, no one ever said, "This isn't the real band." The group was shrouded in mystery.'

A band was hastily assembled by Sesnick. Joining Yule were drummer Rob Norris, George Kay and Mark Nauseff. Nauseff was hired via a tour agency. Norris and Kay had played in The Red Rockets, along with Billy Yule, who were another Sesnick-managed band. At one point he'd tried to persuade Moe Tucker and Sterling Morrison to join the band but that fell through. The new group flew to London in November 1972 and Sesnick was supposed to meet them at Heathrow. However, he never arrived and Yule has never seen him again. The band were in big trouble: no money and nowhere to sleep were the immediate problems. No manager to liaise with promoters and sort travel arrangements in a foreign country were more long-term issues to be resolved.

Luckily, Rob Norris had a good friend who let them sleep on the floor of his apartment for the first night, then Yule tracked down one of his sisters who was studying in the capital and they stayed with her for a while. It was a cold November and the band were left sleeping on a freezing floor and cursing their supposed manager. Within a few days, Yule had managed to locate the promoter, who was sympathetic to their situation and arranged for them to loan some equipment and helped with the travel.

While sitting around in London, Norris and Yule talked about Sesnick a lot. It transpired that he'd tried to use his 'divide and conquer' tactics with The Red Rockets just as he had with The Velvet Underground. 'You take four people who are basically insecure and very hungry for something and you feed each one what they want to hear,' explains Yule. 'You keep them from talking to each other by telling them that the other people are against them and keep them isolated from the group. I would be told by him that I was better than Lou and that the others were not really my friends, I should not confide in them. And he did that to everybody. That way, your only source of information becomes him and he can tell you whatever he wants because you're not talking to other people. His whole scam collapsed on The Red Rockets because they started talking to each other. The Velvets never talked to each other: he kept them apart and we never communicated much.'

The tour visited such out-of-the-way rock venues as the Malvern Winter Gardens. The Winter Gardens were past their best when the Velvets played there in the basement room, which had two bars. The likes of Hawkwind, Mott the Hoople and Black Sabbath were other early-1970s' visitors to the venue. It was a long way from Andy Warhol's *Exploding Plastic Inevitable*. On 26 November, a hassle over whether the promoter was going to pay the money before the show in Cardiff almost led to an ugly situation. A stand-off of 'no money equals no gig' developed. 'We were in the dressing room and this real sleazy, low-brow guy with the club went on-stage and got these skin-head types all revved up,' recalls Rob Norris. 'He was saying, "Well, they're here but our money's not good enough for them." They came after us and tried to bang down the door. It was George Kay who said, "Shit-ass punks aren't gonna bother us: we're gonna go out that door, we're gonna get in the car and get out of here, and they're not even gonna touch us." We formed a "V" with the guitar cases, burst the door down and moved through the crowd, and they didn't bother us. But I was fearing for my life.'

Melody Maker reviewed the 2 December show in St Albans saying, 'Old faithfuls like "Waiting For My Man" and "Sweet Jane" harked back to the days when Lou Reed was in the band. Half the audience were there to see a group which must be legend now. The other half were there to rave, so everybody was happy. The Velvets had been jamming in the dressing room for two hours before they came on stage – they obviously like playing.' Four days later at St David's University College the gig was recorded and the tapes actually show an improvement on the previous year's shows, with a slightly different choice of material. George Kay and Mark Nauseff's rhythm section worked well together and propelled along the songs like 'White Light/White Heat' that had struggled the year before. Though this was billed as the 'Squeeze tour', they hardly featured any *Squeeze* songs in the set list. They sounded like a garage outfit, which was fine. If they didn't have the baggage of the glorious past, a casual observer might have said they were a decent up-and-coming band with some good, if raw-sounding, songs. The tour ended at the tiny Northamptonshire Cricket Club. By the end, Doug Yule knew they were touring under false pretences and he didn't like it. 'But it meant I was working, and it was tough to turn down,' he admitted. 'We never had an audience react negatively.'

To all intents and purposes, The Velvet Underground was over. With Sesnick conspicuous by his absence, Doug Yule felt lucky to have got back from England in one piece and had set up a covers band with his brother Billy, George Kay from the final Velvets' line-up and Don Silverman, a friend of Kay's from California. The unnamed band played a healthy sprinkling of Velvets' songs but did their best to stay away from any promotional links to the previous band. They played a few gigs in the late spring of 1973, but the promoter insisted on billing the group as The Velvet Underground. 'He was supposed to bill us as "Featuring Doug Yule from The Velvet Underground,"' explains Yule. 'But he wasn't supposed to say it was *The Velvet Underground*. We played next to Boston's Fenway Park [baseball stadium] in Kenmore Square, that was probably our second-to-last show.' That show at Oliver's, on 27 May, was recorded and now highlights a band that was a pretty good Velvet Underground tribute outfit, which just happened to have one of The Velvet Underground in it. They played more non-Velvets' tunes than they did songs by the band they were advertised as being. The final shows came days later. Doug Yule: 'At some ski-place in Vermont: we drove in, saw "The Velvet Underground" and said, "That's the last straw."

Plus, the place turned out to be a real dive. It was one of those places you hear [puts on whiny voice] "Can you turn down? Can you play 'Louie, Louie?'" We didn't even play the second night – the guy asked us to leave.'

Chapter 15
1972–1974
Hand in Hand with Myself

'I love Lou but he has what must be a very fragmented personality, so you're never too sure under any conditions what you're going to have to deal with. Will he be boyishly charming? Lou is very charming when he wants to be. Or will he be vicious? And if he is you have to figure out what's stoking the fire.'

Sterling Morrison

While Doug Yule was extinguishing the final embers of The Velvet Underground, the original band members were heading in vastly different directions, both personally and musically. John Cale garnered a reputation as a supreme producer on some of the 1970s crucial albums, got divorced and remarried; Lou Reed set sail on a solo career while publically flirting with homosexuality; Moe Tucker got a job and started a family, while Sterling Morrison turned to academia. Yule himself headed west to become a carpenter. But while the principal players scattered away, the band itself continued to grow in stature.

John Cale spent the first half of the 1970s being as inquisitive as ever. After Nico's *The Marble Index* he worked with her again on her *Desert Shore* album in 1971, while also eclipsing Lou Reed's prolific output by recording seven of his own albums (all studio albums rather than concert) before 1975. Somehow he also found the time to work as a staff producer for Warner's and produced Patti Smith's classic album *Horses* and the Modern Lovers' eponymous debut album.

Though Cale's sterling production work put him in the spotlight by the middle of the 1970s, it had begun a few years earlier when his work on Nico's *The Marble Index* for Jac Holzman's Elektra label opened the door for him to work with another Elektra signing, The Stooges. The Stooges and lead-singer Iggy Pop (real name James Osterberg) had been inspired by seeing another Elektra band, The Doors, in concert at the University of Michigan. The Stooges made their debut in 1967 and were signed to Elektra when Danny Fields went to see the MC5 but ended up signing both bands to the label. The Stooges soon whipped up a reputation of being enthusiastic and often outrageous live performers, and John Cale had the difficult task of trying to transfer that overflow of intense energy onto tape for their debut album in 1969. 'I thought I'd have a problem capturing this very visual performer on record,' said Cale. 'In the end, we recorded in a tiny room – just wheel them in, and off you go. It was the same thing recording the Modern Lovers – get them in a room and press record.'

Cale's next production only began to be mentioned many years later, when Nick Drake suddenly became popular in the 1990s after two decades of being a fringe cult figure. It was in London in 1970 that Cale met the doomed folk singer and was asked to produce a couple of songs for the *Bryter Layter* album. 'I think

Nick was slightly bemused by Cale,' said Drake's musical mentor Joe Boyd. 'In retrospect he may have felt that John took over "Fly" and "Northern Sky", but everyone loved the tracks so much he didn't say anything.'

'Drake's stuff was so wide open, you could build deep landscapes behind him,' said Cale. 'It was very gentle, sensitive music but it accommodated an enormous amount of colour. I got on with him but he was obviously incredibly fragile.' Drake would only record three studio albums before his premature death from an overdose in 1974 at the age of 26. Looking back in 2007, Cale said: 'I didn't know about [his] other problems, he was just very shy and very withdrawn. I was just trying to work out what the choruses were, but there weren't any. And now every time I go to Starbucks, I hear it.'

In 1971, Cale and Betsey Johnson divorced. Shortly after this he met Cindy Wells, who had been a member of The GTOs, a Frank Zappa offshoot band. After several months they married and Cale moved to the San Fernando Valley to set up home. 'Whatever the professional drug takers were in New York, there were about ten times more of them in LA. I got involved in a different kind of drugs scene.' As well as all of his production work, Cale was prolific with his own material. His early solo work of *Church of Anthrax*, *Vintage Violence* and *The Academy in Peril* covered classical music to jazz, and most points in-between. Most of it was purely instrumental. 'I couldn't make my mind up whether I wanted to write them or invent them on the spot,' reveals Cale about his songwriting. 'I was a classical musician playing catch-up with everyone around me. I was a little embarrassed and I was constantly trying to prove myself against Lou's work.'

His marriage to Wells started to come unstuck when her GTOs' bandmate 'Miss Christine' died of an overdose in

November 1972. She suffered, in Cale's words, a complete mental collapse. On the advice of Wells' psychiatrist, Cale had her committed, then sank into a morass of drink and cocaine to blot out his marital problems and lack of commercial success.

In 1973, his next project, *Paris 1919*, proved that he could stand up against Reed's solo work. An album of defined beauty, it was also the one he was most prepared for. 'Everything had time to percolate,' said Cale. 'Everything else I've done has been off the cuff, but on *Paris 1919* I went into the studio with complete pieces.' On the album Cale successfully fused rock and roll and his avant-garde classical leanings, using Little Feat as the backing band and bringing in the UCLA Symphony Orchestra for the string sections. 'It was an example of using the nicest ways of saying something really ugly,' said Cale.

He moved back to London, taking Cindy Wells with him, and signed for Island Records in 1974 (here, he blossomed as a songwriter. Cale brought in Roxy Music's guitarist Phil Manzanera and keyboard maestro Brian Eno to aid his quest to record a rock album. 'When I got to Island the main point was to keep on doing the stuff that Lou had refused to keep doing in The Velvet Underground,' he said. 'It certainly helped to have people the quality of Eno and Manzanera there to continue that. Phil's one of those musicians who can respond to whatever's going on around him, always an invaluable trait.'

Though Cale is listed as producer and arranger for his three Island albums, *Fear*, *Slow Dazzle* and *Helen of Troy*, the impact of the Roxy Music contingent was comparable to the Bowie/Ronson effect on Lou Reed's *Transformer*. Cale was a lot less successful commercially, but he was never going for mainstream acceptance. It was just not part of his modus operandi. Critically these three albums were some of the best of his career.

Fear covers a lot of musical ground. Many of Cale's songs were piano based on his trademark all-out style and his distinctive vocals work well in this environment. He wasn't afraid to slow it down on tracks like 'Buffalo Ballet' and the ballad 'Emily' shows that he can evoke the atmosphere of waves breaking on a beach much better than Reed on 'Ocean'. He even rocked out on tracks like 'Gun'. As ever, Cale was producing the kind of music that interested him at a particular time, irrespective of any commercial benefits.

Lou Reed was also exploring new sonic vistas, but was being critically (and commercially) rewarded for it. Buoyed by the successful Paris show with John Cale and Nico in January 1972, he headed back to London, to complete work on his first solo album at Morgan Studios. He felt it was really important to break away from his musical past in New York and take a breath of fresh air in London where he didn't really know anyone. He could start afresh and not be distracted by friends and parties. The music scene in London was one of confused transition. Many genres fought it out for airplay and shop window displays. The metal of Led Zeppelin's *Led Zeppelin IV*, the folk of Simon & Garfunkel's *Bridge Over Troubled Water* and the pumping glam of T-Rex's *Electric Warrior* all rode high in the album charts. Not far behind were the monolithic progressive acts like Yes and Emerson, Lake & Palmer. Where Lou Reed was going to fit into all of this was anyone's guess.

Reed had spent most of the time out of the spotlight at his parents' house, recording snippets of song ideas on his home cassette machine, writing poetry and dating a pretty blonde he'd recently met, Bettye Kronstadt. Like Reed, Kronstadt was Jewish and had grown up on Long Island. By all accounts she was well-dressed and stylish, the kind of girl his parents would undoubtedly have approved of. She'd flown to England with him in December 1971. In London, Reed and co-producer Richard Robinson had assembled a strange mix of musicians and personalities to play as the studio backing band. Rick Wakeman and Steve Howe were members of Yes and Caleb Quaye had played with Elton John. The album was recorded at Morgan Studios in London.

Reed dove back into the unreleased Velvet Underground archives for over half of the album, simply titled *Lou Reed*. 'I Can't Stand It' (with vocal changed from 'Shelly' to 'Jenny'), 'Walk It And Talk It', 'Lisa Says', 'I Love You', 'Love Makes You Feel', 'Ride Into The Sun' and 'Ocean' were all re-recorded. 'Ocean' was the most radical of the re-workings as the Yes contingent whipped up an atmospheric storm around Reed's vocal. Too literal perhaps, but interesting nonetheless.

Of the new songs, 'Going Down' was a souped-up piano ballad with strong harmony vocals provided by Helene Francois and Kay Garner, 'Wild Child' was a forgettable mid-tempo rocker while 'Berlin' was destined to become a classic, but only after he later re-recorded it for the album of the same name.

'I don't think anyone who has been following my stuff is going to be surprised by what I've done with this new album,' said Reed at the time of its release in May 1972. 'And I think the general audience will find it more accessible.' Unfortunately, it disappeared without trace for most of the next 30 years. Within months Reed was disowning the record, saying, 'There's just too many things wrong with it.' His label, RCA, agreed and were very disappointed with the production and overall quality of the songs. Reed would be on probation for his next album and they saw his choice of producer as being key to the direction his career was going to take.

Reed, having been lauded in the press by David Bowie (who himself was riding a wave of critical and commercial fame with his Ziggy Stardust character), was receiving more attention than he ever did while in The Velvet Underground. He was getting a relative degree of fame in the UK without actually doing anything himself. Bowie was covering 'White Light/White Heat' and 'I'm Waiting For The Man' in concert and talking up Reed's songwriting abilities when anyone would listen. In July, Reed made his first appearance on a UK stage when Bowie invited him on to play 'White Light/White Heat', 'I'm Waiting For The Man' and 'Sweet Jane' at a charity show at the Royal Festival Hall. Reed donned a black sequined jacket and gold shoes for the occasion, while a fully glammed-up Bowie was compared to Danny la Rue in *Melody Maker*.

Bowie had proved himself as a studio guru by the production work he'd carried out on his last two albums, *Hunky Dory* and *Ziggy Stardust*, so RCA were happy about Reed asking him to help out with the next album. In this atmosphere of expectation, Reed found himself at Trident studio in August to record his second solo album of the year, with Bowie and guitarist Mick Ronson acting as producers. The trio were the perfect fit for the material that Reed had written and the era it was being recorded in. Glam Rock was taking off in a big way and this album, *Transformer*, would contain the anthems of that movement. This was the album that Reed had threatened to make with *Loaded*. Packing a commercial pop feel with more of the ballads that he'd wanted to do at the end of Max's run back in 1970, and benefiting from Ronson's skilful arrangements, it captured the scene of New York's pimps, transvestites and misfits. It was The Factory. Holly Woodlawn and Candy Darling, a couple of transvestites from The Factory, appeared in a song called 'Walk On The Wild Side' and comments that Andy Warhol had made formed the opening lines of 'Vicious'.

Reed hadn't used up all of the unreleased Velvets' songs that he'd written, and both a slower version of 'Andy's Chest' and a re-worked 'Satellite Of Love' were recorded. The arrangement of the latter showed how Mick Ronson's piano work could trans-form an average guitar tune into a classic. The song also featured David Bowie's vocal talents at the fade-out after Reed had put in an inspired performance.

'Perfect Day' shows Reed's sentimental side and again, Ronson's piano lifts the song to new heights, as does his string arrangement on the chorus. It wasn't all sweet little piano pieces, though. Chugging T-Rex rhythms drive 'Hangin' Round' and 'Wagon Wheel', 'I'm So Free' is a hard-nosed rocker, despite the over-the-top comedy backing vocals, and 'Goodnight Ladies' hits ridiculous depths of pseudo-New Orleans jazz. The most telling song on the album was 'Make Up', in which Reed sings of 'coming out of his closet'. The hamming up of the song as a *Cabaret*-style bisexual opera fitted and defined the Glam-era. 'People like Lou and I are probably predicting the end of an era,' said Bowie. 'And I mean that catastrophically. Any society that allows people like Lou and me to become rampant is pretty well lost. We're both pretty mixed-up, paranoid people, absolute walking messes.'

Transformer was released in November 1972 and Reed began playing US shows for the first time in 27 months. On Boxing Day he played a live radio session before an enthusiastic studio audience on WLIR-FM in Hempstead on Long Island, just miles from his family home. As was the norm on these sessions he played an hour's worth of songs with a short interview mid-way through the set.

His choice of material was interesting. Of the 11 songs he performed, five were from his Velvets' days, two were from *Lou Reed* and four were from *Transformer*. During the interview he was asked if he'd moved to England as he'd been gone for so long, but he reassured his hometown listeners that New York was still his base. When asked about the ex-Velvets, and in particular Doug Yule (who at the time was recording *Squeeze* in London), Reed replied with playful sarcasm. 'So, where's Doug Yule?' asked the interviewer. Reed replied, 'Dead, I hope.' Amid 'oohhs and aahhs' from the studio audience, the clearly shocked DJ countered, 'You can't say that!'

'Well, I can, but I didn't mean it', said Reed. Talk turned to the new album and when asked about David Bowie, he said: 'I loved working with David, he had terrific empathy', which caused theatrical 'whoos' from the crowd. 'Not that way!' laughed Reed. The set continued with 'Heroin', which Reed introduced by saying, 'In the original days, not only was this banned but they wouldn't take advertisements for our album because of it. Now here we are doing it over the radio.' This change in attitudes towards the content of rock songs soon allowed Reed to have his first, and to date biggest, hit single. 'Walk On The Wild Side', without listening closely to the words, was a great piece of bass-driven acoustic pop. The melody was catchy, combining Reed's almost-spoken vocal with great female harmony vocals. It sounded fantastic and received large amounts of radio airplay. In 1973, it became a Top 20 single.

To Lou Reed this was hugely ironic based on his past experience of having songs banned from the airwaves for, in his view, trivial reasons. 'Did anyone actually listen to and understand the lyrics to "Walk On The Wild Side"?' he mused. While 'Venus In Furs' and 'Sister Ray' were banned, 'Walk On The Wild Side' narrated a graphic travelogue of transvestites ('shaved her legs and then he was a she'), drug use ('Little Joe never gave it away') and oral sex ('she never lost her head/even when she was giving head') in just over four minutes. Candy Darling was again referenced as being 'everybody's darling' in the back room at Max's Kansas City. The radio stations suddenly didn't mind these things being aired or, more likely, they just hadn't listened to the words. Either way, it gave Reed a hit.

To follow up his commercial breakthrough, he returned to London to put down the basic tracks for his next album. Again he brought along Bettye Kronstadt, whom he'd surprised everyone by marrying in February 1973.

The new material took a general concept of being the story of two amphetamine misfits on either side of the Berlin Wall. Reed wasn't writing about what was popular at the time, he just wrote about issues. Whether people actually wanted to listen to some of them in a song was a different matter. Bob Ezrin, who'd worked with Alice Cooper, produced the album and along with Reed, took substance abuse to new lows, resulting in some stories that have gone down as legend in rock history. For the introduction to 'The Kids', Ezrin (according to Mark Spitz in *Uncut* magazine) locked his children in a cupboard, told them their mother was dead and taped their screaming.

Berlin addressed things head on in his most simple lyrical approach to date. 'You didn't have to be high to figure out what was happening, or be super hip or anything,' said Reed 'It was to-the-point, whereas some of my other albums and songs had puns or double entendres. In other words, the difference would be, in "Heroin" I wrote, "It makes me feel like Jesus' son." Now if the Berlin guy had said that, he'd say, "I take heroin." That's the difference. Like in "Heroin" I say, "I wish I was born a thousand years ago." The guy on *Berlin* would say, "I don't dig it here." You can go through the whole album and he's always approaching things that way. He's consistently saying very short, straight, to-the-point, unmissable things.'

But emotional devastation of the record was not liked by the critics. *Rolling Stone* called it 'a disaster' and similar notices were printed throughout the rock press. 'I had to do *Berlin*,' said Reed. 'If I hadn't done it, I'd have gone crazy. It was insanity coming off a hit single, but it was all written. If I hadn't got it out of my head I would have exploded. I think I've gone as deep as I want to go for my own mental health. If I got any deeper, I'd wind up disappearing.' In hindsight it became apparent that much of the anguish on the album had spilled over from his personal life. His marriage was falling apart almost before it had begun. 'If people don't like *Berlin*, it's because it's too real,' snapped Reed. 'It's not like a TV program where all the bad things that happen to people are tolerable. Life isn't like that, and neither is the album.' That comment seemed to echo what was happening with his marriage to Kronstadt. She'd made a suicide attempt in a hotel bathtub. Reed had regressed while back on tour, taking speed and shutting her out of his life. She couldn't take any more and the marriage was over.

In December 1973 he recorded a live album at The Academy of Music on East 14th Street in New York. Of the seven songs that were released on the *Rock 'n' Roll Animal* album, four were Velvet Underground songs. The album sold well, no doubt because a wider audience could now hear how good some of the old Velvet Underground songs actually were. The only other purpose that the album really served was to highlight the superb guitar player that Reed had evolved into, but the heavy metal versions of some of the songs are overblown. The album was in shops just six weeks after the show. Reed was totally committed to his work again.

In 1974 Reed's life took another turn when he met 'Rachel' at a Greenwich Village club. 'Rachel', a Mexican/Indian transvestite was previously known as 'Tommy', the couple were together for four years before a trial separation became a permanent one. A famous on-the-road incident occurred when a hotel maid was terrified when she spied that 'Rachel' actually had male genitalia. 'I enjoy being around Rachel', said Reed. 'Whatever it is I need, Rachel seems to supply it, at least we're equal.'

Continuing in a prolific vein of composing form Reed was already well into writing his next album, *Sally Can't Dance*, which he recorded at Electric Lady Studios in New York during March and April 1974. In the true up-and-down nature of his 1970s solo work, Reed turned out a surprisingly commercial record that sold well. He also, in a surprising turn, brought Doug Yule back into the fold. 'He called and he thought that my particular style of bass playing would work on the song "Billy"', recalls Yule. 'I think he was right, I really like the playing on that song. That was the first time we'd spoken since he left the band. In my mind, playing with Lou was just an extension of the Velvets, it was a great band that year. So I did that and then he called me a little later and said, "Listen, do you want to come and play?" So I said, "Sure, of course." I was working at a lithography plant, not what you want to do if you can help it. So off we went touring with the 1974 band "The Music Police".'

Sally Can't Dance turned out to have strong autobiographical links. The heroine of the album was a one-time model who sleeps with folksingers, a thinly veiled portrayal of Nico. 'New York Stars' is a look back at the Andy Warhol scene, and 'Kill Your Sons' is a graphic recollection of the electroshock therapy Reed had had to undergo as a teenager. The album went straight into the Top 10 in the USA.

Keen for a quick follow-up, RCA decided to release the second half of the 1973 live album, simply titled *Lou Reed Live*. The six tracks included his best-known solo work ('Vicious', 'Satellite Of Love' and 'Walk On The Wild Side'), the Velvet's 'I'm Waiting For The Man' and a near 11-minute version of 'Oh, Jim'. Chrissie Hynde, writing for the *NME*, was less than impressed with the Lou Reed live experience. 'He looks like a monkey on a chain, court geek,' she wrote. 'Damaged and grotesque, huddled in rodent terror.'

Reed had garnered a reputation for being a party animal on tour during the 1970s and while Doug Yule admitted he hadn't really followed Reed's solo career, he was a little apprehensive about what his off-stage antics might entail. 'From what I heard from his handlers,' said Yule, 'from people who had been with him at the time was, that they would basically walk him out to the stage, holding him up all the time, walk him out and let him go in front of the microphone and pray that he didn't fall over. Then he would perform and they would come out and take him back, and walk him back to his dressing room. He was in pretty bad shape, I guess – drinking a lot and taking a lot of drugs. But the 1974 tour in a lot of ways was very much like being in The Velvet Underground. Except that he was more separate, he was less social. But musically, it was like the Velvets: there was a lot of onstage spontaneity. I remember being on stage with him when he turned around and said in front of 5,000 people, 'Follow me.' And he played a new song I'd never heard before. He did it, and it worked. I mean, his songs were simple enough that you could do that. They were basic, not a huge amount of chord changes and you could pick it up pretty quick and you could go with it, basic melodies that you could learn quickly and follow.'

With Lou Reed and John Cale well on their way with their solo careers, Doug Yule temporarily out of the music business, and Sterling Morrison and Moe Tucker seemingly out of it for good, The Velvet Underground name still held some cachet. As the decade progressed, their shadow seemed to lengthen as a trickle of posthumous releases continued to add to their reputation as godfathers of punk and to introduce younger listeners to their back catalogue.

The seeds of this legacy can be traced back to the early 1970s. With Bowie's patronage and a slow series of releases, the record-buying public began to think they might have missed out on something and the younger bands that were listening to the albums were taking note and looking at ways of emulating the Velvets.

The 1972 posthumous album release came via Brigid Polk. She was persuaded by Danny Fields to let Atlantic have a listen to the mono recording she'd made of Lou Reed's last show with the Velvets at Max's Kansas City. Polk finally agreed and was paid $10,000, which she split with Fields. Atlantic did little to the tape apart from clean up some of the background hiss. They left in the between-song conversations from the table that Polk was sitting at, giving the listener a real sense of being at the show. This became one of the first legitimate releases of a bootleg.

To necessitate a single LP they cut out four songs ('Who Loves The Sun', 'Cool It Down', 'Candy Says' and 'Some Kinda Love'), all of which were unreleased from the (at the time) forthcoming *Loaded*. The cover showed a simple photograph of the venue, and the sound quality was surprisingly good. 'I'll Be Your Mirror' has Doug Yule taking over Nico's vocal duties, while Lou Reed does the same on 'Femme Fatale' (which was an audience request) and he also sings Moe Tucker's part for the show-closing, country-tinged 'After Hours' – an apt choice for the final song of his Velvet Underground career. The album is often overlooked in the Velvets' back catalogue but it's a vital piece of the band's history and an engaging insight into the Max's residency too.

Two years later, Mercury Records bought the rights to a series of live recordings by Robert Quine and collected together the best as a double album release under the title *Live 1969*. It appeared that these tapes had been shopped around various labels and when Mercury contacted the band, it became apparent that they were in fact the property of the band. Mercury consequently confiscated them.

Lou Reed was keen to get the tapes released, but Morrison and Tucker weren't so enthusiastic. 'I listened to the tapes and I thought, "Oh man! I can't see this selling ten copies,"' said Sterling Morrison. 'I signed the release for a pittance. Meanwhile, Mercury had moved ahead with production. That's why I wasn't listed anywhere on the record, because I wasn't co-operating.' It had already been decided that Lou Reed should have his name on the cover as he was now a saleable name with a successful solo career. Mercury coerced Reed into calling Morrison to convince him to sign the release papers. 'We had to sign our consent for, like, $200,' adds Moe Tucker. 'Then this agent was calling and said, "How about 300?" I said, "What, are you crazy? I broke my ass for seven years – $300? Go to hell!' Sterling and I held out for more. We said, "We're not signing for anything less than $1,500", which even then was stupid. $1,500, which we foolishly signed for.'

The April 1974 US release (it wouldn't be issued in the UK

until 1979) showcased 17 songs from two shows. The first of these was the End of Cole Ave. club in Dallas, Texas (19 October 1969), and the second was from the Matrix season in San Francisco, the following month. The radically different, slow version of 'Sweet Jane' was recorded on the same day as it was written in Texas. Doug Yule's extended organ playing considerably stretched the songs and the style of The Velvet Underground at that time is well documented. 'Lisa Says' and 'Ocean' had been re-recorded as Lou Reed solos by the time the live LP came out. Other treats for fans included the then-unreleased songs 'We're Gonna Have A Real Good Time Together', 'Sweet Bonnie Brown' and 'It's Too Much'. Later CD versions also added a second version of 'Heroin' and 'I Can't Stand It'. Bizarrely, the CDs were sold as two separate single CDs rather than as a double-CD set.

'I think the club tapes show a different side of the band,' said Doug Yule. 'The "End Of Cole" was similar to Max's except maybe we were not as much of a house band. Still, we were staying close enough to the place so we would walk and we were hanging out and jamming afterwards. And two shows per night as I recall and fairly intimate. Much more than "La Cave", which was a club, but it was a vast basement. Even beyond where the people sat, it just seemed to go on forever. It was a different side of the group.'

David Bowie aside, the early bands that championed the Velvets' legacy came from Boston and Cleveland – two cities that the Velvets had regularly visited. Jonathan Richman and the Modern Lovers from Boston eventually approached John Cale to produce them. Cleveland's Peter Laughner was at the centre of that city's alternative music scene: 'When I was younger, The Velvet

Underground meant to me what the Stones, Dylan, etc, meant to thousands of other Midwestern teen mutants.'

In New York, the first Velvets' acolytes were Alan Vega and Martin Rev in Suicide. An early piece of theirs was titled 'Sister Ray Says'. Vega was inspired by the Velvets, saying, 'The first time you heard The Velvet Underground, you could no longer say you were the same person anymore.'

By the middle of the decade New York City had produced a music scene like never before. Where a decade earlier the Velvets had ploughed on alone, now there were bands everywhere. The New York Dolls had been pumping out their own brand of Stateside punk since 1971 and by 1975/6 The Ramones, Patti Smith, Television and Blondie were all making names for themselves. At the centre of this maelstrom was Lou Reed, raised up by the bands' appreciation of the Velvets and bolstered by his current uncompromising solo outputs. Television's Tom Verlaine moved to New York in 1968, citing the Velvets as one of his favourite bands, and in 1974 Patti Smith was using the Velvets' riff of 'We're Gonna Have a Real Good Time Together' to open her shows. As these New York bands gained fame around the world, the Velvets would come up in conversations and interviews. Their name was starting to spread.

Chapter 16
1975–1978
Hey White Boy

'My expectations are very high, to be the greatest writer that ever lived on God's earth. In other words, I'm talking about Shakespeare, Dostoevsky. I want to do that rock and roll thing that's on a level with The Brothers Karamazov. I'm starting to build up a body of work. I'm on the right track.'

Lou Reed

In 1975 the musical landscape on both sides of the Atlantic was changing. Disco and punk were two polar opposites, but they'd soon come to dominate the airwaves for the next few years. It was in this climate of diversity and change that Lou Reed recorded the most experimental work of his career. It made 'Sister Ray' look like a nursery rhyme. *Metal Machine Music* has come to be one of the most loathed rock albums of all time. Even in the liner notes Reed penned he said, 'Most of you won't like this, and I don't blame you at all.' With no lyrics, no words and just over an hour of guitar feedback it was a miracle that RCA agreed to release it at all. Critics and fans alike were stunned. The review in *Cream* simply repeated the word 'no' 816 times.

Reed later said he didn't record an hour of noise to be an album, he just did it for 'fun'. That fun was split into four 16-minute sections and issued as a double LP. He overlapped four screaming electric guitars and cleanly split two each into each stereo channel. Listening on headphones could send a listener crazy. Maybe that was the intention. Reed didn't want a steady tempo, he didn't have a key and he pushed it as close as he could get to Ornette Coleman's free jazz, but in a rock format. He had two tape recorders which he went back and forth between, overlaying tracks before ending up with one Scotch tape of the whole thing. Then he played the whole thing backwards and pumped that in one channel with the original forward-playing tape on the other in order to make a stereo recording. Some thought this was a deliberate contract-breaker of an album, others believed he'd lost his mind and a small minority liked and understood it. 'They [RCA] took *Metal Machine Music* off the market in three weeks and said they'd never carry a Lou Reed record again,' snarled Reed. 'I'm sure if you'd check some lower level music magazines and the morons who work there you'll find a review!'

In just over three years he had released a mind-boggling seven albums, and maybe *Metal Machine Music* was just the palette cleanser he required. But if Lou Reed was spinning dangerously out of control with *Metal Machine Music*, he had regained some composure by 1976. His *Coney Island Baby* album proved he was still a fine songwriter when the mood took him, though some songs here did date way back. RCA had told him to go and record whatever he wanted, so long as it wasn't *Metal Machine Music II*. Whether it was just because the new album was eminently more listenable than its predecessor or whether they really liked it, the critics welcomed *Coney Island Baby* with open arms.

It was somewhat strange that in 1976 Reed was featured on the cover of Legs McNeil's groundbreaking magazine *Punk* with the headline 'The Godfather of Punk'. Just as the punk movement was gathering momentum, he was putting out decidedly non-punk music, though obviously *Metal Machine Music* and the Velvets' early albums had been influential on the likes of The Ramones. By the mid-1970s, in the aftermath of *Metal Machine Music*, Reed had slipped back to the periphery of the rock scene. The end of his RCA deal showed nothing but diminishing record sales. He went on to spend four years with Arista, a move that stabilised his career and allowed him to grow again, starting in 1976. Reed was back in the studio and all over the press that autumn to promote his new album, *Rock and Roll Heart*. His latest work was musically diverse with horns, chugging guitars, piano-led ballads and loud rock stompers. It was the sparse nature of the lyrics which connected the songs across the album. Either Reed felt he had less than usual to say, or he wanted the listeners to fill in the blanks for themselves. Despite lots of promotion and a tour to match, the album received only an average reception and sales.

The following year, 1977, marked 10 years since *The Velvet Underground & Nico*. It was the first year that none of the ex-Velvets issued an album. Reed returned with *Street Hassle* in 1978, but times were changing. Punk had well and truly taken its place in mainstream culture and while being part of New York's rock scene, Reed as the solo artist was being questioned over his late-1970s output. The *NME* was especially disparaging, with Julie Burchill writing that 'Lou Reed is apathetic, empty and defeated, like 99 per cent of rock these days. Maybe Arista should stop Lou making records and make him write a problem page instead.'

Prolific as ever, Reed just kept turning out the albums. 1978's *Street Hassle* featured the title song about the death of Eric Emerson, a re-working of the Velvets' 'Real Good Time Together' and a guest slot from Bruce Springsteen. Later in the year Reed's penchant for live albums was evident again, this time a patchy album called *Take No Prisoners*. More of a lecture than a concert; Reed took every opportunity in between songs to have a dig at anyone and everyone who'd crossed his path. Swipes at critics and the audience illustrated an artist unsure of himself.

By 1975 John Cale was also changing his musical output. That year's *Slow Dazzle* album showed him drifting away from his classical roots and towards rock and roll: 'Dirty Ass Rock 'n' Roll', as one song was titled. His cover of 'Heartbreak Hotel' was a real down-and-dirty re-working that rendered the original almost unrecognisable. On *Helen Of Troy* he'd pushed even further and turned in an album of sparse despair that could quite easily sit alongside *Berlin* or Neil Young's *Tonight's The Night*. He was coming to the end of his marriage to Cindy, and his personal and professional lives were overlapping.

During the recording of this last album Cale was hunted down by a young New York writer and singer, Patti Smith. Smith's manager, Jane Friedman, tracked him down in London and oblivious to the five-hour time difference got him out of bed to talk to Smith on a long-distance line. Smith had released a single, but was pretty naïve about the workings of a recording studio and held Cale in high regard. He agreed to fly over and work on the album, not really knowing how difficult she could be. 'I was very, very suspicious, very guarded and hard to work with, because I was so conscious of how I perceived rock 'n' roll,' admits Smith. 'It was becoming over-produced, over-merchandised and too glamorous. I was trying to fight against all of that. We had a big, hard battle. I had all these ideas, and no one before or since has ever been as patient about them as John. I'd have seven different poems I'd want to put on different tracks, sometimes I only wanted three words from one, or two lines from another. I was creating a sort of William Burroughs' cut-up. Instead of throwing his hands up or being pissed at me, John got even crazier and more obsessive. It was like having two crazy poets dealing with showers of words; it was a great experience. I drove us all crazy but I think we can look at it and say, we did this body of work together, it's intact, there are no compromises in it. There's a certain beauty in it that wouldn't have happened without John.'

'Patti was doing something for women that nobody else was,' responds Cale. 'She was really setting a role for a poetess, taking what Dylan had done and extending it.' Cale was also intrigued by an unlikely link he saw in her vocal style that took him back to his childhood. 'She has the rhythms of a Welsh Baptist preacher,' he explained. 'That way of starting with the text and getting worked up. She steps outside of herself every night on stage.'

The songs Smith had ready for her album put forward songs from a woman's viewpoint, but not as they had ever been heard before. Her use of everyday language was raw and, like The Stooges, her live performing energy and visionary improvisations were hard to nail on tape. Cale found this to be one of his greatest musical challenges. 'I really tried to capture the band,' he explains. 'I think she was really enthralled by the possibilities that came out at the end. I think she was happy with how different it was.'

Horses became a cornerstone of the emerging New York punk scene and has been hugely influential. For his part, Cale was able to take away a new enthusiasm for rock music that Smith's passion for music had awakened. 'She struck me as someone with an incredibly volatile mouth who could handle any situation,' said Cale. 'She could also turn any situation around from a lethargic to an energetic one. But I think it was a very different experience for her going from being a band onstage to working in the studio. It immediately throws you back on yourself. All her strength and instinct was there already, and I was trying to provide a context for it. It wasn't easy. It was confrontational and a lot like an immutable force meeting an immovable object. Still, something creative came out of it. There was push and pull.'

Throughout the 1970s Cale proved to be something of a musical enigma. He could veer from using his educated background to mix classical Greek references (Helen of Troy and Archimedes) with quotes from films and books (Dylan Thomas). *Paris 1919* was influenced by the French Surrealist writers of the time, *Slow Dazzle* was regarded as 'art rock', *Honi Soit* was punk, while *Wrong Way Up* was pure electro pop. In 1977, as an Island recording artist, he'd caused a mini-outrage when he beheaded a chicken on stage at the Croydon Greyhound with a meat cleaver, but he confessed the bird was already dead as he'd wrung its neck backstage beforehand. It was some way over the line from planting an axe into a piano.

John Cale and Lou Reed apart, little had been heard of the ex-members of The Velvet Underground. Doug Yule's last major musical project occurred in the mid-1970s when he was a founder member of the almost-super group American Flyer. In 1976 he teamed up with Steve Katz, whom he'd met on the *Sally Can't Dance* sessions, Craig Fuller (who had sang with Pure

Prairie League, a Cincinnati-based folk band) and Eric Kaz, who had written hit songs for Bonnie Raitt and Linda Ronstadt. The brains behind the line-up was Dennis Katz, Lou Reed's lawyer and the brother of Steve. 'We put together 10 songs and played them live in Dennis' living room for several record company presidents,' explains Doug Yule.

With soaring harmonies and a folk-rock sound they generated a buzz among the record labels partly because they were all well-established musicians in their own right and were offered a hefty advance by United Artists to record an album. Not only that but George Martin, The Beatles' producer, was signed up to produce it. Maybe they could be the next Eagles.

The eponymous debut album was recorded in Los Angeles amid great hope. Not much recording was done on the first day in the studio – the band just sat down and demanded that Martin regale them with Beatles' stories, and the Englishman didn't disappoint.

Doug Yule recalls a conversation he had with George Martin, where he asked the producer about his expectations for the album. 'I said, "You mean, you wouldn't have picked this project if you didn't think it was going to go gold?" He looked at me and said, "Of course not."' Stylistically similar to the mega-successful Crosby, Stills and Nash, the album featured trademark Martin string arrangements across a strong set of songs highlighted by 'Let Me Down Easy'.

With hindsight Yule believes that despite Martin's vast experience and ability he was actually the wrong producer for American Flyer. 'The other leading contender for the job was Phil Ramone, who is a hands-on, active producer,' explains Yule. 'Whereas George Martin says, "Show me what you've got and I'll bring it out." We needed someone to kick ass and say,

"You're all going to sit here and play it until it's done!" Whereas George was like, "You don't want to play anymore? Well, let's get together tomorrow."

The sessions never really helped the band to gel and soon people started jockeying for position, knowing that the more songs you had on an album the more money you could make. 'That took it away from being a group to be more a bunch of people trying to get a record out so they could make a living,' said Yule. 'That wasn't something I was good at.'

The problems really began when they decided not to tour because they had just an album's worth of material. Consequently it didn't sell as well as they'd hoped, and by the time they recorded the follow-up, *Spirit of A Woman* in 1977, the momentum was lost and the band were bickering among themselves. They folded soon afterwards. 'It was apathy,' said Fuller. 'I think everyone, having had some degree of success, wasn't willing to put much effort into it. This wasn't a band that came together as a band and worked hard and struggled together: this was more of a business deal.'

The second album was only really completed due to a contractual obligation, the president of Universal had already been replaced and the new one wasn't interested in it at all. For Yule, the disappointment of the outcome was exacerbated when the time came for him to sign his portion of the publishing deal for the band with ASCAP. For the publishing rights, a writer can expect to receive an advance against earnings, but Yule didn't. It turned out that Steve Sesnick in his capacity as manager, had signed on his behalf when he'd recorded *Squeeze*. 'They said I'd received an advance of $500,' he laments. 'Of course I never got it.'

Sterling Morrison would have nodded knowingly if he'd been told of the problems that Yule now faced. Since leaving the

Velvets, he had been at the University of Texas, teaching as an assistant professor and working on his PhD in Medieval Literature. 'I was delighted not to be involved in music in the 1970s,' said Morrison. 'It was the most reactionary period in music. All the record companies were so fed up with all the money they'd wasted on 1960s' loonies, they tried to get control over everything. A&R departments got real strong, there was a general purging. It was really a dreadful era.'

Chapter 17

1979–1987
Out of Nowhere

'I would've thought it was a kiss of death. If anyone wanted to get signed and they said to a record company that they were influenced by The Velvet Underground they would be stupid. The last thing that a record company would want is to have another Velvet Underground.'

John Cale, 1985

It was an unusually warm and sunny autumn day in Athens, Georgia. Peter was walking to work at Wuxtry Records, the college-town's hippest, and best, record store, where he'd worked for most of 1979. As usual on delivery days like today he would spend the morning, or as much of it as he could wangle, looking through the new arrivals and putting aside albums for himself. The price would be docked from his wages of course, but it was one of his favourite perks to have the first chance at the new stock. Today he was especially glad to find a copy of *The Velvet Underground & Nico*: he knew someone who would appreciate an original copy with the peelable banana on the cover. Sure enough, that friend came in later that afternoon.

The two had often talked about the merits of the Velvets, and this shared love of many bands was what had convinced Peter to try and form a band with his new friend Michael. That band would be R.E.M. and like many acts to emerge during the late 1970s and 1980s, it was the Velvets who played a large part in their love of what would come to be known as 'indie' music.

By the mid-1980s The Velvet Underground had grown to be a large cult band. 'It was during the mid-1980s that people started calling me up for interviews,' said Doug Yule. A generation of music fans that hadn't been born when the band were at their artistic peak could now rattle off the names of the Velvets and talk in detail about each of the albums. The late 1970s' scene in New York had featured David Byrne of Talking Heads, The Ramones, Patti Smith and Blondie all paying their dues to the Velvets, either directly in the press or stylistically. In the UK, Joy Division covered 'Sister Ray' and enjoyed a similar aesthetic in their original material; the Jesus and Mary Chain took the drones from the Velvets' first two albums to an extreme of feedback and confusion. In fact the Velvets were almost more revered across Europe than in the United States. Bands in the UK, France, Italy, Holland and the Krautrock movement in Germany paid their respects. R.E.M. were all fans and covered Velvets songs from their earliest gigs. Lead singer Michael Stipe was particularly impressed with the debut album. 'When I was 15 and listening to that stuff, I knew what "heroin" was, but I had no experience with it,' he said. 'It did seem very underground.' On British television the respected ITV arts vehicle *The South Bank Show* devoted a whole show to the band in 1986 and interviewed the principal players and members of The Factory scene.

With more bands citing The Velvet Underground as influences in interviews, and more acts covering Velvets' songs, the record labels began trawling their archives for material to cash in. The most bountiful find was the cache of songs that the band had recorded for the never-released fourth MGM album. Though Lou Reed had subsequently re-recorded many of the tracks for his solo albums, the original Velvets' versions were surely worth issuing.

'They got in touch with me to come out and listen to the tapes,' said Reed. 'It sounded pretty good at first and they said I could be involved in the production of it. Then after listening to the whole thing, I said, "I don't think it should come out."' Reed was worried about the hype surrounding the 'great lost album' and didn't want the bunch of outtakes and leftovers to be the missing link in the Velvets' evolution. He was underestimating the quality of the songs though and Sterling Morrison was called upon to assist in the assembly of not one, but two albums' worth of material.

Morrison made suggestions about what was in the vault and what could be used. He found a vocal-less take of 'Guess I'm Falling in Love' when it was discovered that the vocal take master had been damaged. None of the original recordings had been mixed so that task was carried out in June 1984 under the key eye of producer and compiler Bill Levenson. Levenson would become a major player in Velvet Underground issues and re-issues over the next two decades.

The two albums that were collated were *VU*, issued in 1985, and *Another View*, which came out a year later. The material that was unearthed was pulled in from further afield than just the 1969 sessions. On *VU* a version of 'Stephanie Says' is included that dated from 13 February 1968, a good six months before

John Cale's exit from the band. 'Temptation Inside Your Heart' was recorded a day later and both songs show the band's pop side. *Another View* included two versions of the exceptional 'Hey Mr Rain', both of which featured Cale's viola to full effect. These songs, when taken together, show that during the last sessions Cale played with the band the material was split into two camps and ultimately his yearning to follow the 'Hey Mr Rain' path was ousted by Reed's desire to go elsewhere. The ever-growing popularity of the band was clearly indicated when *VU* made it to number 85 in the US charts, considerably higher than any of the original albums had reached. In the wake of *Another View* the band members all renegotiated, via their lawyers, new royalty percentages that stand to this day.

Like Sterling Morrison, Moe Tucker had been absent from the public gaze since leaving the Velvets. She had completely withdrawn from the music industry, moving first to Arizona in 1978 and then to Georgia. Tucker married a systems analyst, had five children and no plans to restart a career in music. Her daughter Kerry was born in 1970, followed by Keith in 1975, Austen in 1976, Kate in 1978 and then Richard in 1981. Being away from it all meant she hadn't followed the Velvets' spreading shadow of influence and thought that her former band had just evaporated into obscurity. Then in 1980 she received a phone call out of the blue.

An independent label in Boston had got hold of an early 1970s' tape of Moe and Jonathan Richman (of the Modern Lovers) singing 'I'm Sticking With You' and they called for permission to release it as a single. She said it was fine. Then a couple of days later they called again to ask if she would like to record a b-side. Though she wasn't sure about it, Moe plugged in a four-track tape recorder she owned and recorded a cover of the Shirelles' 'Will You Still Love Me Tomorrow?'. She liked the tape so much that she decided to issue it on her own label. 'That's when I realised what was going on as far as young fans,' recalls Tucker. 'When I was selling my little single, I was calling up record shops around the country from my kitchen. I had my little speech set up, I was going to say, "My name is Maureen Tucker, I used to be in The Velvet Underground." I figured they wouldn't know who I was, but before I got to "Velvet Underground", as soon as I said "Maureen Tucker", they knew who I was and that really surprised me.'

Tucker had been working for Wal-Mart in the billing department. Her ethical views and feisty determination to say what she thought was right and wrong kept her in and out of the boss's office for the duration of her employment. One of her favourite stories concerned one year's Christmas bonus. 'I like to work,' said Tucker. 'I don't mind working when you can do your job and when you get paid properly. The first year I was there, we were all in the office, six or eight women, and our boss came out and said, "Oh ladies, the bonus cheques are coming this week, the Christmas bonus checks." So I ask how much and he said, "Five dollars." And I wasn't looking at him and I just thought that he was joking. I turned around and everyone was saying, "Ahh", a happy "Ahh", and I was like, "Five dollars!" I was speechless. Keep in mind, this is the first year that Mr Walton, the owner of Wal-Mart, was declared the richest man in America: he had eight billion dollars. The other girls were just sitting there perfectly happy. I was always griping about things so they thought, "Oh, she's bitching." But this was an insult. So our supervisor, another "Ms Wal-Mart", hoping to climb through the ranks, said, "Well, Maureen, it's better than nothing." And I said, "Verna, that's exactly why it's five dollars, because that's your attitude." Better than nothing! When he brought out the cheques, I said, "I don't want it." He thought that I was kidding and he came over and said, "Here's your cheque." I said, "I don't want it. I'm insulted. Keep it."'

The low-key success of her solo single, and the realisation that The Velvet Underground had actually meant a lot to people and that more and more fans were discovering the band, prompted Tucker to record a whole album that she called *Playin' Possum*. She wasn't confident about her writing at this stage so she chose a selection of her favourite covers and recorded them at home. Playing every instrument herself, she burrowed through rock history to produce stunning interpretations of songs by Bo Diddley, Chuck Berry, Bob Dylan and even the Velvets' 'Heroin'.

Since leaving Island Records in 1976, John Cale's solo career had been patchy, to say the least. A series of average solo albums (*Honi Soit*, *Music For A New Society* and *Artificial Intelligence* were just three) over a chain of different labels. In 1978 his plan to issue a single called 'Jack the Ripper' was shelved when the Yorkshire Ripper case was terrorising northern England. Cale would often take to the stage wearing bizarre overalls and ice-hockey masks (pre-dating Eminem by 20 years), or a surgeon's outfit. He later admitted in his 1999 autobiography that his life was clouded by alcohol and drugs for the first half of the 1980s, a period when he met his third wife, Rise Irushalmi, who had been an extra in Woody Allen's *Stardust Memories*. They married in 1981. Cale's father asked why on earth he was getting married again. His son replied that he wanted to have a child. 'However,' wrote Cale, 'I still had a lot of darkness to pass through first.'

Music For a New Society, in 1983, produced some of the most positive critical reaction he'd seen in quite a while. Cale had holed himself up in a New York studio and churned out 30 improvised tracks in just five days. 'If I can't get excited by whatever groove I'm in, I have to move on,' he said of his rapidly changing styles. 'Luckily, I've found enough different grooves.' In 1985, John and Rise had a daughter, Eden. It was the cue for him to clean up his act. Drink and drugs were jettisoned in favour of healthy living and playing squash. 'It's a game you don't win', said Cale. 'It's a game you play until your opponent loses.'

Guitarist Nils Lofgren made an appearance on Lou Reed's *The Bells* in 1979 to form an unlikely working partnership. The album cover pictured Reed holding up a mirror, signalling a decade of autobiographical writing. Musically, Reed used a range of styles, from deep grooves to gritty guitars. Snatches of spoken conversation pop up, giving a whole that was arguably his most experimental solo work to date (*Metal Machine Music* notwithstanding).

The following year's *Growing Up in Public* cemented Reed's period of autobiographical writing as he approached 40 years of age. He certainly felt as if his life had been under the microscope from his teenage years and now in middle-age he decided the time was right to address his hopes and fears and wax lyrical on what he'd learnt. This self-centred work would be his last for the label, as he moved back to RCA for 1982's *The Blue Mask*, which he dedicated to the memory of Delmore Schwartz. The two-year gap between albums was unusual for the normally prolific Reed: perhaps it was because he'd married for the second time, on Valentine's Day in 1980. His new bride was Sylvia Morales, a half-Mexican scenester at CBGBs, 14 years his junior.

She would become his manager, increasing his profile and profits, before they divorced in 1994.

After the two-year recording break Reed called up the Voidoids' Robert Quine to play guitar on the *Blue Mask* album in 1982. It was a testing time for Quine, who found his previously very good relationship with Reed coming under strain. Despite their personality clashes, Quine would tour with Reed for several years. 'Musically, the first week and a half was really great, out of the four years,' said Quine. 'We did *The Blue Mask*. It's a record that I'm really proud of. There was no rehearsing, no overdubs, no punch-ins for mistakes: the exact opposite of the Voidoids. I inspired and encouraged him to play guitar again. I didn't have a lot of fun with him but at least it's out there and I'm proud of that. By the time we did *Legendary Hearts* in late 1982, he was much more of a control freak. He was rejecting ideas that I brought in; he was feeling pretty precious about his career. His biggest weakness is that he wants to be regarded as a poet. The more conscious he is of this, the worse songs he writes. It could have been a pretty good record. It wasn't going to be as good as the last one: the songs weren't as good. The atmosphere was really uptight – it's impossible to be friends with him.'

Quine's friendship with Reed hit rock bottom when he heard the final mix of the album. Reed, as he had done before with The Velvet Underground, had gone back into the studio and remixed the whole album without anyone else knowing. As usual, he had pushed his vocals and guitar playing to the front of the mix and buried Quine's stellar guitar work to the point of not being heard. When Quine heard the tape, his reaction was to smash it with a hammer.

Despite the problems, Quine continued to tour with Reed for a while longer and is philosophical about the time they spent together, although the resounding animosity is clear to see. 'From the greedy professional angle, I've had three things that have made people interested in who I am,' he admitted. 'The Voidoids' things, the Lou Reed thing and Matthew Sweet. On a personal level, Reed was a guy who really influenced me and I had a chance to give something back to him. Encouraging him to play guitar again was digging my own grave. But I would have done it again because I owed it to him: this guy changed my life. If I did something to put him back in the right direction, I wish that it would have gone on with the level of something like *The Blue Mask*. Everything else after is pretty lousy. He never found anyone else to replace me except The Velvet Underground and he had to ruin that. I hate him because if I had my way, we'd still be playing. It was good steady work. He didn't tour often. I hate his guts because he made it impossible to play with him. There was nothing in it for me. He was not going to give me any space for any creativity.'

Reed's later 1980s' albums included *New Sensations* in 1984 and *Mistrial* in 1986, each with decreasing sales figures, but he would bounce back at the decade's end.

The closest Sterling Morrison came to the music industry was when he started in the mid-1970s, playing in a bluesy covers band called The Bizarros, usually at roadhouses on the weekend. Martha Morrison describes the music as 'dancing bar music' and recalls that 'when they made money, he would always give it to me, the $20 or whatever it was. I loved to go and see The Bizzaros, they were terrific. Those guys wanted to be serious and professional but Sterling didn't, he just wanted to enjoy it.'

By the 1980s his leisure time was taken up by more civilian pursuits as he trained and gained a licence as a tugboat captain, sailing up and down the Houston ship canal. At first he would work on the boats during the summer while he was attending graduate school. 'He started out as an ordinary seaman and ended up as captain of the tugboat,' said Martha Morrison. 'He was really interested in making big money. He had his seaman's papers because his mother had helped him get them, way back on Long Island when he used to work on a ferry there. The thing with him was money, because we didn't have any! He was really smart and he studied, so he got his captain's license. They used to call him the professor on the ship canal. He was really good at it.'

He'd been tracked down for an interview in 1987, at which point he was still dead set against any involvement in the music world. 'The corporate foolishness in record companies astounds me,' he said. 'It's assumed that if a particular course of action will result in more money, that you will naturally pursue it. We didn't swallow it so much, which made them think we were either crazy or hard to work with.'

Morrison finally gained his PhD in Medieval Literature in 1986. By then the Morrisons had two children: Marianne was born in 1975, and Tommy followed a decade later. It was then that Martha wanted to move back to New York. Sterling looked for work in the academic world but he wouldn't take any old job, so Martha and the children settled in New York and Sterling said it would take him six months to relocate. But he never found a position in the Northeast and instead opted to commute between there and Texas. 'It was kind of a stupid way to live, but there was a big money worry,' said Martha. 'Sometimes we'd get a royalty cheque, just a nice little surprise every now and then.'

By 1986 the Velvets' back catalogue was controlled by Polygram, but it was in a mess. Various compilations had been released around the world and no one quite knew what was what. The ex-band members agreed that all royalties should now be paid into a central pot, which they would then divide among themselves. Different contracts with different band members at different royalty rates confused things further. But now with the agreement with Polygram, it should all have been a bit easier. The first cheques arrived, covering years of sales. They were for $1,500.

Chapter 18

1987–1992

Gonna Try to Make it Right

'Lou and I were both at the party following Andy's memorial service, with 150 of the most famous people in New York plus Andy's family. It was the first time we had really spoken to each other for some time. We had bumped into each other a lot of times but he wasn't interested in communicating, probably because I was drinking. A few days later, Lou and I started to discuss doing a collaboration.'

John Cale

As the 1980s drew to a close, things were to change irrevocably in the sphere of the Velvets. The twentieth anniversary of their debut album was approaching, and Andy Warhol was ill. On 22 February 1987, Warhol was being treated in hospital recovering from a routine gall bladder operation. He was scared of hospitals and had put off the operation for almost 15 years. It had got to the point where his doctor had told him that if he didn't have the operation then, his gall bladder would rupture and he would die. In the face of this stark ultimatum Warhol checked himself in using the pseudonym 'Bob

Roberts'. The operation went as planned and he was returned to his room that night. A nurse was stationed outside his room, but during the night he suffered a heart attack and an hour of resuscitation attempts couldn't save him.

The ex-members of The Velvet Underground were stunned. 'I read about the death of Andy Warhol in the *New York Times*,' said John Cale. 'I was shocked – I had not even known that he was ill. Despite the fact that the theme of all Andy's work was death, we had all presumed that he would outlive us, his life force was so strong.'

John Cale and Lou Reed met at a memorial service for Warhol at St. Patrick's Cathedral, New York on 1 April and had their first long chat for many a year. They agreed that they should write something in memory of Warhol. Cale came up with some music, played it for Reed and he added the words. The two then locked themselves away in a rehearsal facility until it was finished.

The album they recorded was called *Songs For Drella*. 'Drella' was a nickname that Warhol had been given back in the 1960s for being a cross between Dracula and Cinderella. Though presented as 'a brief musical look at the life of Andy Warhol' and 'entirely fictitious', the songs had been written from the pair's recollections of Warhol the man, not the popular image he often hid behind. 'It was an elegant piece of reporting how misfits get together and create art,' observed Cale.

The songs were moving and affectionate without being overtly sentimental. It was a dignified way to temporarily bury the hatchet, and the *NME* reported that it was 'gripping yet troubling'. A video of Cale and Reed performing the album at the Brooklyn Academy of Music was filmed in December 1989, though a tour was vetoed by Reed. Cale was unhappy over the decision and thought it would have been a great success. The album had been partially intended to act as a healing and grieving aid for the two men, but evidently Reed had healed more quickly than Cale.

In 1988 the world lost another member of the Factory scene when Nico died at the age of 49. Since the John Cale-produced album *The End* in 1974, she had struggled against various addictions while producing a series of poor albums (*Drama of Exile*, *Do Or Die!* and *Camera Obscura*). Despite health problems she still toured and her static on-stage persona, heavy make-up and high cheekbones had endeared her to the emerging Goth movement that styled itself after her. Ironically, her last concert had been in Berlin. During her solo years she'd been unfairly called a 'foghorn' and fairly described as a 'junkie diva'. She'd always wanted to do 'I'm Waiting For The Man' and finally did so on her 1981 solo effort, *Dream Of Exile*. It was her cover versions that were becoming more interesting than her own songs. In all, she recorded eight solo albums, most of which were overlooked.

In 1985 she told the *NME* that, 'I would rather take drugs than be in a nuthouse.' This attitude led to her being placed on a methadone maintainance programme while living in Manchester. In July 1988, Nico and her son Ari flew to Ibiza for a holiday. On a baking hot day she went out for a cycle ride, as part of the exercise regime she was following on the methadone maintenance programme. During the rise she suffered a brain haemorrhage and collapsed. It was hours before she was discovered at the side of the road. On arrival at the local hospital she was pronounced dead. Her ashes were buried in Berlin beside the grave of her mother. Alan Wise had been her manager for the last seven years of her life and made the following announcement to the press: 'She went to the exact opposite of what we would have considered the appropriate moment to shuffle off this mortal coil. We suspected she'd end up some cranky woman in a home, outliving all of us.' Reed and Cale were in the studio working on *Songs For Drella* when they were told the sad news of another death.

After her early 1980s' dip back into music, Moe Tucker had continued working a day job, but was now writing the occasional song herself. This culminated in a humorous and earthy album, *Life In Exile After Abdication*, in 1989. She admitted that the writer's block had for a long time been a simple case of not knowing what to write about. It was the untimely death of Andy Warhol (which inspired her first song, 'Andy') that gave her some subject matter. Soon the songs were flowing out of her as she realised that she should write about her own experiences – domestic life and the struggle from one pay cheque to the next. Never have songs of domesticity been so poignant and humorous at the same time, such as 'Spam Again'. Again she covered a Velvets' song, this time it was 'Pale Blue Eyes': 'The Velvets' songs I do because I really like them. "Pale Blue Eyes" I think is one of the most beautiful melodies. Also, a big factor when I decide if I want to cover something is if I can actually sing it and not murder it. My version of "I'm Waiting For The Man", I think, is really interesting and fun. I try to make them a little different than the originals.'

To promote the album, Tucker took a big step. She quit her secure job and decided to go touring. By now she had divorced her husband and had five children to support, so the financial and timing implications had to be addressed. Her new booking agent went away to look into the kind of money she could earn and they calculated that six weeks of touring every year would provide the same income as she was earning at Wal-Mart. Six weeks was also the longest she wanted to leave the children, so it worked out perfectly. 'I was lucky to be able to get back into music,' she explains. 'I had to quit my job, which was a very big decision. This is a small town and the kind of place where if you have a job you hang onto it because there aren't many others. I was with my mother at her house with all my kids and the opportunity came to tour in Europe and she was all for it, and she watched the kids while I toured Europe.'

The small-scale European tour that followed was well-received, helped by the fact that there were some well-known guests appearing on *Life In Exile After Abdication*. 'All the people who have played on my records do it on a volunteer basis,' she explains. 'I've never asked anyone because I can't pay anyone and I'm embarrassed. Lou volunteered to play on that. I'm sure he realised that it would get a little more attention if he was on there. He stopped by one night and I knew which songs I wanted to do so we'd be ready for him. When we were going to record that, I didn't have a band at the time and we didn't have a bass player. Kate Nesser knew Kim Gordon [from Sonic Youth] and asked if she would want to play with us, so she came and played.' Sonic Youth had long been fans of the Velvets and the collaboration was natural.

On completion of *Songs For Drella*, Lou Reed immediately headed right back into the studio. He had a strong body of songs written for his next album and he needed to get it out of his system as quickly as possible. The album was *New York*, arguably his finest solo work. He used his well-known lyrical insightfulness to beautifully meld with a newly-found social commentary and spare musical backing. The album was a tour de force of Reed assessing the state of his town. 'Dirty

Boulevard' and 'Last Great American Whale' are two of the best songs of his career and addressed social and environmental issues respectively. Reed had managed to re-invent himself again.

At the start of the 1990s it wasn't just The Velvet Underground who were being given their dues. Lou Reed's solo career had now reached almost 20 years and in 1991, amid the furore surrounding Nirvana and grunge, Reed had a 3-CD retrospective box-set issued, along with a book of his lyrics. Though his career was far from over he was being seen as the elder-statesman of rock – after all, he was approaching 50 years old. Then in 1992, just as some quarters might have thought it was time for him to take a backseat, he produced yet another landmark album, *Magic and Loss*. Continuing some of the themes of death that he'd started to address on *Songs For Drella*, this was possibly his most focused solo work to date. The album was a cathartic experience for Reed, as the songs poured out of him after two great personal losses in his life: Pomus and a woman he referred to as 'Rita'. Pomus had been a long-time friend of Reed's and had written hits for Elvis, among others, 'Rita' was a friend about whom Reed said: 'I can't tell you her name. It wouldn't mean anything to you. She's not a celebrity, put it that way.' Obviously the album was an extension of *Songs For Drella* and it takes the listener through Reed's mourning process too. It had been a tough few years with Warhol, Nico, Pomus and 'Rita' all disappearing from his life.

Reed's solo reputation was now almost as strong as that of the Velvets. His aged face was like a rock and roll addition to Mount Rushmore, stoically looking down on the new bands forming at his foothills. Back in 1972 it had seemed highly unlikely that a pretty much unknown singer who had just quit an unknown band would become a superstar solo artist. His back catalogue was now seen as a great body of work, a musical version of the Great American Novel. 'Put all the songs together and it's certainly an autobiography,' he said. 'It's just not necessarily mine.'

Before her tour in 1989, Moe Tucker called Sterling Morrison to tell him about her plans. He, like Tucker, was obviously not aware that The Velvet Underground meant so much to so many people and he pooh-poohed her enthusiasm. He couldn't believe that she was actually writing her own songs and was going to give up her job to tour almost 20 years after quitting the Velvets. 'He was just thunderstruck,' recalls Tucker. 'He said, "You're gonna record?! What are you gonna record?!" I got so pissed at him. I just thought, "Oh, you schmuck. The hell with you, I'll never ask you again!" All because of the way he reacted. Then when I was going to do that first tour in Europe, I told him about it. He said, "What are you going to play? Who's gonna sing?" He was really flabbergasted that I was going to try this. He wouldn't have had the nerve to do that and didn't see how I could.'

Indeed, Tucker proved Morrison wrong and then the following summer all four original members of The Velvet Underground were invited to attend an exhibition in France. Arranged by the Cartier Foundation, the tiny town of Jouy-en-Josas (20 miles from Paris) was hosting an exhibition celebrating the life and work of Andy Warhol. Among the exhibits was a room dedicated to The Velvet Underground. After much haggling the organisers managed to get John Cale and Lou Reed to play a selection of songs from *Songs For Drella* on 15 June. With Morrison and Trucker also agreeing to attend, it would be quite a coup to have all four together in one place – no one could remember the last time that had happened.

Once everyone had arrived in France there was talk that Moe Tucker might join them for a surprise encore of 'Pale Blue Eyes' after Cale and Reed had performed their five or so songs from *Drella*. On the afternoon of the show the sun was shining brightly and Sterling Morrison was still resisting all attempts to agree to join the band onstage. Then just before Cale and Reed were due onstage Morrison was spotted with a guitar in the backstage area. Reed smiled, turned to Tucker and asked how her muscles felt. Would she be up to playing 'Heroin' instead of 'Pale Blue Eyes'?

Cale and Reed took to the outdoor stage before 2,500 fans and played their *Drella* set, before Reed announced that he had a little surprise for them. 'After Lou and John came off stage, I was watching from back stage, I was standing there, clapping,' recalls Martha Morrison. 'John went running by and I said, "What are you doing?"

"Looking for mallets!"

"What do you mean mallets?"

"We're going to play 'Heroin'!"

'That was literally how improv it was. I never thought it would happen, we were all happily shocked.'

To the amazement of the crowd, Morrison and Tucker walked out and played a 13-minute rendition of 'Heroin'. No rehearsal, no practice, no sound check. After a 22-year gap they played as though they had never been separated. It was a magical moment. 'All the gang from the old days were there too,' recalled John Cale. 'After we had played it was as if we were inseparable – Andy's gang again. It was really nostalgic and kind of sad in a way, because I didn't know if it would ever go any further.

That night all four went out for dinner and tongues were wagging as news of the reunion spread around the globe. Would anything further come of this thawing of relations or was it just a one-off?

The next sign that a reunion was becoming a realistic proposal was when Tucker began recording her next album, *I Spent a Week There the Other Night*, in 1991. Reed, Morrison and Cale all played on the track 'I'm Not', though they each recorded their parts separately. Sterling Morrison's appetite had been whetted and after seeing that Tucker had carried out a successful first tour, his interest was piqued for her second one. But after his reaction to the first tour she wasn't going to let him off the hook lightly. 'The next time we spoke, I told him that I was going to record and I knew he wanted me to ask him,' she recalled. 'But I didn't! I said to myself, "I'm gonna make him ask me!" So we had a few phone calls and he said, "So, you still want me to play?" So I said, "Sure, if you're interested. But you can't say you're going to do it and not show up because I'm depending on you." When we were recording *Spent a Week*, he was there. He came up to me, being nonchalant as usual, and said: "Am I still invited to tour with you?" I said: "What do you mean? I thought you didn't think it was a good idea."' Joking apart, she was glad to have him along on the tour and the pair had a great time. 'He loved the tour and I'm so glad he did it,' said Tucker. 'Out of all of us, he's had the least recognition, partly because he was hiding in Texas. Until he came with me, he never had the chance to have people say to him what they'd been saying to me: "Wow, you changed my life!" It sure is nice to hear, it's mind-boggling. Playing with me, he did get that opportunity and I'm really, really glad. I know he loved it and enjoyed playing. It was very gratifying for him to hear things like that. We had a great time. I've known him since I was 10 so it was really like we were brother and sister rather than friends.' Soon they would be spending more time together, in a way that most observers had thought to be an impossible dream.

Chapter 19

1993

MCMXCIII

'Whether it turns out to be a good idea or bad idea, we'll find out. It won't leave me crushed either way. So many bands are playing Velvet Underground material, why the hell can't The Velvet Underground once in a while if they feel like it?'

Sterling Morrison

Out at Lake Geneva it was a typical summer scene. The usual holiday crowds of tourists and sightseers swarmed on the shores and the lake bristled with pleasure boats and yachts. Among them was a larger-than-average boat with a more-famous-than-average cargo. On board, Bono, The Edge, Larry Mullen Jr and Adam Clayton were taking their tour crew on a cruise for the day during time off from their world tour. Along for this day's relaxation was also their support band – John Cale, Sterling Morrison, Lou Reed and Moe Tucker. Yes, the original Velvet Underground really were on tour after a 25-year break.

As had been the case during most years since the early 1980s, 1993 saw its fair share of Velvet Underground cover versions being released. It was the year of Brian Ferry doing 'All Tomorrow's Parties', U2 covering 'Satellite Of Love' and Billy Idol taking on 'Heroin'. 'He's done nine remixes of it – he sent them over for me to approve,' revealed Lou Reed. 'It's another world. I won't begrudge him the fun of doing it, and the other people the fun of hearing it, if that's what they're into. It's not what I would do, but I showed you what I would do. This stuff holds up. That's a song from 1967, but there you go, as contemporary today as it was then. I always tried not to use contemporary slang, so the songs could be released tomorrow. That to me is good writing.'

But the difference between this batch of covers and the ones from previous years was that the public were about to get the chance to put them up against the real thing in person because The Velvet Underground were ready to perform their own songs for the first time in over 20 years.

1993 seemed to be a good year for reunions. Those other cult favourites Big Star also chose that year to play their first show in almost 20 years. Elsewhere the musical landscape was very different to the one that the four original Velvets had surveyed the last time they played together, over two decades before. So how would the gargantuan noise of New York's finest fit in with the music of the times? They hadn't exactly tried to follow the latest trends before, and surely they wouldn't really care whether or not they did so now? 1993 was the year when the MTV phenomenon of the *Unplugged* album was all the rage. Bruce Springsteen, Neil Young, Eric Clapton and Rod Stewart all had Top 10 albums of their acoustic live-in-the-studio performances. Even the noise-merchants of Nirvana would record an unplugged performance before the year was out. But how did this seemingly impossible dream of the original Velvet Underground line-up playing a tour on the same stage actually come about?

In November 1992 Cale, Morrison, Reed and Tucker all attended a meeting with Polygram records to discuss the idea of a box-set. Usually their Velvet Underground business meetings were attended by representatives, but this time it was conducted face to face. The label wanted input on what should, and shouldn't be included on the planned set. The talks went well and someone suggested the four band members should go to lunch together. Lou Reed casually dropped a comment into the conversation about how strange it would be if they actually toured together as The Velvet Underground. None of the others said much about it at the time, but as they went their separate ways, each was thinking over the previously insane idea. Was it really a possibility? 'I started to get some calls from my lawyer, saying Lou might be happy to tour,' recalls Moe Tucker. 'It took quite a while to get everyone to happily agree.' By early 1993, though, the foursome had agreed to get together to try and work something out. It was in this atmosphere of cordiality that they began rehearsing in February 1993.

Lou Reed had said in an interview in 1985: 'I'm not interested in reunions at all. I'm very proud of it, but I wouldn't want to go back.' So that was perhaps why in 1993 he was refusing to call the tour a reunion. 'We don't think of it as a reunion: we think of it as a continuum,' he insisted. He made a point of saying that they wanted to play for people who were fans and really wanted to see them after all the years.

Rehearsals began in February 1993 in an old factory building on West 26th Street in New York. The band found that getting back together and playing made it almost seem as though they'd never been apart. The majority of the back catalogue was imme-diately performable and they soon had the task of whittling down a set from a solid three hours of songs. 'Straightaway in rehearsals, the sound was there,' recalled John Cale. 'We were basically a very good garage band that doesn't spend a lot of time trying to balance out the instruments. When we tried "Black Angel's Death Song", everybody was running around trying to get rid of the whistling harmonics on the viola, but with all the technology in the world you won't tame this thing. It's going to be painful, and that's the end of it.'

Within a couple of weeks of rehearsing, something which they rarely did in the old days, they had perfected just about every song in the back catalogue. 'I don't really think that rehearsing is what this band is about,' said Cale at the time. 'What Lou does with his own band, which is to go meticulously over every pore of the music, doesn't work with us. This band works on spontaneity: you couldn't find a more responsive group of musicians, the soul of the band is improvisation. If we can get that on the road, then people are going to see something they've never seen before. And they'll see another side of Lou Reed, up there cranking the guitar and roaring.'

Doug Yule was conspicuous by his absence, having not been invited along. 'I was working in San Francisco and someone read about it in the paper,' said Yule. 'It doesn't affect my life, or my monthly pay cheque. I thought about it a lot, and I denied it a lot. My wife would say, "How do you feel about it?" And I would say, "I don't care." I would have liked to have been asked to come. It's kind of like someone saying, "You didn't really count." And I know that's not true, but it feels that way. I thought about it and even wrote a screenplay about it. I don't know without being asked, but I'm pretty sure I would've said no because I had a two-year-old son and I couldn't imagine leaving him for several months.'

So the original quartet of Cale, Morrison, Reed and Tucker

prepared to face the world. The rehearsals were thorough to say the least and Moe Tucker was typically deadpan in complaining, 'We rehearsed for much too long in New York.' All four had different motives for playing the tour. Tucker was enthusiastic about getting the chance to see all the people who had supported the band over the years, and the money was very welcome. Sterling Morrison was looking forward to playing all of the old songs. John Cale was keen to work out some new songs. No one was sure why Lou Reed had agreed to do it.

'None of us approached this tour as a new Velvets' career,' said Tucker. 'It was to give the people who've been buying the records for all these years and paying the rent the chance to see us play live.' She admitted that the amount of money she was going to earn on the tour was like winning the lottery for her and it would enable her to buy her house and a new car. It's quite likely the Velvets earned more money on this single tour than they did in the whole of their earlier career combined. Tucker wouldn't have just done it for the money, though. 'I wouldn't do it for a million dollars if I thought we'd be bad,' she admitted. 'I value my reputation more than I do money; that's my claim to fame.' She was especially keen to play shows across continental Europe and pointed out that even in the band's darkest days they had always sold reasonably well in Europe and most of those fans had never had the chance to see the band play a show.

At the end of May the tour crew and equipment shipped over to the UK and the tour kicked off in Edinburgh during the first week of June. The Velvet Underground finally made it to the cover of the *NME* with the headline 'Revival of the Hippest'. Three thousand people a night sold out two nights at the Playhouse. The world's press descended for the show and reviews were splashed across papers around the globe. Yes, The Velvet Underground really were on tour.[1] The shows weren't just populated by middle-aged fans, though. A large portion of the crowd was relatively young, proving that the Velvets' music endured, passing from generation to generation like a slightly worse-kept secret at each handover.

'Cale's viola scrapes and screeches and conspires with the guitars and drums to give you a real sense of precisely how out there they once were,' wrote the *NME*. *Melody Maker* reported, 'You start listening harder, gripped by what's happening on stage, and you have to admit that the only thing you've ever heard that sounds anything like this has been on Velvet Underground bootlegs 25 years old and more.'

After two nights in Scotland they played the tiny London Forum, and with the shows coming thick and fast (and only Lou Reed was really used to touring on such a scale), they found themselves playing the vast Wembley Arena the following night. Within the first 13 days of the tour they had played eight shows in five countries. The last of these was in Prague, where a special welcome awaited them.[2]

After Prague, the procession called in at Paris for a three-night stand. The band had always seemed to have a soft spot for the French capital. From the original 'reunion' in 1972 to the Cartier gathering in 1990, and now they had chosen the Paris shows to be recorded and filmed for a live album. Continuing on until 9 July they headlined more shows in France, Germany and Italy, supported U2 and played sets at the Glastonbury and Roskilde festivals.

Things weren't too rosy, though. 'Lou was being a pain in the ass, but we were overlooking it,' said Moe Tucker. 'A pain in the ass in that he doesn't know how to be in a band anymore: he's been the boss for so long, the absolute boss, that he just doesn't know how to be a band member. We really wanted to tour. We wanted him to have a good time, and we wanted to have a good time, so we overlooked a lot of shit and had a very good time just being together.'

As the tour wound its way around Europe the Reed-Cale relationship deteriorated. Cale had already had run-ins with Sylvia Reed, pointing out that she managed Lou Reed and not The Velvet Underground. By the end they weren't even on speaking terms. 'The evenings spent on tour listening to Sterling rant at the treatment meted out by our fearless leader was an aggravation that blossomed into even further recriminations. It meant the end of many things,' wrote Cale in his autobiography. In Italy Reed told one of the techs to unplug Cale's piano during 'Waiting For The Man'. Cale was so enraged he said, 'I was ready to knock his teeth down his throat.'

Cale was deflated by the lack of any new material – just one song, 'Coyote', from six months together. While they were supporting U2, the Edge had suggested that the Velvets record an album in an empty cinema. Cale was all for the idea, especially if they could get one or more members of U2 to guest on it. The chances of that were quite high: U2 were going through an experimental phase having recently worked with Johnny Cash and covered both Frank Sinatra and the Velvets. But Reed wasn't interested. Cale speculated that Reed's increasingly erratic behaviour was a consequence of being a small fish in U2's large pond.

'U2 were super-nice, unaffected guys, I was very impressed', said Moe Tucker. 'They had a boat ride on Lake Geneva with us and the tour crew all day floating around. It was great for me to have that opportunity to be among those types of events and to play in a stadium. I think that's an awful way to play: there's so much money involved, the crowd is so far away they have to watch on a monitor and I'm glad I was never in a band that was so big that I was stuck having to play that way, but it was a good experience for me to go through that and see what it was like. I'd never have had that experience on my own.'

As many observers had predicted, it hadn't taken that long for all the old tensions to resurface on the tour. Morrison and Tucker had managed to keep themselves between Cale and Reed for the most part and they were able to see the European tour through to the end, but problems arose over the post-production of the live album, the proposed US leg of the tour and a possible appearance on the *MTV Unplugged* show. By the time the band flew back to the States they were barely on speaking terms. Reed said he'd only consent to a US tour if he could produce the MTV *Unplugged* show and be paid the producer's fee. Cale wanted a more even distribution of the money. This was still in the days before email and when the conversations failed, the respective band members resorted to negotiation via their fax machines. 'We had a week-long fax fight,' reveals Tucker, 'about how we weren't going to do anything. Every time the fax machine would go off my kids would yell, "Fax fight!" and run to see what he [Reed] had said this time.'

The first casuality of the renewed hostilities was a possible Japanese tour. Then, with no compromise found over the MTV show, the US tour talks stalled and everyone went their separate ways. US fans were understandably disappointed, but those who got to see the European dates witnessed something they had never dreamed would be possible. 'Some people are a little more able to handle democracy than others,' said Sterling Morrison. 'Lou is among the least able. I don't want to make him the heavy, but people evolve or grow in different ways. Lou has sort of become very rigid in his thinking. And he would say in his own defence that, "I'm not rigid. I simply know what's right and that's what I'm gonna do." It sort of pains me: there are a lot of things that we could be doing that we're not doing because of weirdness. Not just Lou's, we're all kind of weird. We always were, and stubborn and verbal, so some very mean things can get said very glibly.'

'The most sadness I had about it falling apart was that it was so nice to have everybody together, being friends again,' said Moe Tucker. 'To see that get blown away, that made me very sad because we had such a good time on that tour. We had not been together, the four of us in one place, in years; I was real happy about that. It was really disappointing to have the fighting start again. In Europe, those were the people who had supported us for all these years and we hadn't played there ever. It was great to go there and play for these people who had been paying my rent. I thought it was going to be great because I knew that they'd be thrilled to death. So, that was my thing – that's what I wanted to do.'

That autumn the live album, called *Live MCMXCIII* and sporting a grey banana on the cover, saw release as a two-CD set, produced as a compromise by Mike Rathke. Taking the best performances from across the three Paris shows, the album opened with 'We're Gonna Have a Real Good Time Together' and spread a mixture of classics and out-takes across the 23 songs. 'Venus In Furs' was superb musically but Reed's vocals didn't quite live up to the task, though he did a good enough job on the more upbeat songs like 'Beginning To See The Light' and 'I Heard Her Call My Name'. Strangely, the band chose to play 'The Gift' and John Cale also sang 'All Tomorrow's Parties', while Moe Tucker took the microphone for 'her' songs:

'Afterhours' and 'I'm Sticking With You'. 'Hey Mr Rain' suffered from overly enthusiastic playing by all and lacked the studio version's poise and atmosphere. With the opening chords of every song drawing a raucous cheer from the partisan crowd, the band could do no wrong. John Cale managed to fight his way through the songs recorded after he'd been sacked from the band and suddenly the encores had arrived. To end the album the band played 'Coyote', the one new song, and a pretty unsatisfactory one at that. After the song ended the cheers finally subsided and it was over. As far as The Velvet Underground being a living, breathing band went, that was the end. The band went back to being a fixture in rock history. In December 1993, Channel 4 in the UK screened a night of programming dedicated to eight hours of The Velvet Underground. Not many bands in the history of rock can claim to have been given so much exposure in one sitting. Introduced by Debbie Harry, the films shown were: *Curious*, the 1993 tour documentary, V*elvet Redux MCMXCIII*, the film of the Paris reunion shows, *Coyote* [live], Warhol's *The Chelsea Girls*, S*ongs For Drella*, *The Gift* and archive film of *Sunday Morning*. From now on that was the only way that fans would be able to see the band. On film.

Chapter 20

1994–2010

Last Night I Said Goodbye to My Friend

'The Strokes definitely drew from the vibe of the Velvets. I listened to Loaded *all the time when we started the band, while I was writing my first songs. For four solid months it was just* Loaded. *A lot of our guitar tones are based on what Lou Reed and Sterling Morrison did. I honestly wish we could have copied them more; we didn't come close enough. But that was cool, because it became more of our own thing. Which is something else I got from the Velvets. They taught me just to be myself.'*

Julian Casablancas, The Strokes

In January 1996 The Velvet Underground were ready to be inducted into the Rock and Roll Hall of Fame in Cleveland, Ohio. Alongside David Bowie, Gladys Knight, Jefferson Airplane, Pink Floyd and The Shirelles they would be officially recognised for their influence on three decades of rock music. But getting the band together was going to be as difficult as ever. John Cale and Martha Morrison (representing the recently deceased

Sterling) were ready to go, Lou Reed had been outside of the band's limited activities since the fall-out in late 1993, but he was also ready to take his place. Surprisingly, the main sticking point surprisingly turned out to be the attendance (or not) of Moe Tucker. When responding to her invitation, Tucker enquired about tickets for her family. She was shocked to find she would only be allowed to invite two guests, but that would be insufficient for her family, let alone any friends. She was helpfully told that she would be able to buy extra tickets . . . for $1,500 a ticket! Tucker pointed out that she only wanted to go if she could share the event with her family and that she wasn't going to pay $4,500 for the honour. The conversation ended quickly, but behind the scenes the Hall was scrambling around to smooth over the problem. A couple of days later, they had managed to magically conjure up some extra seats and Tucker got another call which opened, 'Hello Moe, this is the Rock and Roll Hall of Fame. Now don't tell The Shirelles, but . . .'

The Hudson Valley Philharmonic Orchestra was founded back in 1932 when four string players (who were also businessmen) from Poughkeepsie, New York, got together to assemble local musicians. Two years later they performed their first public concerts and began a long and exhaustive programme of helping to promote local players and perform works by local composers. The emphasis always seemed to be on how they could spread predominantly classical music to a wider audience. When Randall Fleischer became the third musical director of the organisation in 1992, he opened what became known as the 'New Wave' series, which brought in guests such as Natalie Merchant, Bobby McFerrin and Richie Havens. In early 1994 the Hudson Valley approached Sterling Morrison, who lived right on their doorstep.

Fleischer met with Morrison and they sketched out enough music to fill an evening: Fleischer wrote a piece called 'Absolutely' especially for the night and Morrison's daughter Marianne helped her father with piano arrangements. Morrison said it was the hardest musical undertaking of his life. The show took place on 12 February 1994 at the local opera house on a wintry, snowy night.

The show was astounding, taking in everything from the 1700s to the 1990s. Samuel Barber's 'Adagio' sat alongside Frank Zappa's 'Alien Orifice', both greeted by an ecstatic crowd. The idea was to bridge the gap between classical and rock music, and it was carried off beautifully.

'The Philharmonic wore black turtlenecks that night', recalls Martha Morrison. 'It was hard for Sterling because he didn't know music theory and he didn't have the training that Marianne had. He stood up and he just blew the roof off this place, it was wonderful. But as we walked away, he was really mad: he wasn't happy with what he did, it was difficult.'

During the year Morrison had some discomfort around his mid-section and by the time the Velvets were invited to play at the Andy Warhol museum in Pittsburgh that autumn, he was struggling. The museum was to screen two of Warhol's films, *Kiss* and *Eat*, but Lou Reed was conspicuous by his absence. Nevertheless, Cale, Morrison and Tucker all agreed to play and Cale wrote some music to accompany the films. When the trio convened for a week's worth of rehearsals, Cale and Tucker were shocked at Morrison's appearance. He did not look at all well. In fact, he looked positively ghastly. 'Sterling was looking bad and feeling awful,' said Tucker. 'But no one had any idea.' Tucker and Cale insisted that Morrison should see a doctor immediately. The physician he saw in Pittsburgh said he had a pulled muscle, but during the week it was obvious to Cale and Tucker that something was wrong. The guitarist found it uncomfortable to sit or stand for very long, so they laboured on through the show in the knowledge that he had to seek a second opinion, and soon. When he did, their worst fears were confirmed: it was non-Hodgkin's lymphoma and he didn't have long to live. By January, he needed a wheelchair to get around.

Morrison retired to the family home in Poughkeepsie, New York. 'He did the whole chemotherapy thing,' said Tucker. 'The reports we were getting was that he was doing okay. So I was thinking, "Okay, he's very sick, but he's gonna be okay. It's gonna take a while, but he *is* going to be fine." And the next thing I knew I was getting a call saying, "If you want to see Sterling, you'd better get up here now." So even though we knew he was sick for almost a year and fighting it, it was still a surprise when he died. It was a real big shock for me.' Morrison eventually passed away on 30 August 1995.

'Sometimes I thought the Velvets' tour must have contributed to his death,' said John Cale. 'People leave a trace not always visible . . . it was in the impressive dignity he showed as he struggled.'

Cale was late getting to the memorial service for Morrison: he was going to say some words and hoped he would be in time to hear what Lou Reed was going to say. But Reed was not present.

Only weeks after Morrison's passing, the band members all received letters from the Rock and Roll Hall of Fame announcing that The Velvet Underground's induction to the Hall would take place the following January. For Moe Tucker the whole thing got off to a bad start and then just got worse. 'Sterling died in August, and then in September or October we got our letters inviting us,' she recalls. 'I'm not the biggest fan of the

Hall of Fame and I know Sterling would have been thrilled, and it pissed me off because we should have been in it well before that.'

The next thing to upset Tucker was the request that they play a song at the show. 'They called John, and John called me and said, "They want us to play something." I was like, "How the hell can we play something? Sterling just died!" He said, "Yeah, I told them that and they said: well, you can get a replacement." So that's how much they knew about rock and roll and the value of a band member. "Oh you can just get a replacement?"– I was so furious I almost didn't go. The main reason I said I'd go, and I was honoured, but there were lots of things that made me angry, bearing in mind he had just died. Sterling's wife got a letter the same as mine but it said "Sterling" instead of "Maureen". There was not a word of "Mrs Morrison, we're very sorry about Sterling", not a word.'

Martha Morrison had the potentially difficult duty of representing her husband so soon after his death, which seems to have been a cathartic experience for her. 'It was wonderful and really fun,' she recalls. 'I got a little misty because I know how much he would have loved it. It was a room full of people and I knew he would have had their rapt attention and done a wonderful job, that was my only problem really. He would have brought down the house: he was terrific at that kind of thing, he would really have enjoyed it. He really wanted to be in the Rock and Roll Hall of Fame.'

The induction took place on 17 January 1996 and it was some kind of vindication for a band that after being ignored, banned, ridiculed, accused and worn down they were now truly seen as one of the all-time greats. Despite the ill feeling still lingering from the 1993 tour, the Velvets managed to pull together for long enough to write a song in honour of Sterling Morrison. During the induction at, the Waldorf Astoria in New York City, the three remaining band members each sang a verse of 'Last Night I Said Goodbye To My Friend' after being introduced by Patti Smith.

As had become usual during the 1990s, Doug Yule was written out of the story. 'Someone told me about the Hall of Fame thing,' he said. 'David Bowie said the Hall of Fame wasn't appropriate for rock and roll, and for the time I was involved in rock and roll, it really wasn't. In fact, it was the opposite and counter-culture.'

In the meantime, Polygram had finally released the long-awaited five-CD retrospective box-set *Peel Slowly and See* in September 1995. It was something that had been rumoured and whispered about for years, and finally the rumours became reality. The set was extremely well-presented and put together, spanning the years 1965 to 1970. Each album was presented, along with out-takes, demos and live versions to total 74 tracks, while a luscious 84-page booklet with extensive liner notes was thrown in for good measure.

Most of the band, but not Doug Yule, was consulted at some point of the project and John Cale dug deep into his personal tape archives to find some of the rarest recordings in the set. While long-time fans may have baulked at having to buy a whole box-set to get the first four studio albums again, the extra 37 tracks of non-album material must have helped to make the wallet-emptying exercise a little easier to swallow.

Significant work went into the music, so traditionally rough-sounding works like the whole of *White Light/White Heat* sounded better than ever before. Edits that had been made to *Loaded* were reinstated, the closet mix of *The Velvet Underground* was used and the first disc filled with 80 minutes of demos from

John Cale's loft in 1965. A downside was the inclusion of an 'artificial' stereo mix of *The Velvet Underground & Nico*, rather than the original mono. Songs of other historical note included a live track from Doug Yule's first show as a Velvet and the John Cale-aided take of 'Ocean'.

Unlike many of his contemporaries, Lou Reed has continued to write fresh, meaningful music into his 60s. 'One of my rules is never listen to your old stuff,' he explains. 'If you do that, then you're not a musician any more, then you're just a self-satisfied nostalgic idiot who's not interested in inventing anything. I think life is far too short to concentrate on your past. I'd rather look into the future. I don't want to go back to the old records. All I hear is the mistakes. I can like them, but all the time I'm thinking, the cymbal there wasn't right.'

After the dissolution of his marriage to Sylvia, Reed is often seen around Manhattan with his partner Laurie Anderson, the performance artist who is five years his junior. Anderson had performed with the Chicago Youth Symphony and had a hit single with 'O Superman' in 1981. Reed has referred to her, on the rare occasions that he lets his guard down in interviews, as 'The love of my life, my soul mate'. But he'll divulge no more.

Reed now publishes books of his own photographs. He still says he might one day write a novel and he records albums exactly how and when he wants, while making sure they are technically as good as modern technology allows.

1995's *Set The Twilight Reeling* was a critical success and proved that Reed still had the hunger for live performance as he set off on an extensive world tour. Three years later, his *Perfect Night* album captured a night at London's Royal Festival

Hall, in which he performed songs from across the full breadth of his career. The songs sounded like they could have been taken from a single studio album, not written and recorded over more than 30 years. '[That's] because I never cared for trends,' said Reed. 'Music was what bothered me, what interested me. I always believed that I have something important to say, and I said it. That's why I survived because I still believe I've got something to say. My God is rock and roll: it's an obscure power that can change your life. The most important part of my religion is to play guitar.'

The other religion that he was following more diligently as his career progressed was his elusive search for the 'perfect' guitar tone. He has increasingly become obsessed with how intricate parts of albums sound, probably beyond an extent that most listeners would appreciate. But being the perfectionist he is, it bothers him if his music doesn't sound as good as he can get it, even if it's over the heads, or past the ears, of his fans.

The increasing use of compressed MP3 files contributes to his chagrin. 'Why bother to have these special amps and special guitars if so many of the listeners out there are gonna squash it and compress it to death?', he asks. 'And why bother with a true band, why bother with the guitars, why bother with the words and this and that if all you really want is big, heavy bass and a loud drum? People haven't heard good sound and they don't know what it is in the first place, or they don't have equipment that would let them know in the first place. Even over a half-decent set of headphones you get to the point. But if you just want to download it and castrate it, fine. And if you say, "Well, I don't give a shit about your record", well, okay, you're right! you know, it's certainly not meant for you. This record is meant for people who like sound.'

Reed is still pushing himself and gets excited when he finds another hero to play with. On *The Raven*, which was inspired by Edgar Allen Poe, he managed to co-opt the services of jazz great Ornette Coleman. 'We have seven versions with Ornette,' he gushed after the sessions. 'He did one, and I was practically in tears, it meant so much to me; it was so beautiful what he did. I said, "Well, you know, you could stop there." "No, no, no," he said, "now we'll do another one, and this one's gonna be with that guitar player. Then I'll do another one and it'll be the bass player, then I'll do another one, it'll be just with the drummer, then I'll do one with the vocalist. The last one I do will be with everybody." And that's exactly what he did. He has very long thoughts, so it's not like you can take a piece out of take six and put it with take four, 'cause unless you really pay attention to what he's doing, you could really fuck it up. So we chose which one was appropriate.'

John Cale has always been inspired by new music. After his third marriage broke down in 1997 he found himself drawn to Radiohead and Beck. He saw Beck perform 'Loser' on the BBC's *Top of the Pops* and singled out the singer as someone who gave him strength to carry on, with music and arguably with an increased enthusiasm for life, during a difficult period. It was Beck's grandfather Al Hansen who had been a spearhead of the Fluxus movement back in the 1950s and early 1960s. For his part, Beck covered 'Sunday Morning' on tour.

Cale still lives in New York and was close to the unfolding events of September 11. His apartment was only a couple of blocks from the World Trade Center and that morning in 2001 he strolled out to buy a newspaper, went home and logged on to check his emails. A friend had sent him a message saying, 'Get the fuck out! We're being attacked!' Only then did he realise what was happening just down the street. He looked out and saw people running through the thick dust; he managed to call his daughter's school before the electricity went out.

He's now approaching 70 but shows no signs of slowing down. 2010 found him playing the whole of his *Paris 1919* album at the Royal Festival Hall in London, the same venue where he'd presided over a Nico tribute evening in October 2008.

As has happened many times before, many new bands of the twenty-first century are Velvet Underground fans. Karl Hyde from British electro-warriors Underworld said that the conversational way Lou Reed wrote his *New York* album was a belated influence on how Underworld worked: 'With Reed I watch a character and now it makes sense – a lot of the states of mind that appear to come out of this invented persona for the stage makes sense now. What he's really saying is he is talking about the state of mind of the artist.'

The latest wave of bands from both sides of the Atlantic continue to cite the Velvets as an influence. Wilco's Jeff Tweedy picked *Loaded* as one of his favourite albums, while Jon Fratelli of The Fratellis chose 'All Tomorrow's Parties' as one of his five key tracks for the *NME*. Antony Hegarty of Antony and the Johnsons picked 'Candy Says' as the song he wished he'd written. The list goes on. It was also evident in the twenty-first century that the grand old lineage of New York Rockers was again in vogue as The Strokes made headlines around the world. Without the Velvets there might not have been Suicide or Television or The Ramones, then came Richard Hell, Blondie and Talking Heads, who paved the way for Sonic Youth and eventually The Strokes.

US magazine *Filter* brought Lou Reed and The Strokes together in 2004 for a joint chat about the Velvet Underground's history and New York music in general. The Strokes were like a bunch of teenage fans, but Reed threw out a few snippets of Velvet's folklore and they lapped it up. At the time their second record was flagging, but Reed did give a rare compliment to their debut album, saying, 'I thought it was great that bands are making music like that again.' Lead singer Julian Casablancas wrote in *Rolling Stone*: 'The Velvet Underground were way ahead of their time. I couldn't believe that this wasn't the most popular music ever made. I honestly wish we could have copied them more.'

The repackaging of the Velvets' catalogue continues unabated. Deluxe double-CD sets of *The Velvet Underground & Nico*, *Loaded*[1] and *Live At Max's Kansas City* have all been issued since the millennium and the demand is still there for more. Collectors continue to survey record fairs and a few years ago, one fan discovered more than he'd bargained for. In archaeological terms it was like stumbling across the sarcophagus of Tutankhamen for £1. In September 2002, Canadian record collector Warren Hill was visiting New York. At a yard sale in Chelsea he was browsing through some cardboard boxes when he came across an un-sleeved record with a handwritten label that said: 'Velvet Underground. 4/25/66. N. Dolph'. Hill was intrigued, thinking it might be either a test pressing or a bootleg, and paid the princely sum of 75 cents for it. Back in Canada he phoned his friend Eric Isaacson, who ran a record store in Portland, to ask about the record. Isaacson assumed it was a test pressing and offered to sell the record at his store with an $800 price tag. When Hill played it to his friend (which they had to do sparingly because acetates can easily be damaged), the duo discovered they had something more valuable than they had originally thought. The track selection was different to the released album and they heard that these were different versions of the songs. They tracked down Norman Dolph and he confirmed that they had the acetate of the debut album that he'd had pressed at Columbia back, in 1966. As the original tapes have either been lost or destroyed, this is probably the only copy of those takes in existence. The price suddenly jumped even higher. Once word got out about the find, Hill was offered $10,000 for the disc, which he declined, later deciding to sell it on eBay for $25,000.

In recent years, Doug Yule has finally achieved some well-deserved recognition for his part in the Velvets' story. After all, he did play on two studio albums (not counting *Squeeze*) and three live records. In 2001, his later version of the Velvets had a box-set of live recordings issued under the title *Final VU*. He still writes music and finds that compliments from his peers mean more than record sales these days. 'As far as recognition goes, I was sitting in a bookstore with some other musicians,' recalls Yule. 'Sandy Bradley, a local hero in Seattle, asked to hear a song. I played one I'd written in 1996 or 1997, and when it was done she said: "I'm impressed".' To me, that's recognition. Because she's a professional, she knows what she's hearing and she's not obligated in any way to approve or disapprove. An audience is already on your side, so how can you really expect them to hate it unless you're really, really bad?'

Yule has played live only a handful of times over the last decade. At the Crocodile Café in Seattle he was involved in a Velvet Underground night where local bands got up and played one or two Velvets' songs in their own way. He too assembled a band and played a few songs. It was a poignant irony that the forgotten Velvet would end up playing songs at a Velvet Underground tribute night.

Today Yule says, 'The Velvet Underground was an important part of my life, but not the only part. I have an honest job: I have no money, I have lots of fun. I learned how to fly and became a pilot. I still have music in my head but I don't play it anymore, but I do sing it. People think I'm crazy because I sing all the time. I still have strong feelings for the other members in the band. In spite of the Sesnick-created conditions and the periodic animosities which grew out of that, we spent a lot of time together in strange places and strange situations.'

When asked to look back over the past 40 years of the band Moe Tucker said, 'We had a lot of fun and I'm extremely proud of our music and that I was very lucky to be involved.' Today she has unofficially retired from music. She would love to travel and play on tour but having to do everything on her own is tiring. 'I do my own booking,' she explains. 'The thought of going through the whole job of booking, I just want someone to come and knock on the door and say let's go, 'cos my band are up for it and I really want to do it. I'm very busy with my grandson so that doesn't leave much room for smoking cigarettes and playing guitar!'

Lou Reed is content with his life. 'I've become completely well adjusted to being a cult figure,' he quips. And of course New York is still his home: 'I love New York – I can pick up a phone and have anything I want delivered to my door. I can step into the street and have a fight immediately. All the energy, people going crazy, guys with no legs on, rollerskates . . . it's very intense. The energy level is incredible.' Most recently, he has been touring versions of *Berlin* and *Metal Machine Music*.

Cale is still writing as much as ever. 'I got a lot out of The Velvet Underground,' he said, 'but it took me a long time to regain my vitality.' In 2005, he put out the *Black Acetate* album, which was critically acclaimed, and followed it up with a tour.

❋ ❋ ❋

In 2007, *Time Out New York* listed The Velvet Underground as the city's greatest musicians of all time. 'We put a ship in the water, it turned out to be a turbo-powered sub and it took a while for it to land wherever it landed,' said Lou Reed. 'Time was the real judge. The proof was in the work, and the work is on the record.'

'I never stood back and thought our music is revolutionary but I was super-impressed with our music,' said Moe Tucker. 'There were times on stage when I would literally get chills and I thought we were interesting as hell.'

Sterling Morrison once pointed out that although people thought they must be depraved junkies, The Velvet Underground were actually very well-behaved middle-class people who paid their hotel bills and didn't break the furniture. They were ordinary folk who just happened to come together and inspire, each other to make some extraordinary music. The legacy lives on and The Velvet Underground will be influencing bands for as long as people listen to their music. Which figures to be a long time to come.

The final word, as usual, goes to Lou Reed: 'Together we did something that none of us could do alone, and then when you separated us we did things that we would do on our own, but with the added knowledge of what we did before.'

Epilogue
A Velvet Revolution

'When Lou Reed was in Prague as a Rolling Stone *reporter, we threw a party for him. We recounted our story to him, which he had known in an outline. When we told him that had it not been for them [the Velvets] in the 1960s, our band would never exist, he was very impressed and said that in all likelihood The Velvet Underground had been much better known in Prague then than in the USA.'*

Milan Hlavsa (Czech performer)

'Did you know that I am President because of you?'

Vaclav Havel to Lou Reed

Prague is about 4,100 miles from New York City, or around 6,600 kilometres if you prefer. But culturally, at the end of the 1960s during the Soviet occupation, it might as well have been as far as the moon. Take one particular night, and one particular man as an example. On this night our man in question can be seen crossing the River Vltava across Karlův most, the Charles Bridge. Behind him the Royal Palace and St Vitus's Cathedral are lit up against the night sky, projecting a spectacular back drop to the Czechoslovakian capital. A vicious, chilling wind rips along the river and anyone willing to brave the night walks head-bowed through the atmospheric onslaught. Our man has a determined stride and with the collar of his chunky overcoat turned up and one hand holding his hat onto his head, he leaves the bridge, ignores the guards on duty at the impressive gatehouse and walks along the river for a little while. He turns left onto Narodni and then left again into the warren of ancient, narrow streets that make up the Old Town district. Here, it is easy for a man to get lost, and that is exactly what he wants to do. He's pretty sure that he isn't being followed tonight, but you could never be sure.

Soon he reaches his destination, a plain wooden door in an unexceptional building. He knocks twice and looks right and left, while waiting for it to be opened. Inside he is warmly greeted, hangs his coat among many others and descends into the cellar. Muted wall lights give the scene a slightly satanic feel but that is wide of the mark. Shaking hands with people as he works his way through the crowd of around fifty, he collects a drink and turns to a small wooden stage at the end of the room, where a band is setting up. A few minutes later they mumble their greetings and dive into the opening song, a western rock song called 'White Light/White Heat'.

Our man, one Vaclav Havel, smiles as the song blasts out. He sips his drink and wonders what the authorities would say if they knew that an album by a band as revolutionary as The Velvet Underground had been smuggled into the country, never mind what they would do if they knew he was standing there watching a Prague band play a set of Velvets' cover versions. It was a thought that, made him very warm on the inside despite the cold outside.

❖ ❖ ❖

Vaclav Havel initially gained some prominence as a playwright and dramatist before later being imprisoned for his political views. He formed Charter 77, a movement of like-minded Czechoslovaks intent on bringing the government's Human Rights violations to a worldwide audience, and his political ambitions gained momentum at the end of the 1980s as he rose to become the last president of Czechoslovakia during the 'Velvet Revolution' of 1989 and the first president of the Czech Republic.

Havel was born in 1936 to a wealthy family. He and his brother went to private school and had Ivy League or Oxbridge careers laid out before them. But things changed in 1948 when the communists took power and seized much of the family's wealth. With his future plans dashed, he gravitated towards the bohemian theatre set. Throughout his twenties he penned plays that were thinly-veiled attacks on the incumbent regime. *The Garden Party*, *The Memorandum*, and *The Increased Difficulty of Concentration* all permeated the growing sense of liberalisation that spread across the country during the 1960s. The country embraced what became known as 'Socialism with a Human Face'. Café society in Prague was on the upturn, though not back to its pre-war heyday. In 1968, the 'Prague Spring' saw leader Alexander Dubcek attempt to push through more reformist ideas. Moscow was watching, though, and didn't like what she saw. In August, she invaded and removed Dubcek from power. He was exiled to the countryside and replaced by the hardline Gustav Husak. The period of leniency well and truly over, Havel suddenly found his plays banned by the State.

During 1968, before the Soviet invasion, Havel had been allowed to make a trip to New York. 'That was an extraordinarily interesting, fertile and inspiring period,' he said. 'Not only [in Prague], but in the culture of the entire world. Personally, it was a relatively happy time. 1968 was for me just a natural climax of that whole period.' In the United States Havel was given a copy of *The Velvet Underground & Nico*, the debut album of the then largely unknown New York band mainly acknowledged only because of their relationship with pop-artist Andy Warhol. Havel took it home, along with Frank Zappa's debut, and managed to smuggle it through Customs. Soon it was being copied and passed around the Prague underground, influencing the avant-garde set to play secretive gigs around the capital.

One copy of the outlawed album reached Milan 'Mejla' Hlavsa, who formed a band called The Plastic People of the Universe (PPU) the same year. They instantly added Velvet Underground songs to their live set. The sound of The Beatles had reached Prague and jazz was well established, but it was the visit of Allen Ginsberg to the city's Charles University in 1965 and the Velvets' and Zappa albums that really turned some young bands into Czechoslovakia's first psychedelic acts. The PPU would play Velvets' (they even added a viola player), Zappa, Doors' and Captain Beefheart songs, but after the Soviet invasion things became increasingly difficult for them. The Kremlin-led 'normalisation' program that followed the invasion eventually left the PPU in a cultural wilderness as an unauthorised band who were no longer allowed to be paid for performing and who had their right to use state-owned rehearsal facilities revoked.

This period of being a purely amateur outfit severely tested the band but they managed to beg and borrow equipment, build their own makeshift amplifiers and continue to play ever-more bizarre venues and shows. Band member Ivan Jirous was an art critic and still a member of the Union of Artists so he could obtain permits for convention halls. He would lecture on Andy Warhol, show film and slide shows and then the band would 'demonstrate' the songs of the Velvets. Soon the powers that be found out what was really going on and gave the band a blanket ban from playing in Prague.

The band hid out in the countryside, playing in small towns and even forests. Fans would spread the word along the underground grapevine and wander into the woods near small towns around the country. It was a constant game of cat and mouse, but on the days when the police won the game they came down hard. Fans were beaten and arrested, names taken and students were often kicked out of school or college. The last straw came in March 1976 when police raided the homes of many musicians, making 27 arrests including all of the PPU, and putting the artists on trial. As the band sat in the dock, the courtroom was seen as presenting a trial of the very basics of rock and roll. The State cited their music as an anti-social phenomenon. Eventually, the four members of the PPU were jailed for between 8 and 18 months.[1]

The trial inadvertently brought all of Czechoslovakia's dissidents together and on 1 January 1977 they formed Charter 77, which strived to protect human rights. At the forefront of this new organisation was Vaclav Havel. He was the natural figurehead for Charter 77 as his political dissent had grown during the 1970s. In 1975, he had written an open letter to President Husak under the title 'The Power of the Powerless'. 'So far you and your government have chosen the easy way out for yourselves,' wrote Havel, 'and the most dangerous road for society: the path of inner decay for the sake of outward appearances; of deadening life for the sake of increasing uniformity; of deepening the spiritual and moral crisis of our society, and ceaselessly degrading human dignity, for the puny sake of protecting your own power.' This document would prove to be the basis for Charter 77. Like the underground music scene, the writings of Havel were passed among the interested on hand-typed manuscripts or in the form of foreign books smuggled back into the country.[2]

Poland and Hungary had already made moves towards democracy before the Berlin Wall started to come down on 10 November. A fortnight later the Czechoslovak Communist leaders resigned. It was the climax of a week of growing unrest and peaceful protest which had seen almost 500,000 gather in Wenceslas Square. By the end of the year Havel had been elected president. He was instrumental in the splitting of Czechoslovakia into the Czech Republic and Slovakia in January 1993.

By January 2005 Vaclav Havel had retired from politics and it came as a surprise when he took part in a public meeting with Lou Reed in Prague. Moe Tucker had previously played in Prague on a solo tour and met Havel when he attended her show. 'The Czech Republic was cool and having dinner with Vaclav Havel was amazing,' she enthuses. 'The first time he came backstage and was trying to express in English what the Velvets' music meant to him. And he was holding his hand on his chest over his heart but he couldn't express it and that was quite an honour.'

The acknowledged Havel-Reed odd couple first met for a morning press conference and followed it up at the Švandovo Divadlo Theatre to stage a 'public conversation'. The press conference didn't go especially well, with Havel saying little and Reed being as difficult an interviewee as numerous journalists have reported over the years. For the evening event, The Plastic People of the Universe played a short set before the two headliners emerged to a standing ovation.

'It's always dangerous to meet someone you admire,' said Reed. 'I had no idea what to expect.' The two chatted about their respective influences, the Revolution and their love of music.

Towards the end of the evening the moderator asked the two participants to ask each other a question. Settling on a somewhat prosaic subject, Reed chose to ask Havel whether when he wrote he did so longhand, on a typewriter or with a computer. Havel, it turned out, had given up longhand but lived in terror of his new PC, which he described as being 'full of little characters that stick their tongue out at me'.

In turn, Havel asked Reed if he'd ever run for political office. 'I lack certain people skills,' he admitted. 'But I have good instincts. I can think of people who could do a better job. I might bring you in!'

A less than auspicious exchange of notes between two very different undergrounds. As Reed himself warned, admiration is dangerous and, as Lester Bangs counselled, romanticising would be a mistake. But for this post-cold war summit to have proven such a disappointment, is itself telling. Revolutions need heroes. That The Velvet Underground should have inspired the isolated free-thinkers of communist Czechoslovakia, as they themselves were inspired by the Beats, the avant gardists and rock and rollers of 1950s America, is a testament to the enduring energy of pop in the broadest sense; and the test of the Velvets' legacy.

The Velvet Underground story will go on. Despite the recording of their last 'real' album now speeding past the forty-year mark in the rear-view mirror of rock history, the Velvets are as important and influential today as they have ever been. Column inches continue to be filled, internet forums kept abuzz and New York museum retrospectives packed out. Each new generation of bands that comes to the fore has a sprinkling of Velvets' influence. The shadow they cast shows no sign of diminishing.

From the underground, the revolution: the heroes of The Velvet Underground will be with us for a long time to come.

Notes

Chapter 1

1. Long-forgotten acts like Paul Williams, Tiny Grimes and Varetta Dillard, were booked to perform at the 10,000-capacity venue, but after more than 20,000 fans turned out for the show, it was stopped after just one song as the authorities feared a riot might break out.

2. King Curtis had already played with Buddy Holly and The Coasters. He opened for The Beatles at Shea Stadium in 1965, and also played with Aretha Franklin, during a glittering career.

Chapter 2

1. In 1959 the payola scandal erupted. Freed was found guilty of receiving payments to pay certain records ahead of others, though he claimed the money was paid as a 'consultation fee'. He eventually admitted to commercial bribery but his career was on a downward spiral and in 1965 he died a heavy drinking, depressed man. In 1986 he was inducted to the Rock And Roll Hall of Fame.

2 Canadian-born writer Saul Bellow wrote a widely acclaimed novel based around Schwartz's life in 1975. Titled *Humboldt's Gift*, it placed Schwartz as the central character Humboldt von Fleisher. Bellow described the book as a 'comic book about death.' It won the Noble Prize for Literature in 1976.

3 His later compositions often included electronic sound, as in *Bohor* (1962) and *Polytope de Cluny* (1972), or virtuoso percussion, as in *Psappha* (1975), *Rebonds* (1988), and his last piece, *O—Mega* (1997). He was a founder of the Centre d'Etudes Mathématiques et Automatiques in Paris, and of the Center for Mathematical and Automated Music at Indiana University. Xenakis wrote several treatises explaining his various theories.

4 Hansen's daughter Bibbe would be one of the youngest Warhol Superstars at The Factory and her son Bek Hansen is better known as Beck.

5 A young artist by the name of Andy Warhol later claimed to have been at this show and sat through the entire piece.

6 Jeremy Shatan who had played with the Beastie's Mike D in the punk band Young Aborigines shot the photos in April 1989 to capture the hustle and bustle of the Lower East Side, which was then still described as 'gritty'. Now it's a hip hang-out and the thrift stores from the album sleeve have been transformed into upscale boutiques, and Paul's Boutique itself is now a café of the same name.

Chapter 3

1 A follow-up book, *The Velvet Underground Revisited*, was published in 1968, with the cover blurb claiming that the author 'has continued his research and found that things *have* changed – but for the worse.'

2 When John Cale wasn't working with the rest of the band he was always playing and thinking up new sonic schemes with his home tape recorder and viola. Some of these rare recordings were issued in 2000 by the Sandwalking Company. The three discs give a valuable insight into the non-Velvet Underground workings of Cale during the mid- to late-1960s. He is captured on tape with Tony Conrad, Angus Maclise and Sterling Morrison, among others. The quintessential moment comes on a recording of Cale by himself at his apartment: he's squealing away on his viola until he eventually coaxes some response from his neighbours downstairs. At the end of the piece (called 'Big Apple Express'), a distant voice can be heard to shout: 'I don't want to hear this bullshit! If you want to do something, do it far, far away, out in the country.'

Chapter 4

1 Other reasons given over the years for ending the residency at Café Bizarre are that the guests couldn't dance to the Velvets' music, that they refused to work on New Year's Eve and that they got into a fist fight with a bunch of sailors.

2 Delon was a major star in France and was engaged to actress Romy Schneider when he had the affair with Nico.

Chapter 5

1   These takes were thought to be lost for almost the next 40 years until they sensationally surfaced in 2002 at a New York yard sale. Warren Hill paid 75 cents for the acetate disc, which had the songs in a different running order to the released version of the album. The nine-song acetate's running order was, 'European Son' (different take, longer version) / 'Black Angel's Death Song' (different mix) / 'All Tomorrow's Parties' (different mix) / 'Heroin' (different take, alternate lyrics) / 'Femme Fatale' (different mix) / 'Venus in Furs' (different take) / 'I'm Waiting For The Man' (different take, alternate lyrics) / 'Run Run Run' (different mix). In 2006 the acetate was sold on eBay and bids topped a whopping $155,000. However, the winning bidder turned out to be a prankster and the acetate was relisted, reaching $25,000, which at the time made it the most expensive record ever sold on eBay.

Chapter 6

1   Lou Reed's miserable summer got even worse in July when he heard about the death of Delmore Schwartz. Schwartz had meandered through a series of short-lived teaching positions and in his last days he'd been a lonely, dishevelled shadow of his former self. His drinking had increased even more but he'd still managed to work on some writing right up until his death from a heart attack. When his body had taken just about as much abuse as it could handle.

2   In 1967 Maclise moved to the West Coast, where he met and married the painter Hetty McGee. The couple travelled extensively through Asia and finally settled in Kathmandu where they had a son, Ossian. He continued to make music and a

posthumous CD of his work was issued in 1999 entitled *The Invasion Thunderbolt Pagoda*. After a trek through the Himalayas in the summer of 1979, he collapsed and died in Kathmandu.

Chapter 7

1 Just two examples of the high regard for the album are *Uncut* magazine calling it the 'Greatest Debut Album of All Time' and *The Observer* hailing it as the number one in its '50 Albums That Changed Music'.

2 This, the most famous Velvet Underground album, also has the most complicated history as a record. The Eric Emerson legal twists not only caused there to be the original version, the version with a sticker over his face, the version with his face airbrushed out and a version with a different back photograph, but there were also mono and stereo copies of each of these releases, and that was just in the US. Over the years the various re-issues and cover art changes have meant that there are over 30 versions of the album in that country alone. It has also been issued in many other markets: the UK, Germany, Japan, Italy, New Zealand and Mexico are just some of the variations that a completist could spend a lifetime collecting just this one album.

3 Fallon's credits include Van Morrison's *Astral Weeks* and The Rolling Stones' 'Gimme Shelter'. He died in 2005.

4 The film had nothing to do with Nico's album but was over three hours of fairly raw, unedited footage of women staying at the Chelsea hotel.

Chapter 8

1 Like the debut album, *White Light white Heat's* reputation has grown with time. In 2002 *Rolling Stone* listed it at the top of its '50 Coolest Albums of All Time'.

Chapter 9

1 Comprising Dave Guard, Nick Reynolds and Bob Shane, The Kingston Trio are one of the all-time most popular folk bands. Their landmark albums, *The Kingston Trio* and *The Kingston Trio At Large* (which spent 15 weeks as the number one album) opened the door allowing Bob Dylan, Joan Baez and the like to have mainstream success in the 1960s.

2 The Chateau Marmont opened in 1929: 'the Chateau', as it is known by its illustrious guests, is one of rock and roll's most famous hotels. Jim Morrison lived there and undertook adventures on the roof; The Rolling Stones and Led Zeppelin famously stayed there. The latter decided to start the craze of throwing TVs out of windows too. But the hotel is best-known for a tragedy, as John Belushi died there in 1982.

Chapter 10

1 The different mixes from these sessions have caused the upmost confusion for collectors over the years. Lou Reed's claustrophobic sounding 'closet mix' was issued in the USA only. UK and Canadian versions initially used Val Valentin's original mix, but then they were recalled and replaced with a different version of the Reed mix. Various European issues confused things even more: one German CD used mixes from both Reed and Valentin, while a French album managed to have 'Beginning to See the Light' pressed twice on side two.

Chapter 11

1 Ohio-native Robert Quine was almost the same age as Lou Reed and Sterling Morrison, and so they had a lot in common when reminiscing about the music they listened to while growing up. 'I was 12 in 1955 when rock and roll hit,' said Quine. 'It just completely transformed me. I was getting into Frank Sinatra before that. But when that hit, it was all over; it was raw. The first rock record I bought was Frankie Lyman and the Teenager's "Why Do Fools Fall In Love?"'

As well as being famous for taping so many Velvets' shows, he later embarked on a guitar-playing career of his own. A founder member of Richard Hell and the Voidoids, he later worked with Lou Reed (1981 to 1985) and has appeared with the likes of Brian Eno, Lloyd Cole, Matthew Sweet, Tom Waits and Marianne Faithfull.

Chapter 14

1 After his stint with the Velvets, Alexander went on to be described as 'this generation's Kerouac' by the *Boston Globe*, as he found himself at the centre of the city's punk scene in the mid-1970s. His list of bands is impressive and includes The Lost, The Bagatelle and The Boom Boom Band.

Chapter 19

1 Once the first show kicked off there was one fan happier than most. Londoner Neil Chippendale had placed a bet that the Velvets would reform and play a show to a paying audience before the end of 1993. He was given fairly small odds of 20-1, but he took them and wagered £5.

2 The Czech Republic had probably the highest density of Velvet Underground cover bands and groups covering their material.

A Beat played many 1960s' hits and threw in the occasional Velvets' tune; Pavel Bobek recorded 'Zkus Se Zivotu Dal Smat' ('Walk On The Wild Side'); Fiction covered 12 Velvet songs for their album *Neverending Party*; Garaz formed in 1970, regularly playing 'Sweet Jane'; Lexington 125 took their name from the line in 'Waiting For The Man'; The Plastic People of the Universe covered over 20 Velvets' songs over the years; Porybny Stramak covered several Velvets' songs, including some sung in Czech ('Co Se Ji' was 'What Goes On' and 'Kraska v Kozesine' was 'Venus In Furs'). Other bands playing one or two Velvets' songs included Rany Tela, Silenstvi, Spacir Bleu and Ticha Dohoda. The aptly named Velvet Underground Revival Band formed in 1987, playing Velvet's songs around Prague.

Chapter 20

1 The alternate *Loaded* album from the special edition two-CD set, 'Who Loves The Su', starts with a simple drum pattern and ends on a vocal chord, not a fade out. 'Sweet Jane' is the slow version without the echo-y introduction and different lyric. 'Rock & Roll' has a chiming guitar running through it and builds to a chaotic ending. 'Cool It Down' is a simple take, possibly live in the studio; it has different lyrics and a drum intro. Prominent piano part-crescendos with the drums to end the song. 'New Age', very similar to the regular album version, runs a few seconds longer. 'Head Held High' again sounds like a live studio recording. 'Lonesome Cowboy Bill' opens with an acoustic guitar and keyboards. Wailing guitars jump around but the mix sounds 'muddy'. Reed's vocal style is quite different. 'I Found A Reason' opens with a harmonica and the whole song is arranged in a country style and tempo. 'Train Round the Bend' is reworked with different drums,

guitars and vocals. 'Oh! Sweet Nuthin'' has Reed vocal and different lyrics.

Epilogue

1 Prominent dissident writer and PPU lyricist Egon Bondy, who died in 2007, was not one of those arrested, but the band released an album in his honour: 'Egon Bondy's Happy Hearts Club Banned'.

2 After the formation of Charter 77, Havel began carrying around what he called his 'emergency packet'. He would take it with him every time he left his house. It included soap, a toothbrush, toothpaste, laxatives, some paper, a T-shirt and cigarettes. He carried this in case he was picked up and imprisoned by the police, something which became a common occurrence for him – he was jailed numerous times between 1977 and 1989, including 1979 to 1983 inclusive. But in 1989, things began to change.

Appendices

AUTHOR'S NOTES

This book has been a long-time coming – on and off for eight years, in fact. If nothing else, thanks for your patience. Thanks to everyone who has contributed photos, articles, interview time, rare discs of music, anecdotes and just general help to get this book finished. In strictly alphabetical order you are:

Tim Bates, Martha Dargan, Norm Dolph, Gino Farabella, Sam Harrison and all at Aurum, Warren Hill, Carolyn Jovanovic, Paul Lester, Gerard Malanga, Sal Mercuri, Steve Nelson, Rob North, Graham Palmer, Moe Tucker and Doug Yule.

BIBLIOGRAPHY

The following works were consulted during the writing of this volume:

Bokris, Victor, *Lou Reed The Biography*, Random House, London, 1995

Bokris, Victor and Cale, John, *What's Welsh For Zen*, Bloomsbury, London, 1999

Bokris, Victor and Malanga, Gerard, *Uptight*, Omnibus Press, London, 2002

Clapton, Diana, *Lou Reed & The Velvet Underground*, Proteus, London, 1982

DeRogatis, Jim, *The Velvet Underground*, Voyageur Press, Minneapolis, MN, USA, 2009

Doggett, Peter, *Growing Up In Public*, Omnibus Press, London, 1992

Fein, Art, *The LA Musical History Tour*, 2.13.61, Los Angeles, 1998

Harvard, Joe, *The Velvet Underground & Nico*, Continuum, New York, 2004

Heylin, Clinton, *All Yesterdays' Parties*, Da Capo, Cambridge, MA, USA, 2005

Heylin, Clinton, *From The Velvets to the Voidoids*, Helter Skelter, London, 2005

Johnstone, Nick, *Lou Reed Talking*, Omnibus Press, London, 2005

Koestenbaum, Wayne, *Andy Warhol*, Weidenfeld & Nicolson, London, 2001

Kostek. M.C., *The Velvet Underground Handbook*, Black Spring Press, London, 1992

Leigh, Michael, *The Velvet Underground*, MacFadden, New York, 1963

Leigh, Michael, *The Velvet Underground Revisited*, MacFadden, New York, 1968

Malanga, Gerard, *Archiving Warhol*, Creation Books, London, 2002

Mitchell, Tim, *There's Something About Jonathan*, Peter Owen, London, 2000

Mitchell, Tim, *Sedition and Alchemy*, Peter Owen, London, 2003

Reed, Lou, *Pass Through Fire*, Bloomsbury, London, 2000

Reynolds, Simon, *Rip It Up And Start Again*, Faber and Faber, London, 2005

Roberts, Chris, *Lou Reed: The Stories Behind the Songs*, Carlton, London, 2004

Shore, Stephen and Tillman, Lynne, *The Velvet Years*, Pavilion, London, 1995

Stein, Jean, *Edie*, Grove Press, New York, 1982

Thompson, Dave, *Beyond The Velvet Underground*, Omnibus Press, London, 1989

Unterberger, Richie, *Unknown Legends of Rock'n'Roll*, Miller Freeman, San Francisco, 1998

Unterberger, Richie, *White Light/White Heat*, Jaw Bone, London, 2009

Warhol, Andy and Hackett, Pat, *Popism The Warhol Sixties*, Harcourt, Orlando: FL, USA, 1980

West, Mike, *The Velvet Underground & Lou Reed*, Babylon Books, Manchester, 1982

Witts, Richard, *The Velvet Underground*, Equinox, London, 2006

Wrenn, Michael, *Lou Reed Between the Lines*, Plexus, London, 1993

Young, James, *Songs They Never Play On The Radio*, Bloomsbury, London, 1992

Zak III, Albin (ed.), *The Velvet Underground Companion*, Schirmer, London, 1997

Numerous magazines were used for background information and research into The Velvet Underground. Specific articles relating to the band are as follows:

Creem   1975, 'Monolith or Monotone',
                                 Cyborg QX38

Creem   November 1987, 'The Velvet
                                 Underground', Bill Holdship,
                                 Roy Trakin, John Neilson,
                                 Thomas Anderson

East Village Other   15 April 1966, 'A High School of
                                 Music and Art', John Wilcock

Frieze   Summer 1993, 'The Velvet
                                 Underground', Jon Savage

Guardian   23 May 2003 'Velvet goldmine',
                                 Ed Vulliamy

Los Angeles Times   5 May 1966 'A Far Out Night with
                                 Andy Warhol', Kevin Thomas

Melody Maker   29 May 1993, 'Notes From The
                                 Underground', Allan Jones

Melody Maker   12 June 1993, 'Déjà Vu', Allan Jones

Mojo   July 2002, 'The Velvet Underground
                                 & Nico', David Bowie

Mojo   March 2004, 'The Speed of Sound',
                                 Phil Alexander/'Heart of Darkness',
                                 Victor Bokris/'The Model', Will
                                 Hodgkinson/'Cooking for One',
                                 David Sheppard

Mojo	February 2007, John Cale, Paul Trynka
New York Times	14 January 1966, 'Syndromes Pop at Delmonico's', Grace Glueck
NME	30 July 1988, 'Last of the Bohemians', Michele Kirsch
NME	5 June 1993, 'Survival of the Hippest', Keith Cameron and Steven Wells
NME	12 June 1993, 'White Light/White Hair', John Harris
NME	20 September 2003, 'Why I Love', Tim Jonze
NME	10 January 2004, 'Why I Love', Paul McNamee
NME	22 May 2004, 'Heroes', Mikel Jollet
Observer Music Monthly	March 2007, 'Soundtrack of My Life', Will Hodgkinson
Q	July 1993, 'Party On, Dudes!', Mat Snow
Record Collector	August 1989, 'The VU on CD', Clinton Heylin
Record Collector	September 2001, 'The Velvet Revolution', Peter Doggett
Rolling Stone	15 April 2004, 'The Velvet Underground', Julian Casablancas

Uncut	April 2007, 'Anyone Else Would Have Broken Both Her Arms', Marc Spitz
Uncut	December 2009, 'The Velvet Underground', Allan Jones
Vanity Fair	November 2002, 'Rebel Nights', Lisa Robinson
Vox	July 1993, Max Bell
The Word	May 2007, 'Face Time', Jude Rogers

DISCOGRAPHY

Velvet Underground Albums
The Velvet Underground & Nico 1967
White Light/White Heat 1968
The Velvet Underground 1969
Loaded 1970
Live at Max's Kansas City 1972
Squeeze 1973
Live 1969 1974
VU 1985
Another View 1986
Live MCMXCIII 1993
Peel Slowly and See 1995
Final VU 1971–1973 2001
Bootleg Series Volume 1: The Quine Tapes 2001

John Cale Studio Albums
Vintage Violence 1970
The Academy in Peril 1972
Paris 1919 1973
Fear 1974
Slow Dazzle 1975
Helen of Troy 1975
Honi Soit 1981
Music For A New Society 1982
Caribbean Sunset 1983
Artificial Intelligence 1985
Words for the Dying 1989
Walking on Locusts 1996
HoboSapiens 2003
Black Acetate 2005

Nico Studio Albums
Chelsea Girl 1967
The Marble Index 1969
Desertshore 1970
The End 1973
Drama of Exile 1981
Camera Obscura 1985

Lou Reed Studio Albums
Lou Reed 1972
Transformer 1972
Berlin 1973
Sally Can't Dance 1974
Metal Machine Music 1975
Coney Island Baby 1975

Rock and Roll Heart 1976
Street Hassle 1978
The Bells 1979
Growing Up in Public 1980
The Blue Mask 1982 .
Legendary Hearts 1983
New Sensations 1984
Mistrial 1986
New York 1989
Magic and Loss 1992
Set the Twilight Reeling 1996
Ecstasy 2000
The Raven 2003

Moe Tucker Albums
Playin' Possum 1981
Life in Exile After Abdication 1989
I Spent a Week There the Other Night 1991
Dogs Under Stress 1994

Doug Yule Albums
American Flyer * 1976
Spirit of a Woman *1977
Live in Seattle 2002
Hard Times **2009
* with American Flyer
** with RedDog

Index